IMAGES
*of America*

# Robert Allerton
## His Parks and Legacies

**On the Cover:** Employees and their families pose near the dipping pool in 1912. John J. Borie III's gates appear in the background, and beyond that, the peaked gable of the icehouse. From left to right are James Shield (with the hose), John Aldt, James and John Shield (sitting at pool), Emma and Waneta Ashby, Jessie Shield, A. McNaughton, James Louis, and Albert Priebe. (Allerton Park and Retreat Center, University of Illinois.)

IMAGES
*of America*

# ROBERT ALLERTON
## HIS PARKS AND LEGACIES

Maureen Holtz

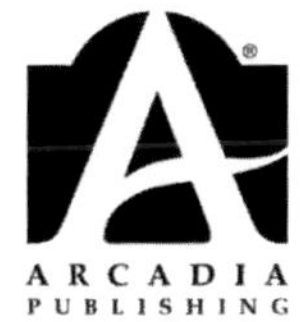

ISBN 978-1-4671-0618-4

Published by Arcadia Publishing
Charleston, South Carolina

Printed in the United States of America

Library of Congress Control Number: 2020943210

For all general information, please contact Arcadia Publishing:
Telephone 843-853-2070
Fax 843-853-0044
E-mail sales@arcadiapublishing.com
For customer service and orders:
Toll-Free 1-888-313-2665

Visit us on the Internet at www.arcadiapublishing.com

*This book is dedicated to my wonderful husband, Michael, and to my parents, who instilled in me a love and appreciation of history.*

# Contents

# Acknowledgments

This book would not have been possible without the assistance provided by Allerton Park and Retreat Center. I particularly want to thank director Derek Peterson and volunteer archivist Connie Fairchild. Additional gratitude goes to, among others, Juanita Gale and Lisa Winters, from Monticello, Illinois; Stormy Cozad, from Kauai, Hawaii; Lynne Stanton and Rosina Rand (granddaughter of Ellen Emmet), from Salisbury, Connecticut; William H. Tyre, from Chicago's Glessner House; Denyse Cunningham, from Fort Lauderdale's Bonnet House; Delia Akaji, from the Kauai Historical Society; and Valerie Langfield and Tim Miller, in the United Kingdom. Each image's source is shown at the end of its caption, using the abbreviations listed here:

| | |
|---|---|
| AO | Author image |
| APL | Courtesy of Allerton Public Library |
| APRC | Courtesy of Allerton Park and Retreat Center, University of Illinois |
| BH | Courtesy of Bonnet House |
| CT | Public domain, *Chicago Tribune* |
| GH | Glessner House, Chicago, Illinois. Reprinted with permission. All rights reserved |
| JG | With kind permission of Juanita Gale |
| KHS | Courtesy of the Kauai Historical Society |
| LL | Laird & Lee, *Glimpses of the World's Fair. A Selection of Gems of the White City Seen Through A Camera*, Laird & Lee Publishers, Chicago, 1893 |
| MH | With permission of Michael Holtz, all rights reserved |
| RR | With kind permission of Rosina Rand |
| SC | With kind permission of Stormy Cozad |
| TM | By kind permission of Tim Miller |
| UI | Allerton Family Collection, University of Illinois Archives, Record Series 31/13/20, Box 1 |
| VL | By kind permission of Valerie Langfield |

# INTRODUCTION

Today, many Central Illinois communities around Monticello, Champaign, and Decatur know the name of Robert Allerton only as the former owner of Allerton Park and Retreat Center outside of Monticello. Some people may also know of his Kauai, Hawaii, paradise called Lawai-Kai, today part of the National Tropical Botanical Garden. But few people today are aware of his history.

The only son of Samuel and Pamilla Allerton, Robert was born on March 20, 1873. His sister, Kate, was 10 years older. By then, his father's reputation as a savvy businessman—a founder of Chicago's Union Stock Yards and the First National Bank of Chicago—was firmly established. Samuel Allerton participated in several historical events, including helping organize the 1893 World's Columbian Exposition. At the same time, he ran for the position of Chicago mayor. He lost—fortunately for him, as the winner was assassinated four months later. In 1896, he turned down the post of secretary of agriculture under president-elect William McKinley.

Robert Allerton grew up on Chicago's Prairie Avenue, nicknamed "Millionaire's Row" and "the Sunny Street that Held the Sifted Few." The area was home to approximately 20 millionaires, including the Marshall Field family across the street from the Allertons, and Robert Allerton's best friend, Frederic Clay Bartlett, down the street. As expected, *Chicago Tribune* columnists closely followed the movements of these families and the others—the Pullmans, Armours, Swifts, and Glessners.

When Robert Allerton and his sister were young, they and their mother, a sickly woman, contracted scarlet fever. Sadly, Pamilla died, and the children recovered but remained hearing-impaired for the rest of their lives. Two years later, Samuel married Pamilla's shy sister Agnes Thompson.

Samuel Allerton's foray into Illinois farmland ownership began in 1863 after he purchased 1,280 acres in Piatt County at $10 per acre. He used the land as a feeding station for hogs and cattle heading to the Chicago stockyards. He continued buying Piatt County land steadily until 1918, eventually accumulating approximately 12,000 acres countywide, with more acreage throughout other parts of the United States.

In 1893, after viewing the artwork displayed at the World's Columbian Exposition, Robert Allerton and his friend Frederic Bartlett persuaded their parents to pay their expenses for five years of studying art in Munich and Paris. In 1897, after deciding he had no talent to succeed in the art world, Robert burned his paintings and returned to Chicago. Soon, he decided to manage the family farmland in Piatt County and build a home there.

Construction of his mansion commenced in April 1899 and was completed by the end of 1900. The *Chicago Tribune* extolled the beauty of his property, the novelty of his swimming pool, and the many beautiful gardens and statues across his estate, named the Farms. Allerton was generous with his home, inviting friends to use it as a retreat for their cultural pursuits. The mansion's current dining room, once part of the stables, often served as a library/studio for writers, composers, painters, sculptors, and others.

Around 1922, Allerton met a young man from the University of Illinois who became his future companion and the man to whom he would refer as his "adopted son," John Wyatt Gregg. Upon Gregg's graduation with a degree in architecture, Allerton arranged for him to work in the office of an architect friend, David Adler. When the Great Depression and Adler's despair after the death of his wife forced the business to close, Gregg moved to the Farms to help Allerton manage the estate and enhance the gardens.

While making his estate a wonderful haven, Allerton also focused on Chicago's Art Institute, one of his favorite philanthropies. By 1960, after he had donated over 6,000 pieces of art to the museum, it named him its greatest living benefactor. In 1968, it named its main building after him.

A turning point in Allerton and Gregg's lives came in February 1938. While returning from a trip to Australia, they discovered the perfect location for a winter home on the island of Kauai. They named the property Lawai-Kai for "valley of plenty." There, they worked alongside gardeners who taught them about the native plants not listed in any books. They learned to limit the use of a bulldozer because it could change the natural landscape. They left undisturbed the flowers and vegetation that Queen Emma had planted: a species of mesquite, tamarind, ferns, rose apple, and bougainvillea that still drape the cliff behind their home.

During most of World War II, they stayed on the island, assisting with the war effort and finally deciding that, after the war, they would make Lawai-Kai their permanent home. They planned to donate Allerton's Monticello estate to the University of Illinois but keep a house (now demolished) near the current music barn, to enable a yearly return to Illinois.

In October 1946, Allerton deeded 5,500 acres of his property to the university to be used as a public park and research center for wildlife and plant life, as well as an example of landscape architecture. He also gave 250 nearby acres for the Illinois 4-H Memorial Camp. Although Hawaii became their main base, Illinois remained their legal home.

In 1960, after Illinois passed a new law allowing adults to adopt other adults, 87-year-old Robert Allerton officially adopted John Gregg. However, Gregg did not add Allerton as a last name until after Robert's death.

During the 1960s, Allerton joined with four other men in petitioning Congress to issue a charter for a nonprofit tropical botanical garden that would be dedicated to tropical plant education, research, and conservation. In August 1964, Congress passed Public Law 88-449, which incorporated the Pacific Tropical Botanical Garden (later renamed the National Tropical Botanical Garden). Allerton's assistance was generous: he contributed $75,000 in startup funds and further endowed it with $1 million.

On December 20, 1964, Allerton fell and fractured his hip. Two days later, at the age of 91, he died of a heart attack. Following Allerton's last wishes, Gregg had his remains cremated, dusting them over the bay off Lawai-Kai beach.

John Gregg lived another 22 years, dying in May 1986. His body was cremated, and the ashes were scattered over Lawai-Kai bay. A portion of his estate went to the Honolulu Academy of Arts and the Art Institute of Chicago. Lawai-Kai was placed in trust for the National Tropical Botanical Garden. Gregg endowed the National Tropical Botanical Garden with $6 million for its maintenance, leaving another $3 million for research and educational purposes.

Allerton's artistic efforts have been recognized since his death. In 2007, the Illinois Bureau of Tourism designated Allerton Park as one of the Seven Wonders of Illinois, while the Department of the Interior has listed the property in the National Register of Historic Places. It also appears on the American Institute of Architects' list of 150 Places in Illinois.

A century after he burned his paintings because of a perceived lack of talent, Robert Allerton can be proud that the Farms and Lawai-Kai proved to be his ultimate canvases.

# *One*

# Family and Influences 1873–1895

When Robert Allerton was born, his father, 45-year-old Samuel Waters Allerton (1828–1914), was already a well-known Chicago multimillionaire and president of the St. Louis National Stockyards, with a hotel near the yards named after him. The youngest of nine children, Samuel had struggled for over three decades, renting and purchasing farms with his brother Henry, eventually drifting to Illinois to enhance his role in the livestock industry.

Early during the Civil War, he learned that the Union army was paying top dollar for pork. After obtaining financing, he purchased every hog in Chicago to sell to the army. With his fortunes rising, he bought his first farmland in Piatt County, at $10 an acre. His holdings of pasture land in Piatt County eventually became a feeding station where they fattened up livestock in order to obtain the best possible price at Chicago's stockyards. Eventually, Allerton owned over 78,000 acres throughout the Midwest.

At the age of seven, Robert Allerton lost his hearing after suffering from scarlet fever. He battled embarrassment all his life, trying to discern what people were saying. It caused him to withdraw within himself and, in time, learn to read lips.

Allerton and his sister grew up on Chicago's Prairie Avenue in a servant-filled mansion a block from Lake Michigan. Their father bought the property in 1879 from fellow First National Bank director Daniel Thompson. Although tutored for most of his childhood, Robert briefly attended the nearby Harvard School for Boys and then boarding school in New Hampshire with his friend Frederic Bartlett. Later, the two of them, captivated by art at the 1893 World's Columbian Exposition, decided to become artists.

To avoid the noise and dirt of Chicago, the Allertons, Bartletts, and other neighbors summered in Lake Geneva, Wisconsin, or Charlevoix, Michigan. Wherever they were, their social occasions were mentioned in newspapers, including attendance at costume parties, plays, and the opera. Meanwhile, the businessmen all hoped their daughters would marry well and their sons would be successful, following in their fathers' footsteps, and become equally rich.

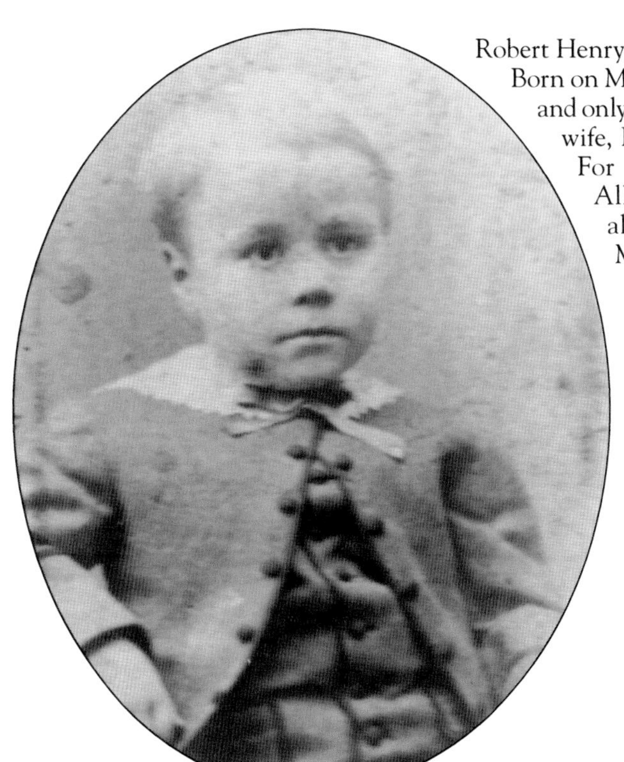

Robert Henry Allerton is seen here around age two. Born on March 20, 1873, he was the second child and only son of Samuel Waters Allerton and his wife, Pamilla Wigdon Thompson Allerton. For his son's seventh birthday, Samuel Allerton gave him 280 acres of farmland along the Sangamon River outside of Monticello, Illinois. (APRC.)

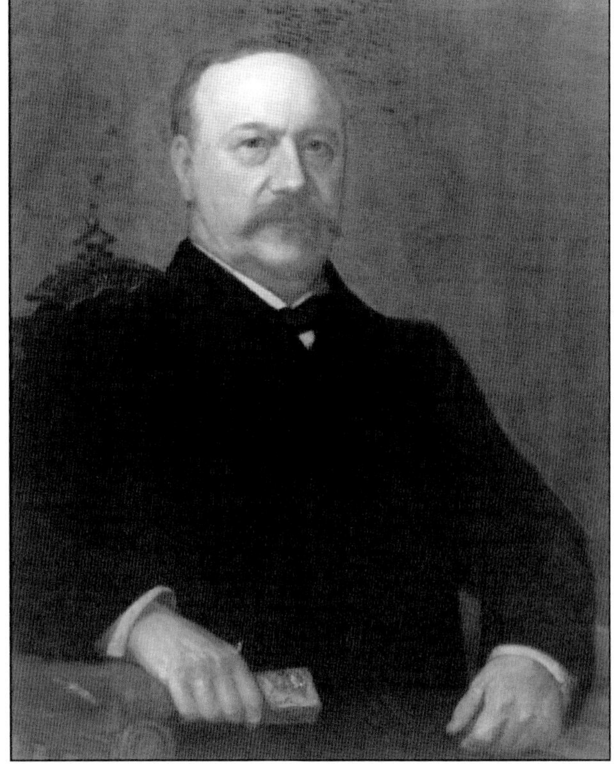

Samuel Allerton's first wealth came from trading livestock in 1855. By the late 1880s, a congressional report claimed that he and four meatpackers fixed beef prices. In 1893, he ran and lost the race for mayor of Chicago. In 1888, he published a history of the Allerton family, descending from Isaac Allerton, the richest *Mayflower* pilgrim, fifth signer of the Mayflower Compact, and lieutenant governor of Plymouth Plantation. (APRC.)

Samuel Allerton and several other investors pooled their money, raising $250,000 to establish the First National Bank of Chicago, which opened on the southwest corner of LaSalle and Lake Streets on July 1, 1863. Edmund Aiken served as president. While the building suffered from effects of the Chicago Fire, the safe's contents were unaffected. Samuel Allerton served on the board of directors until his death. (APRC.)

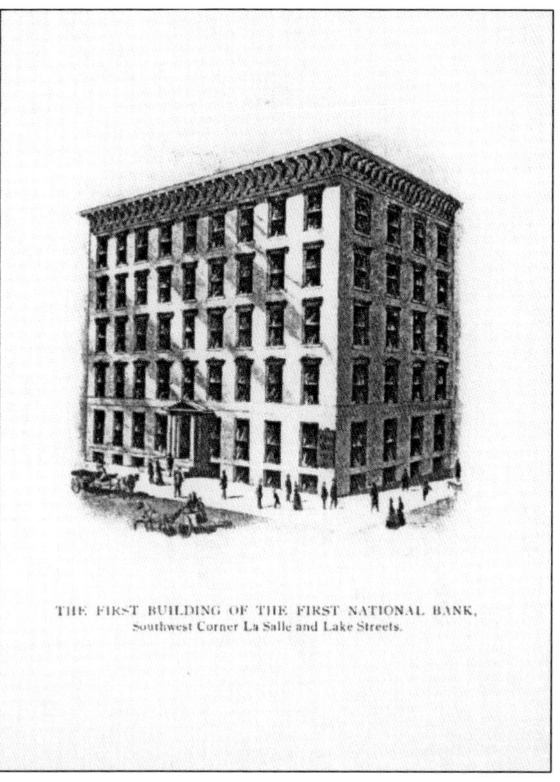


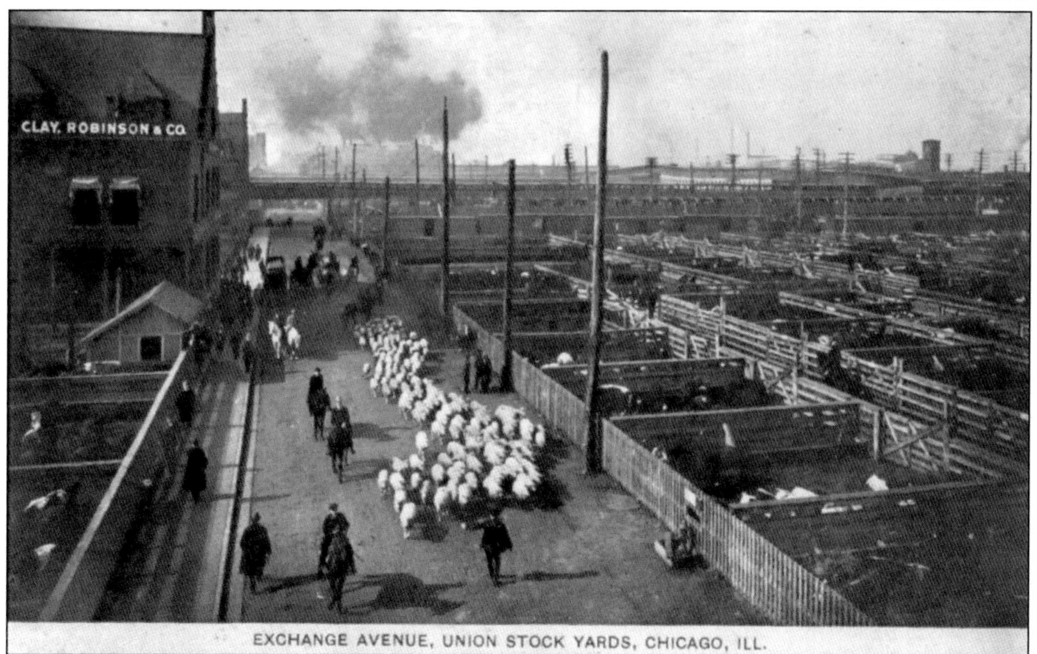


In the 1860s, Samuel Allerton managed a Chicago railroad's stockyard. By 1865, he helped consolidate all stockyards into one entity, the Chicago Union Stock Yards, seen in this photograph. In addition to controlling Pittsburgh's stockyards, yards in Baltimore, Jersey City, Omaha, St. Louis, and Philadelphia, he was one of the first to export cattle to England. (AO.)

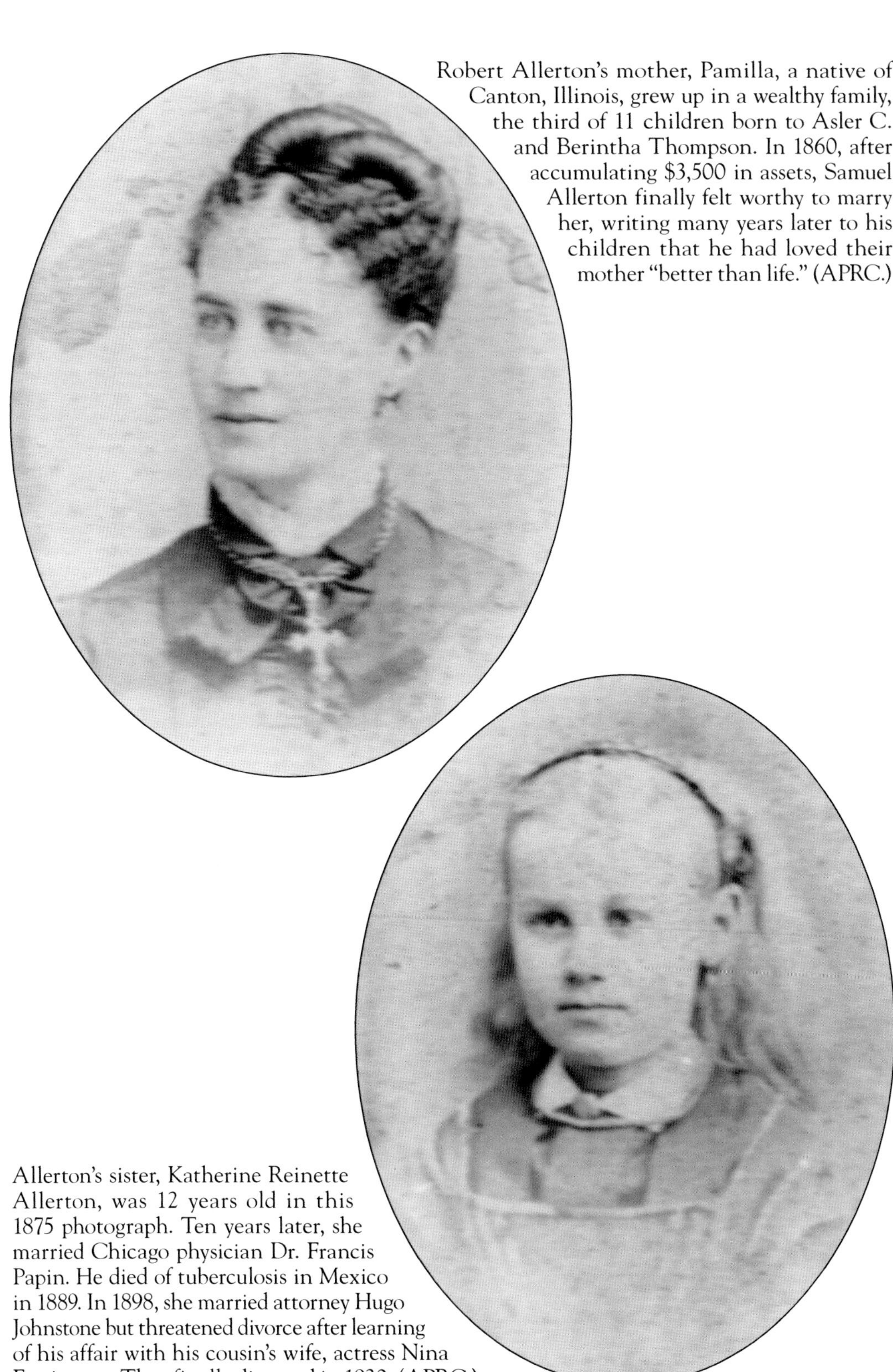

Robert Allerton's mother, Pamilla, a native of Canton, Illinois, grew up in a wealthy family, the third of 11 children born to Asler C. and Berintha Thompson. In 1860, after accumulating $3,500 in assets, Samuel Allerton finally felt worthy to marry her, writing many years later to his children that he had loved their mother "better than life." (APRC.)

Allerton's sister, Katherine Reinette Allerton, was 12 years old in this 1875 photograph. Ten years later, she married Chicago physician Dr. Francis Papin. He died of tuberculosis in Mexico in 1889. In 1898, she married attorney Hugo Johnstone but threatened divorce after learning of his affair with his cousin's wife, actress Nina Farrington. They finally divorced in 1930. (APRC.)

The aftermath of the Chicago Fire, which started on October 8, 1971, is seen in this photograph. At the time of the fire, the Allerton family was living at 644 Michigan Avenue. Their house made it through the disaster, but just the week before, a fire blazed through Allerton's leased warehouse on Sixteenth Street, killing a man. (AO.)

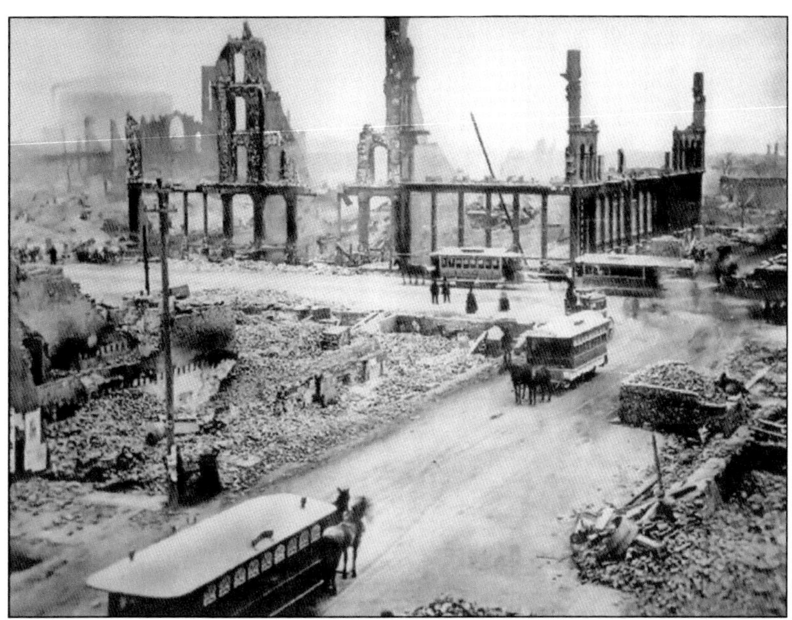

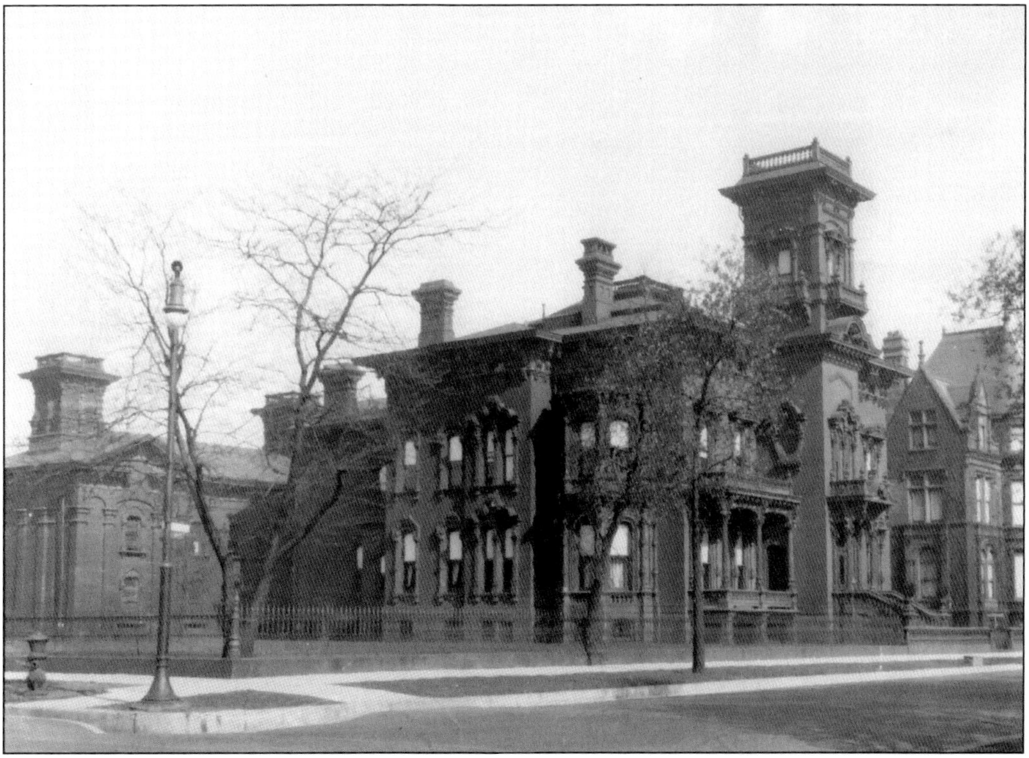

In 1879, Samuel Allerton bought a mansion with a two-story barn and stable at 1936 South Prairie Avenue. The first $100,000 house on Chicago's South Side, its frontage was the neighborhood's largest. The mansion's 70-foot tower offered a view of Lake Michigan. About Prairie Avenue, the *Chicago Tribune* wrote that at the "beginning at 16th Street, you could hardly throw a stone . . . without hitting a millionaire." (APRC.)

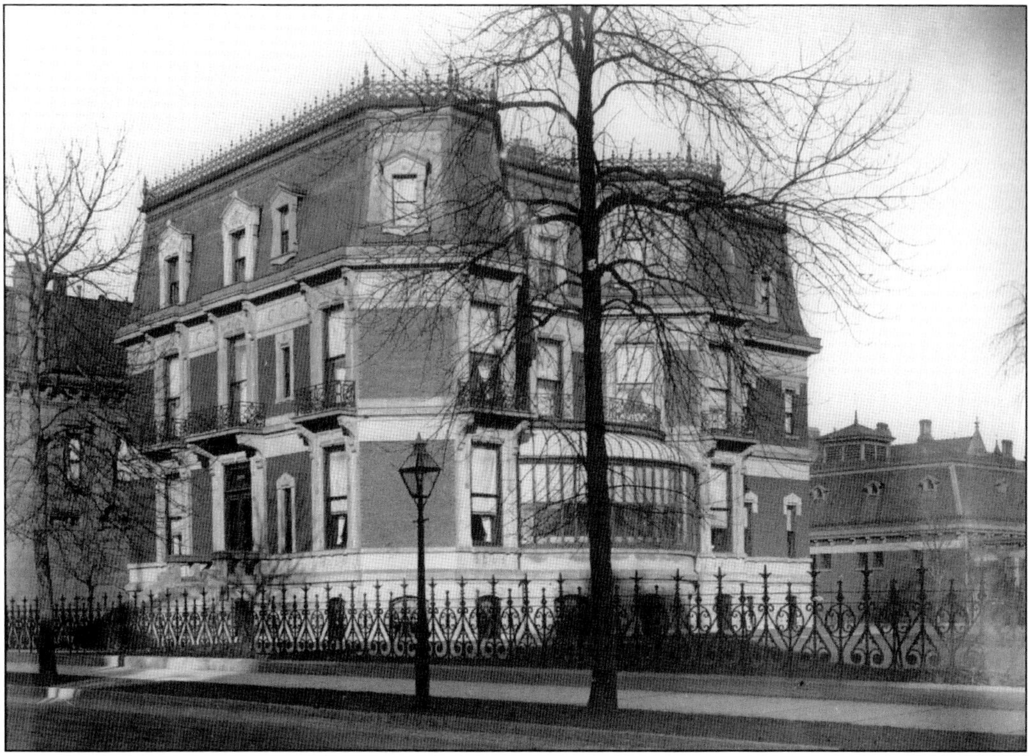

The east side of Prairie Avenue is seen in 1888, looking north from what is now Cullerton Street (at one time Twentieth Street). The center of the photograph shows Marshall Field's home at 1905 Prairie Avenue, designed by New York architect Richard Morris Hunt. The Fields' house is one of only 11 original homes remaining today. (GH.)

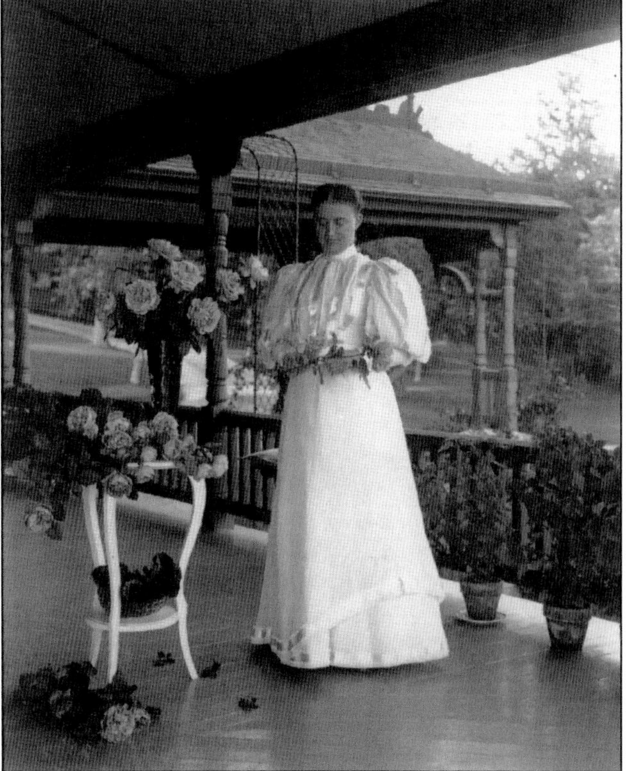

In March 1880, soon after Samuel Allerton bought the Prairie Avenue house, his wife and the children fell ill from scarlet fever. Sadly, the illness killed Pamilla Allerton. Although the children survived, they suffered serious hearing loss for the rest of their lives. Two years later, on March 15, 1882, Samuel married his wife's sister, Agnes, who was 30 years younger than he. (APRC.)

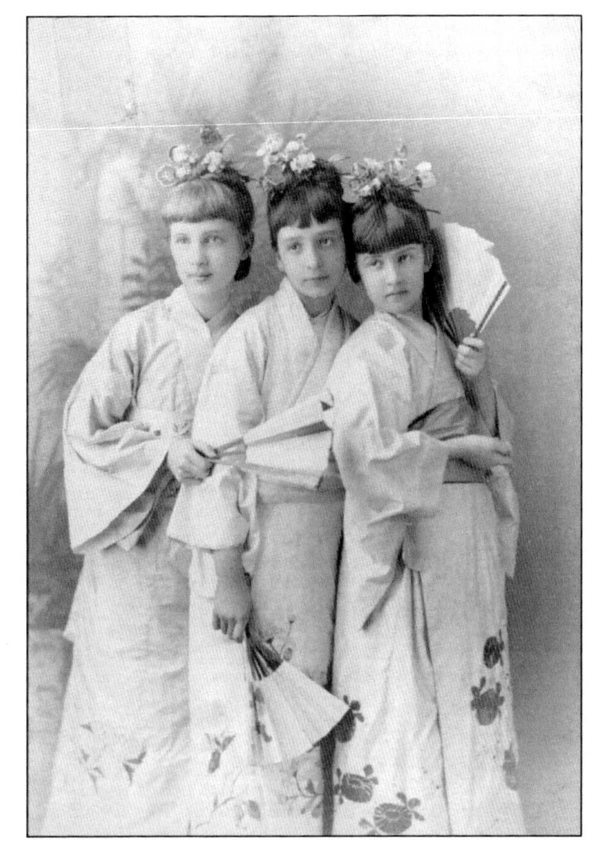

On January 1, 1886, Marshall Field's wife, Nannie, threw a holiday party for her teenage children, decorating her home's first floor with sets from the opera the *Mikado*. The party cost approximately $75,000 and included 400 friends and neighbors, a famous Chicago orchestra, and renowned photographer Mathew J. Steffens. Appearing as "Three Little Maids" are, from left to right, Alice Keith, Ethel Field, and Florence Otis. (GH.)

The Vermilion County town of Twin Grove Farm changed its name to Allerton after Samuel Allerton deeded farmland to it in 1897. He gave the town right-of-way through his land and established a grain company with Joseph Sidell. Allerton also established the town's first private bank in 1892, seen here in 1906. Later, he tried unsuccessfully to get a county (to be named Allerton) created around the town. (APRC.)

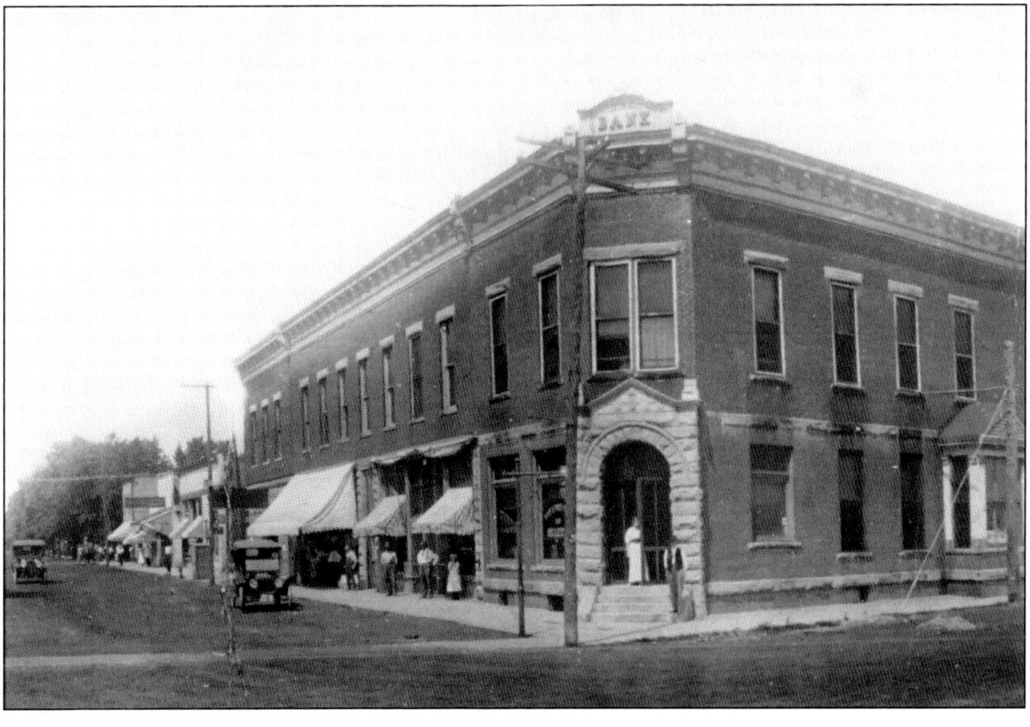

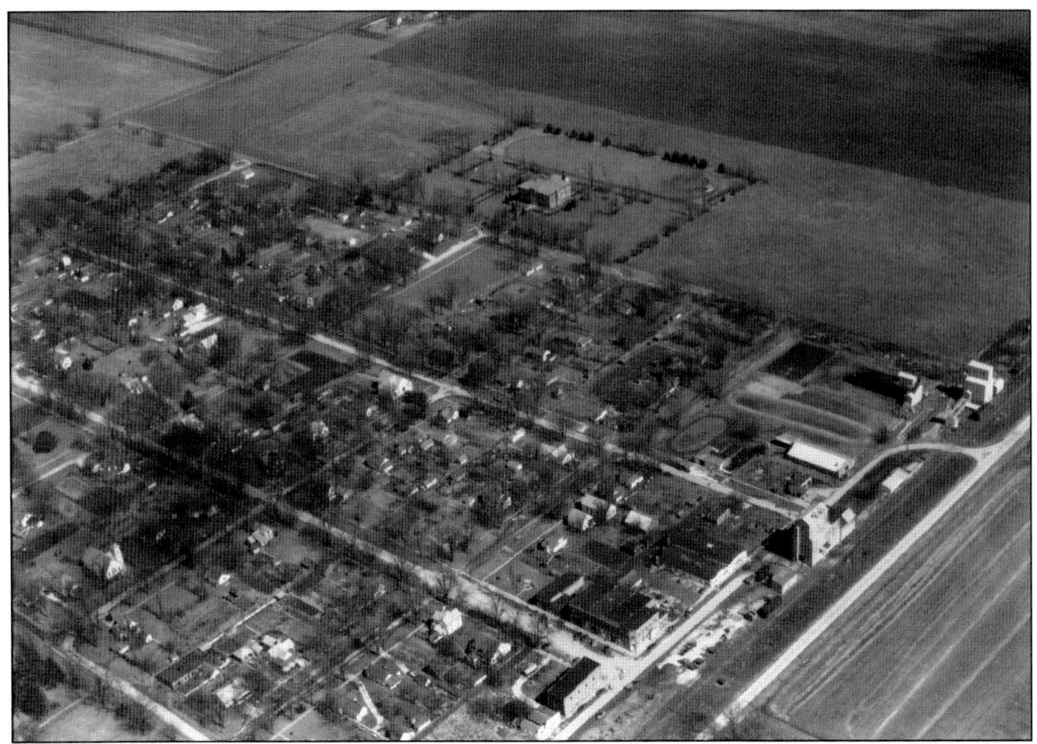

For the Allerton, Illinois, high school, in 1893, Samuel and Agnes Allerton donated funds toward its construction and equipping of the domestic science room. Agnes also employed its first teacher. Other donations included money for a water system and materials for sidewalks. In 1903, Samuel deeded land for the town's park. The school, demolished in 1975, appears surrounded by farmland at top center. (APRC.)

HAZEN'S COMPLETE SPELLING-BOOK.

LESSON 85.

"Famine shall *devour* him." What *disposition* make of his property? "When he heard this filled with *concern'*." "That is none of your *con* "The *concern'* went into bankruptcy." Iron *co* as it cools. Did you make a *con'tract?* The *co* of the proposition is true.

| | | | |
|---|---|---|---|
| in fe lic'i ty | an ni'hi late | so lic'i tude | crys'tal |
| dis pos'al | con verse' | re verse' | ca the'd |
| pul'ver ize | re ver'ber ate | re sound' | cor po r |
| in ter sect' | pat'ron age | el e va'tion | cor re sp |

LESSON 86.

| | | | |
|---|---|---|---|
| ar mo'ri al | bar ri cade' | car'da mom | ar o mat |
| car'i ca ture | ef fem'i nate | dem'a gogue | de mar c |
| de mur' | fruit'age | glyc'er ine | ef fer ve |
| fraud'u lent | fu ne're al | grav i ta'tion | gra tu'i t |

As a young boy, Robert Allerton briefly attended painting and drawing classes at the Art Institute, studying heads, figures, and still life. This copy of *Hazen's Complete Spelling Book* from 1884 (possibly from his time at Chicago's Harvard School for Boys) shows an artistic eye in sketching the ideal Gibson girl. It is assumed to be his work. (UI.)

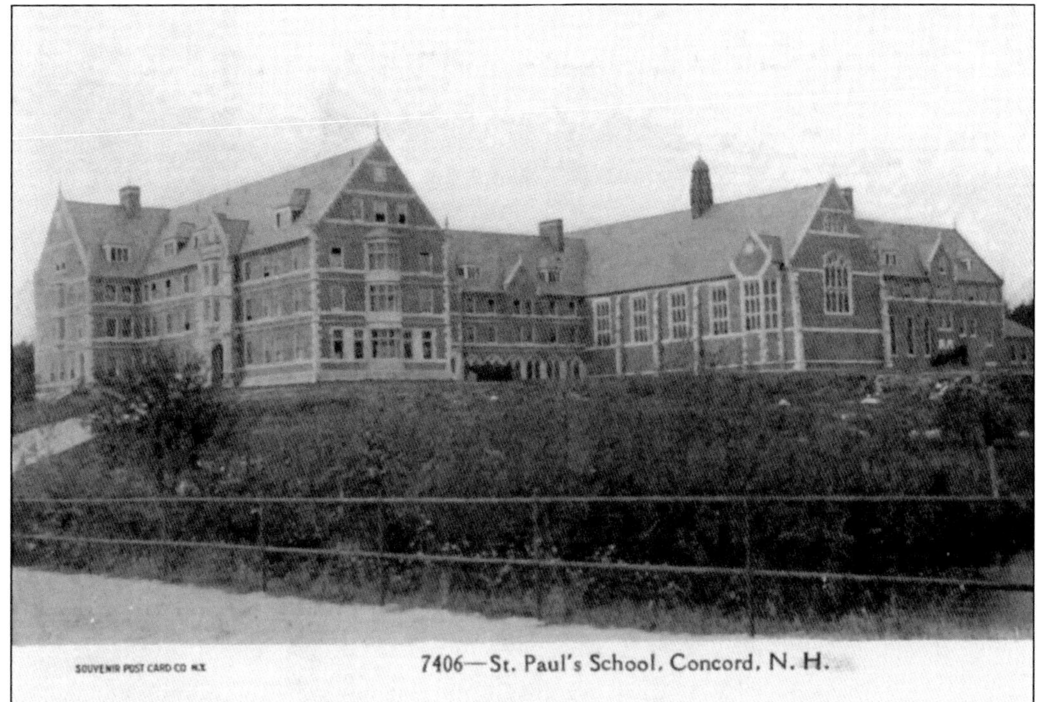


In 1889, Robert Allerton joined his friend Frederic Clay Bartlett at St. Paul's School, an Episcopal boys' school in Concord, New Hampshire, seen here in 1907. Boys learned sciences, religion, languages (Latin, Greek, French, and German), music, and liberal arts. They were encouraged to spend as much time outside in nature as possible, surely shaping Allerton's love of the outdoors. (AO.)

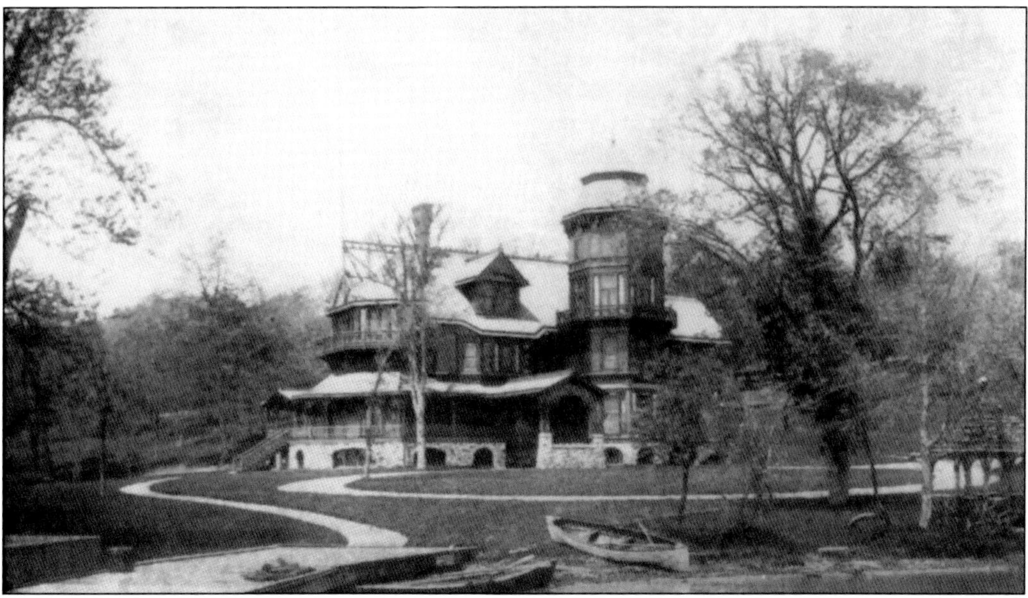

For $15,000, in August 1883, Samuel Allerton purchased the Forest Lodge estate in Lake Geneva, Wisconsin, located on 26 acres at Manning's Point. The original architect, Henry Lord Gay, drew up plans to enlarge the house after moving it out of the way of a tree that Samuel wanted to keep. Agnes Allerton referred to the house as "the Folly." (APRC.)

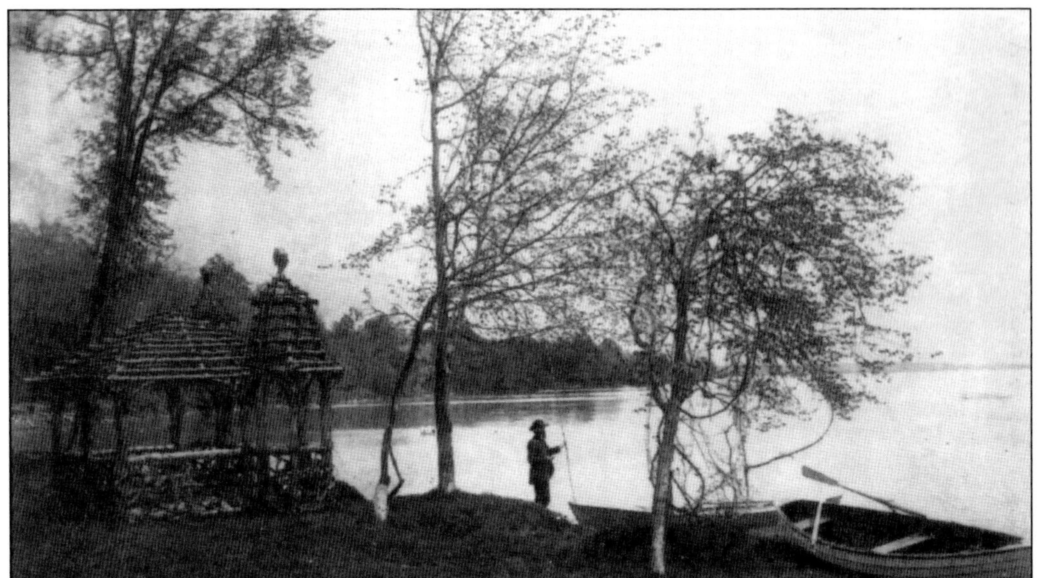

Over the years, Samuel Allerton added 80 more acres to the property at Lake Geneva for gardens. The man with the fishing pole near the boathouse is assumed to be Robert Blackwood, the gardener who helped Agnes Allerton win prizes for her chrysanthemums in 1914 and for peonies in 1917. (APRC.)

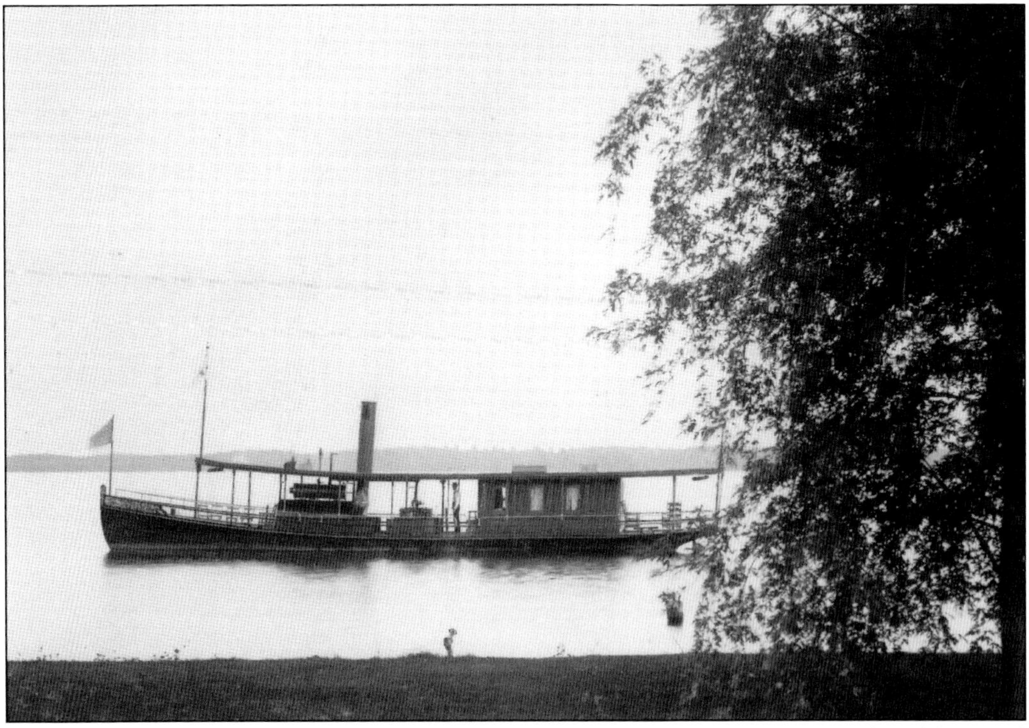

To get around Lake Geneva, most residents—and members of the Lake Geneva Yacht Club—used their boats whenever possible. They would race their neighbors to the railroad station. Samuel Allerton's steam launch, the *Time*, was photographed by Chicago photographer Leo D. Weil. The yacht sank after a tornado destroyed it in July 1885. (APRC.)

In 1895, photographs were taken of the Allerton family on the Folly's porch. Samuel Allerton and his second wife, Agnes, are seated. Twenty-two-year-old Robert Allerton stands behind his stepmother. Behind Samuel stands his widowed daughter, Kate Allerton Papin. Three years later, she would marry Hugo Richards Johnstone, a friend of her first husband. (APRC.)

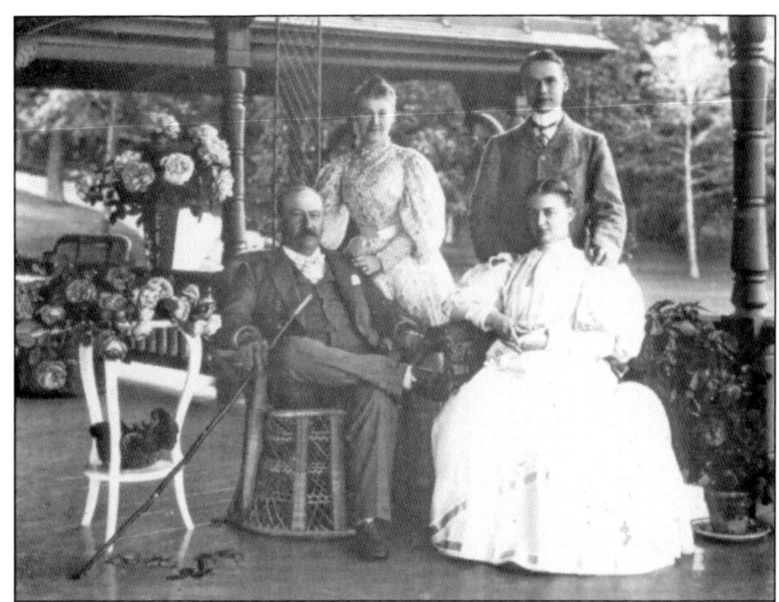

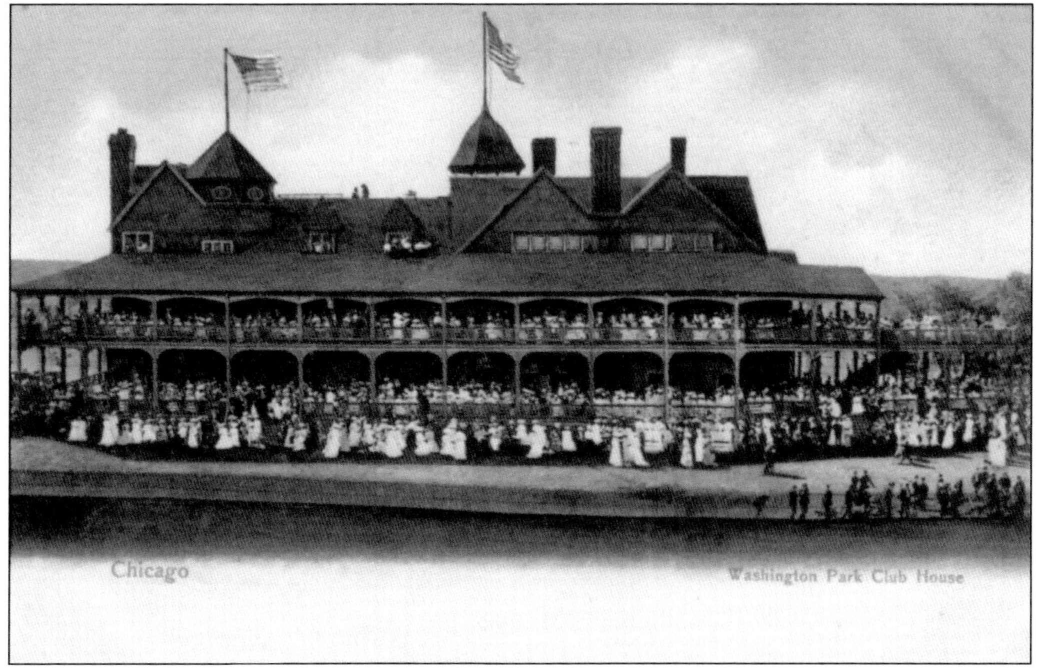


The annual Derby Day at Chicago's Washington Park Club brought out members in their carriages, parading down Michigan Avenue. In June 1891, a newspaper described Samuel Allerton's new custom-built coach as "primrose yellow, with panels, boots, moldings of black, vermilion running-gear, and black irons . . . Robert Allerton handled the ribbons over four handsome, high-stepping bays." (AO.)

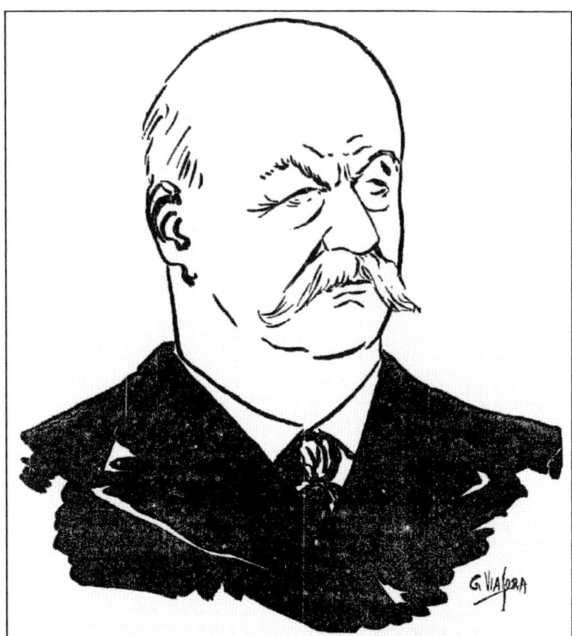


This caricature of Allerton drawn by G. Viafora appeared in a 1907 issue of the *Chicago Tribune*. In 1896, the newspaper named him the third richest man in Chicago, following Marshall Field and Philip Armour. A man sensitive about his bald head, he preferred being seen in public with his toupee, but later, he liked to place it on his son's bust of Julius Caesar as a joke. (CT.)

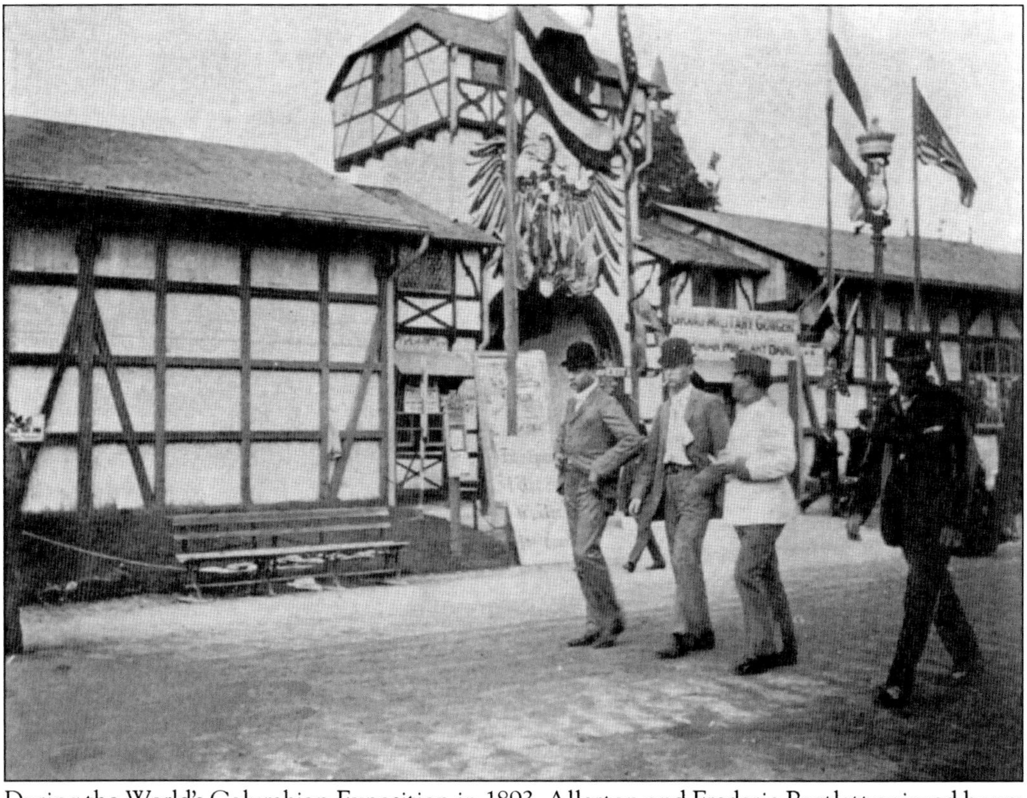

During the World's Columbian Exposition in 1893, Allerton and Frederic Bartlett enjoyed hours listening to waltzes at the German Pavilion. There, according to Bartlett's memoir, *Sortofa Kindofa Journal of My Own*, "We drank great steins of Munich's priceless gift to the world, and with all the passion and ardor of youth, we again sold our birthright, and swore eternal friendship." (LL.)

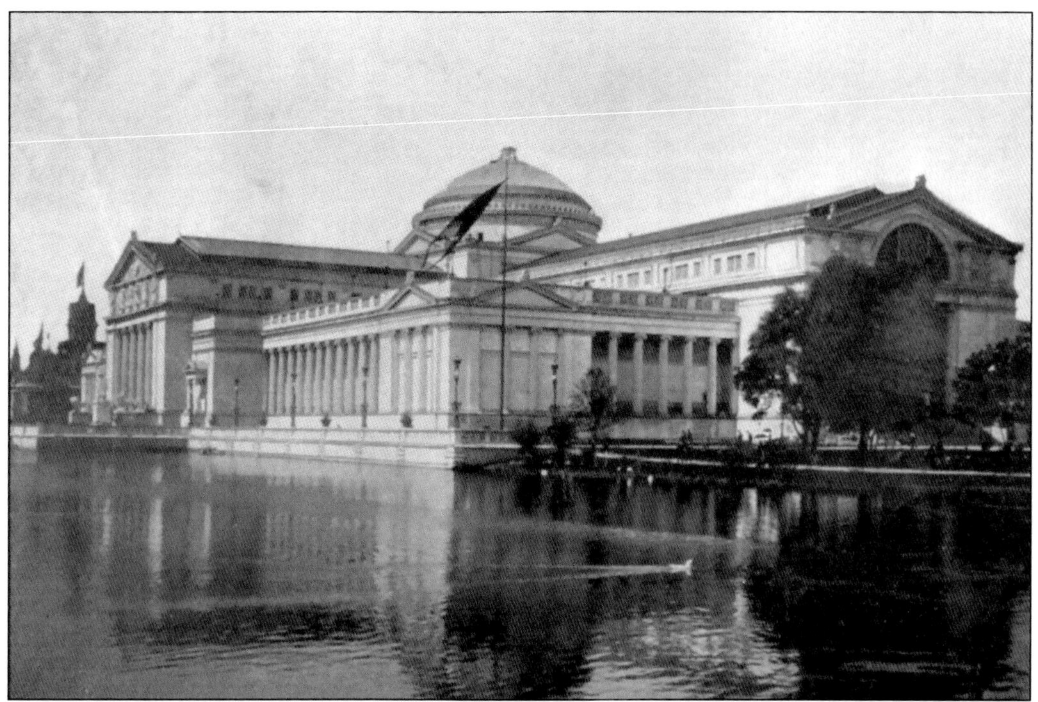

The Columbian Exposition's Palace of Fine Arts, built of brick under layers of plaster, showcased artwork loaned by prominent Chicagoans. Some of the artists included Camille Pisarro, Édouard Manet, Edgar Degas, and more. When the exposition ended, the building housed the Field Museum and now is home to the Museum of Science and Industry. (LL.)

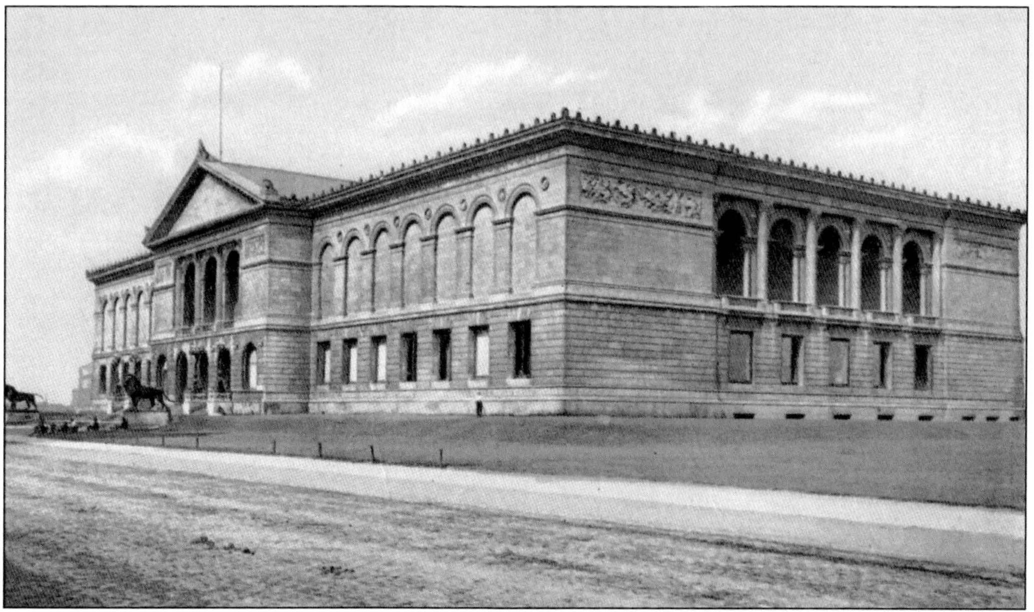

Chicago joined with the Art Institute to construct a new, expanded home in 1893 for the museum, long constrained at 81 East Van Buren Street. During the exposition, the World Congress Auxiliary occupied the structure. The 1907 photograph shows an unpaved road running in front of the new Art Institute. Robert Allerton later served as a trustee and vice president of the Art Institute. (AO.)

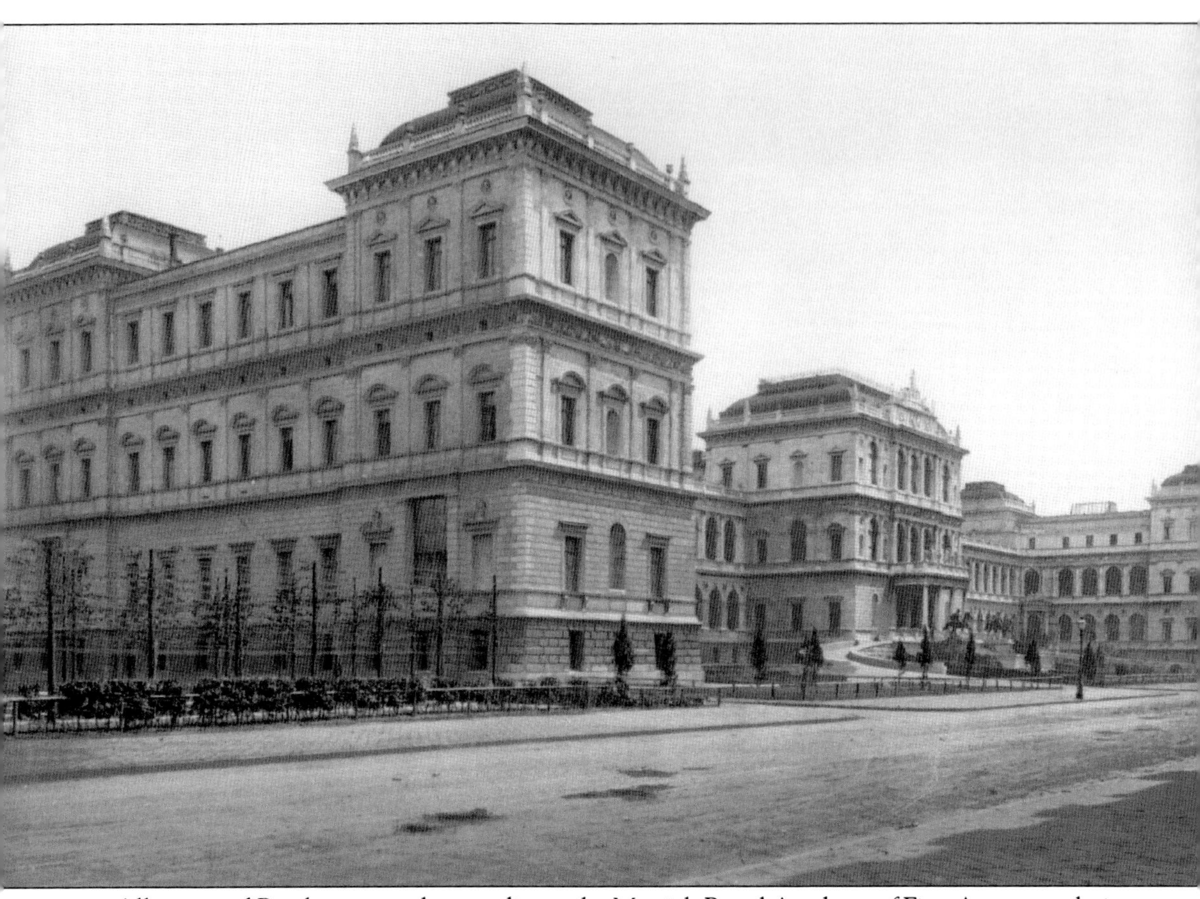

Allerton and Bartlett pursued art studies at the Munich Royal Academy of Fine Arts, completing their studies in spring 1896, then moved to Paris in the fall. Morning drawing classes in Paris were held at École Collin, afternoon classes at Aman-Jean School of Painting, and nude figure-drawing during evenings at Académie Colarossi. There, they also spent a second year, 1897. (AO.)

# *Two*

# At Home in Piatt County 1898–1920s

After returning from his art studies overseas, Robert Allerton agreed to manage the family's Piatt County property but wanted to live there, not visit the land from time to time like his father. His father agreed to fund construction, rationalizing that if Robert had his own home, he would not choose to live overseas. He suggested that he and his architect friend John Borie III travel to Europe to find the perfect mansion to use as a model. They left in October 1898 and soon found what suited Robert in England: Ham House.

In mid-April 1899, with an architectural design available, construction began on what local residents called Robert Allerton's summer resort. Over 150 men labored on the project, some coming from as far away as Chicago. A year later, the mansion exterior was completed, and plasterers were hard at work, finishing by the time summer arrived.

Over the decades, local residents created stories or rumors about the mysterious young Allerton, his guests, and his estate. One story made it to national newspapers in July 1917 after Allerton's butler, Stanley Gollop, claimed he was attacked by a lion roaming the property, with scratch marks to prove it. One newspaper reporter slyly wrote that this situation involved " 'SOME lion'. . . . Or some lyin'." At least 1,000 men volunteered to track the creature, with one hunter telegramming Theodore Roosevelt to suggest he join the hunt. Eventually, it was learned that one of Allerton's maids had caught the butler peering into a window while the maids were changing their clothes. His injuries were caused by the rake she used on him.

Several unfounded stories continue to this day. One was that Allerton shipped rattlesnakes to Monticello via a railroad boxcar, using them to scare away trespassers. Yet another story insists he was responsible for the building of Chicago's Allerton Hotel. In reality, the hotel was built by a company headed by James Cushman, a descendant of *Mayflower* Pilgrim and Isaac Allerton's daughter, Mary Allerton Cushman. Cushman merely preferred using the Allerton name instead of his own.

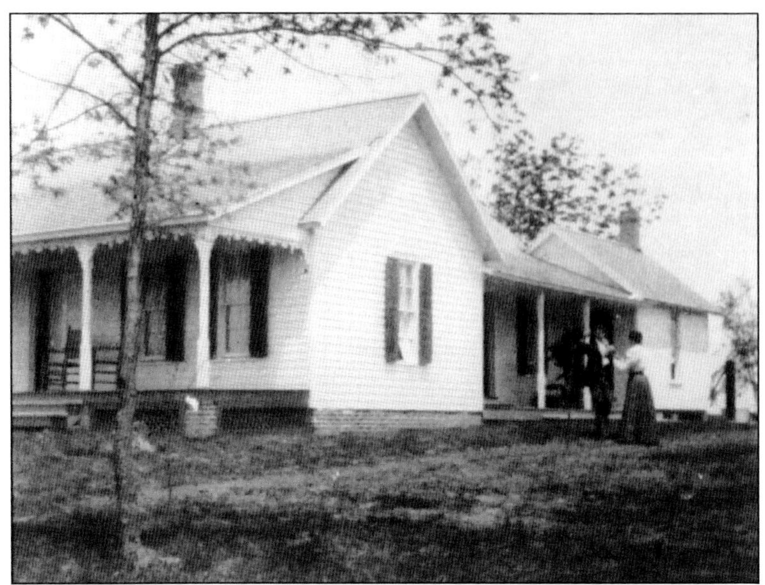

When Robert Allerton decided to manage his father's Piatt County property, he relocated a tenant farmer cottage closer to the spring and decorated his outdoor privy with French posters of Toulouse-Lautrec paintings. He lived in the cottage during the summer of 1898 while determining his needs. He is pictured here with his stepmother, Agnes Allerton. (APRC.)

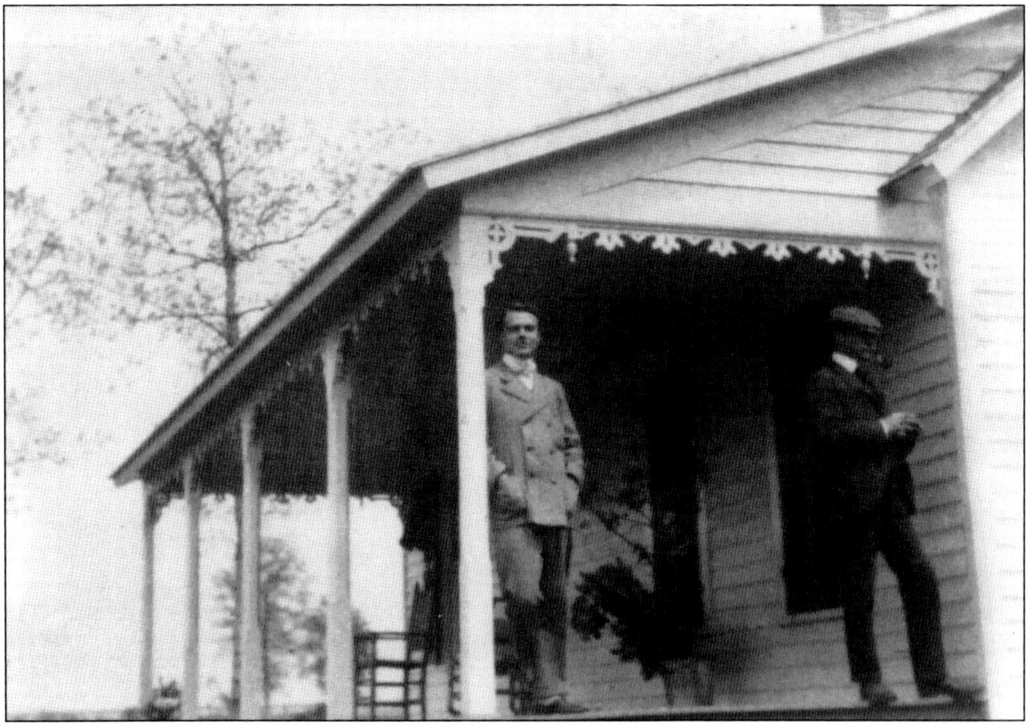

Planning to build his home on the knoll opposite the cottage, Allerton (left) built a dam in the spring between the knoll and cottage, creating a pond. Before leaving in October 1898 for England to seek architectural inspiration with his friend John J. Borie III (right), Allerton attended his sister's marriage to Hugo Johnstone in New York City. (APRC.)

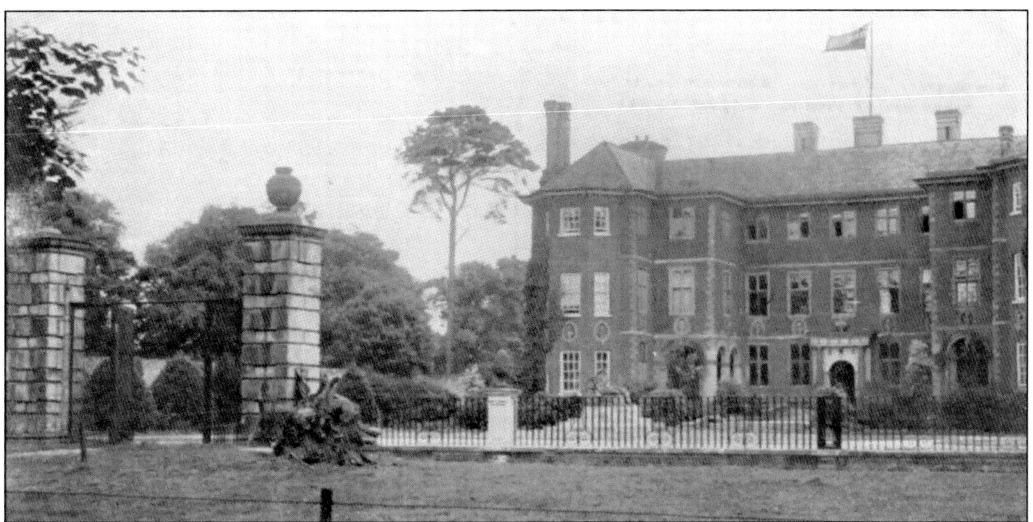

Allerton and Borie discarded several designs for his mansion—Queen Anne, Georgian, and Jacobean—but eventually chose to use a Stuart-styled mansion in Surrey overlooking the Thames River as the model. Only 10 miles from central London, Ham House was built in 1610 for King James I. It boasts formal gardens and the oldest orangery in Britain. (AO.)

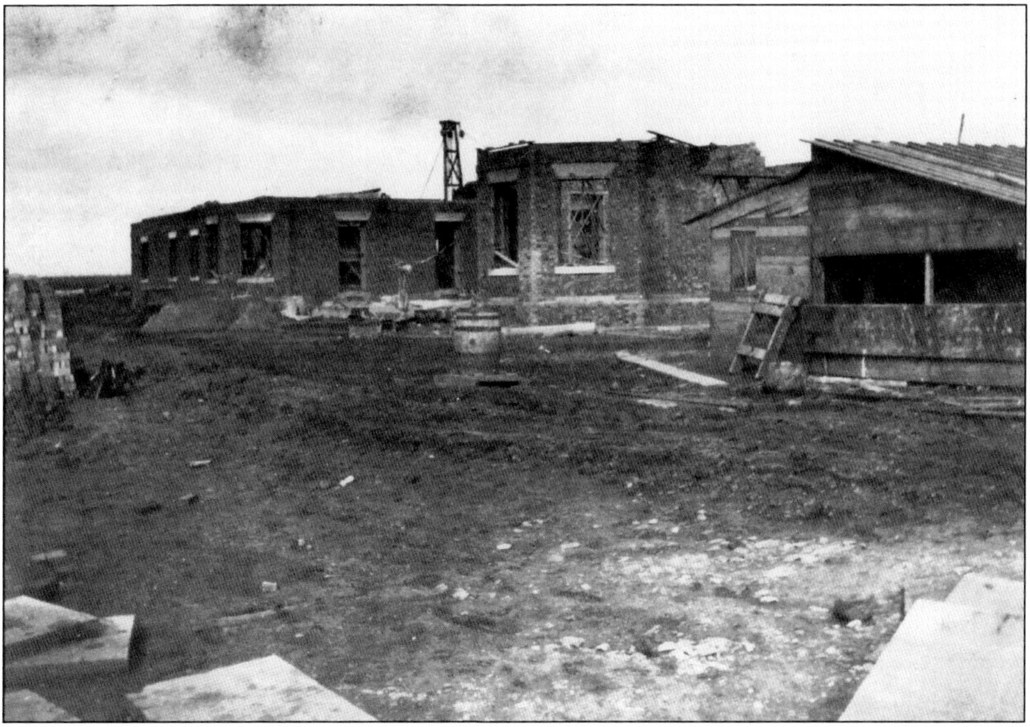

The southwest façade of Allerton's mansion is seen here, with the first floor under construction. At right stands a wooden construction shack. In October 1899, a shed near the house containing 2,000 pounds of dynamite caught fire. Several of the men were able to extinguish the blaze before the dynamite exploded. Blasts were heard as far as 15 miles away. (APRC.)

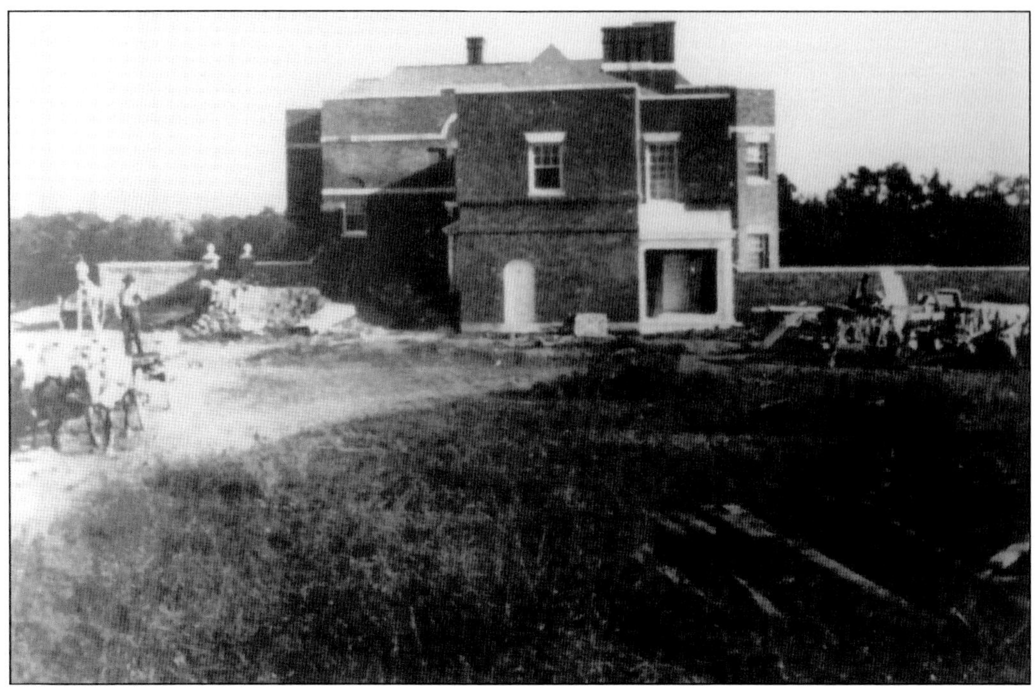

The servants' wing on the north side of the mansion is pictured in 1899. The meadow lies to the right. Individually wrapped bricks used as ballast on a ship from Holland were used to build the mansion. Materials also included custom-tinted mortar. In September 1899, Allerton, his parents, and several friends celebrated the placing of the cornerstone. (APRC.)

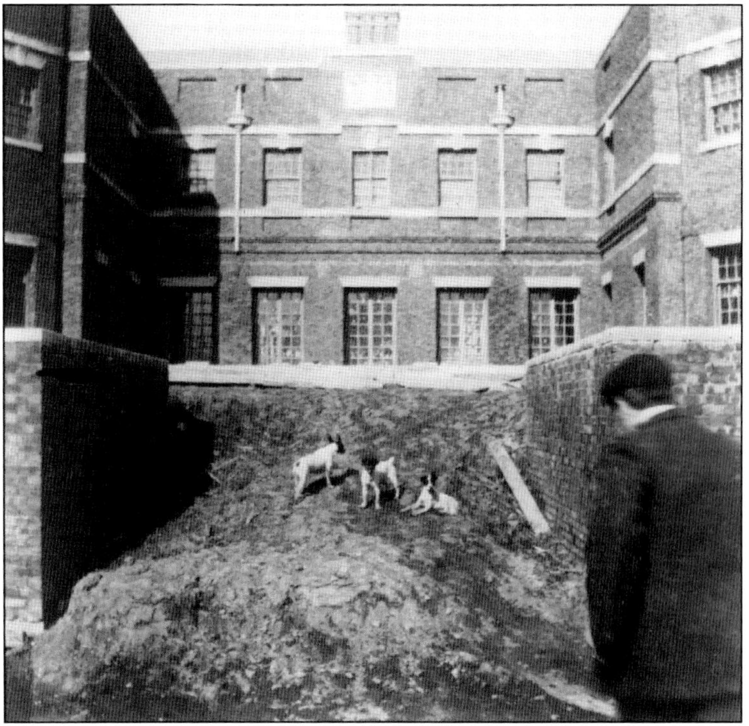

The front of the mansion at the upper terrace and an unidentified man—possibly Allerton—with several dogs are seen here in 1900. This eventually became the pool area outside of the conservatory. Allerton departed in January to spend the winter overseas, returning in April as the construction on the exterior was nearly completed. During his absence, the laborers' boardinghouse on the premises burned down. (APRC.)

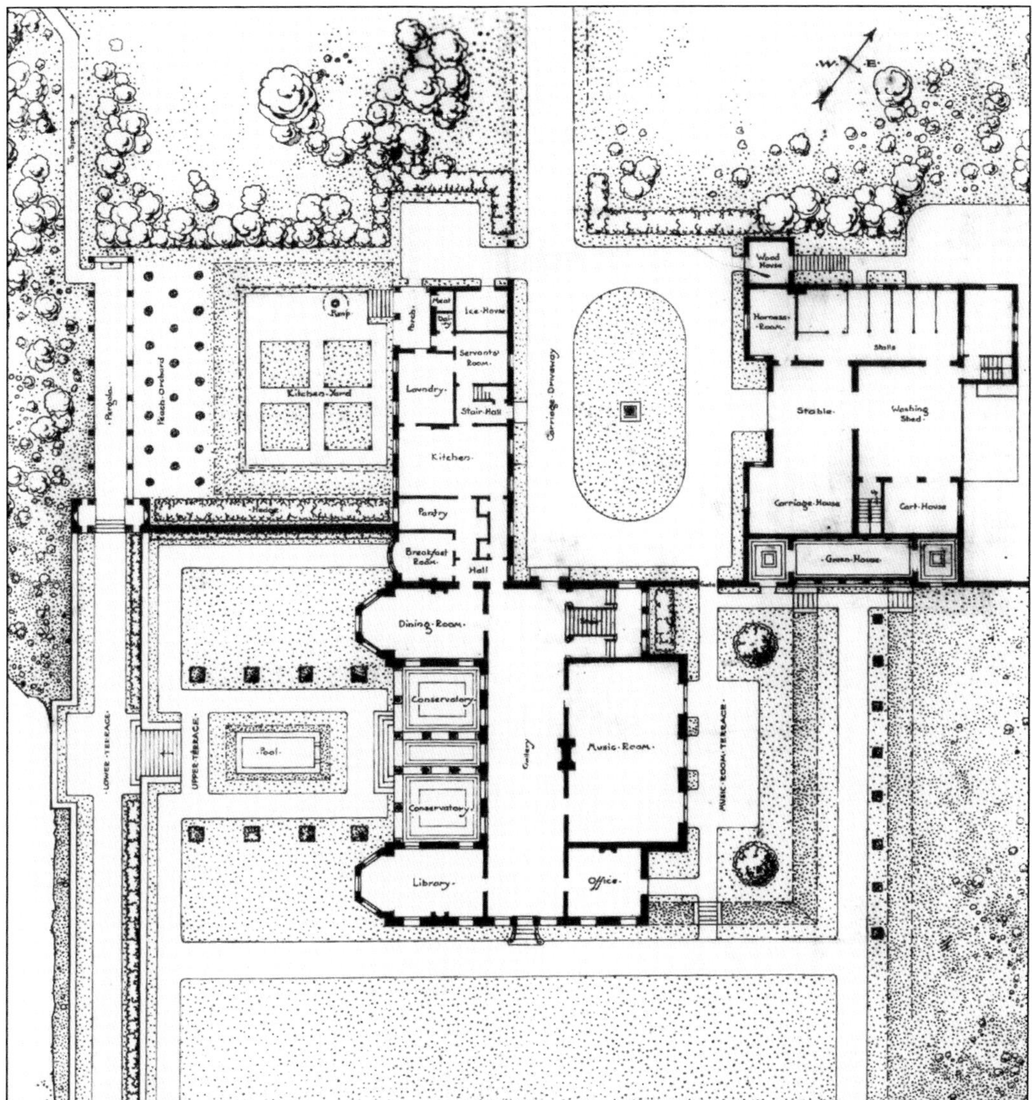


One of John Borie's renderings from 1899 shows details of the first floor of the mansion. From the outside entry court, visitors would enter directly into the gallery. Stairs to the left led to the second floor and the basement. The music room lies beyond the stairs, while farther down on the left is the office. The library is across the gallery. From the gallery, guests could enter the conservatory and view the pool, the pond, and the meadow. As guests returned toward the entrance, they would see the dining room, next to the conservatory. A small corridor led to a breakfast room, a pantry, and the kitchen. Across from the stairs were the laundry, a room for the servants (such as for a dining area), the icehouse, the dairy room, the meat room, a porch, and steps leading down to the kitchen yard. (APRC.)

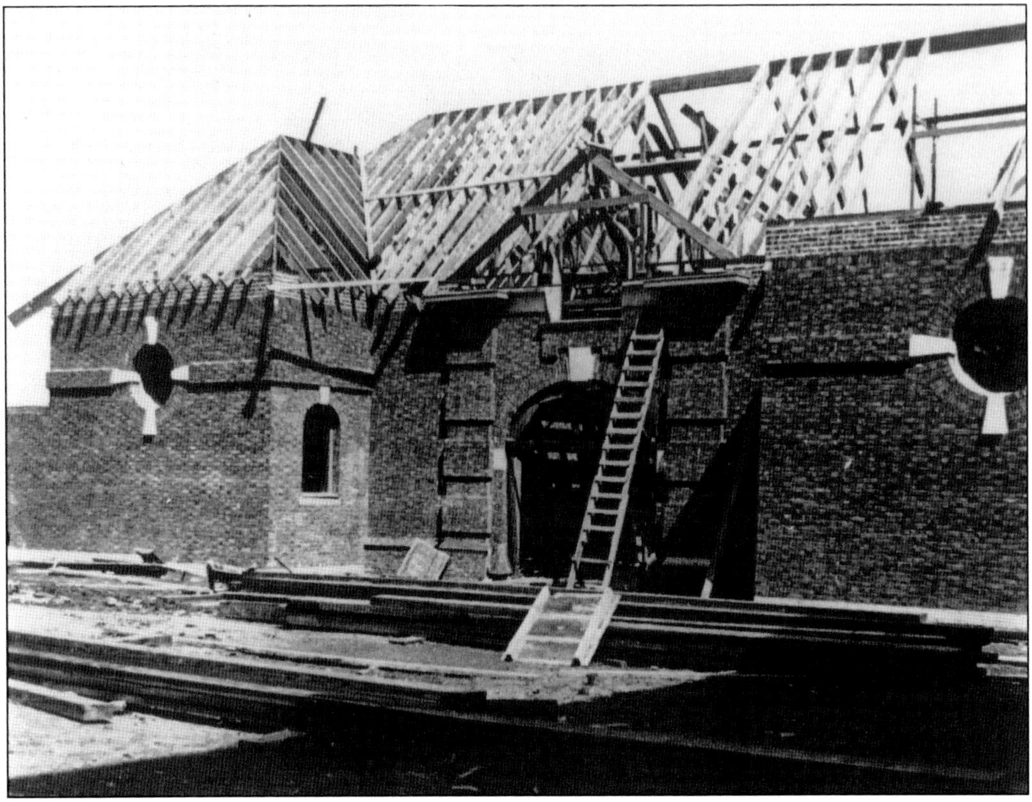

Stable construction began in 1901 by hauling 400,000 bricks from the Monticello train depot, six miles away. Borie's slowness on the project prompted Allerton to write about him: "All work has been stopped here owing to his sending us new plans. . . . I am furious with him." One worker stands above the stable entry. (APRC.)

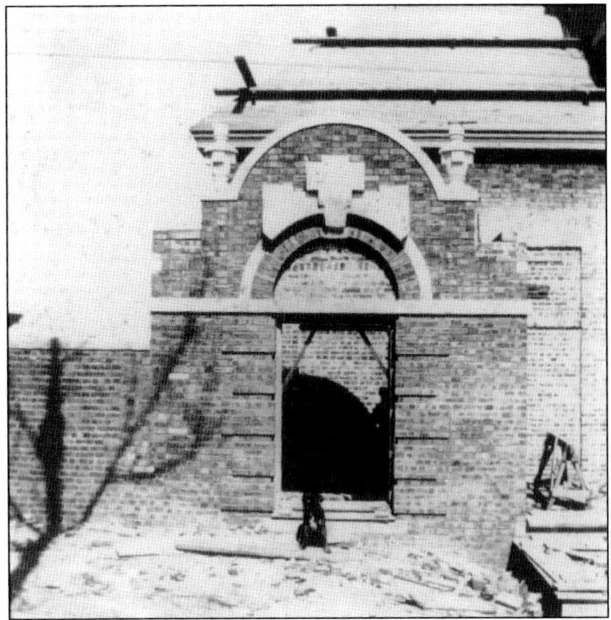

This 1902 photograph, taken from what is now the library terrace, formerly the music room terrace, shows the conservatory section of the stable under construction. A mask of Pan, the Greek god of nature, would eventually be placed above the window. One of Allerton's dogs sits at center, facing the camera. (APRC.)

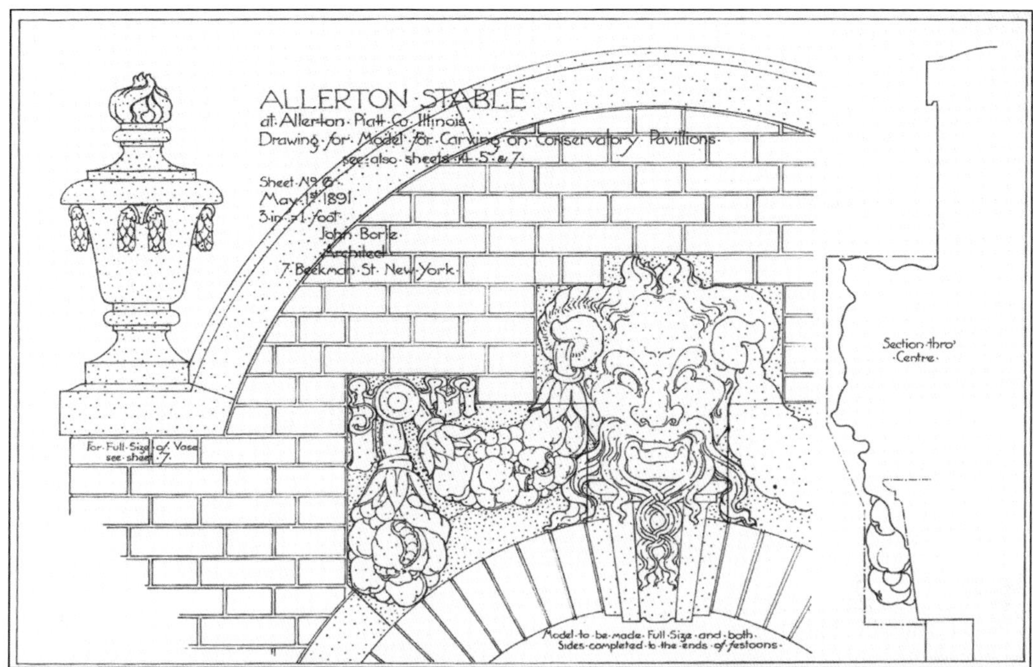


Borie's gargoyle sketch includes a mask of Pan and vase for the stable conservatory. The actual date was 1901, not 1891, as written. Unlicensed in Illinois, Borie asked architect James Gamble Rogers to stamp the drawings. Borie's delays with the stables resulted from helping his sister Emily Ryerson on her estate in New York. (APRC.)

Seen in 1905, the newly completed stable included a cupola, uncommon in Central Illinois. Beyond the building lies bare farmland and pasture. Borie's plan for the stable included a wood house, harness room, six horse stalls, washing shed, carriage house, cart house, hayloft, and three second-floor staff bedrooms. (APRC.)

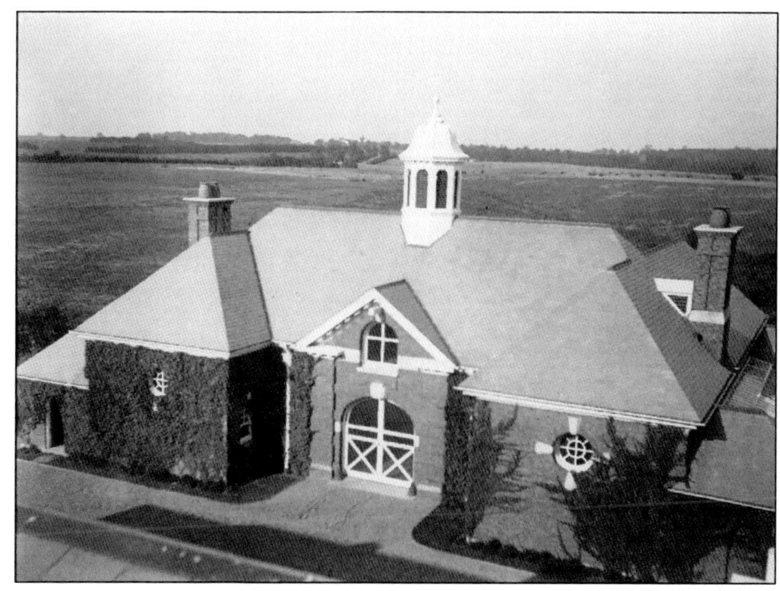

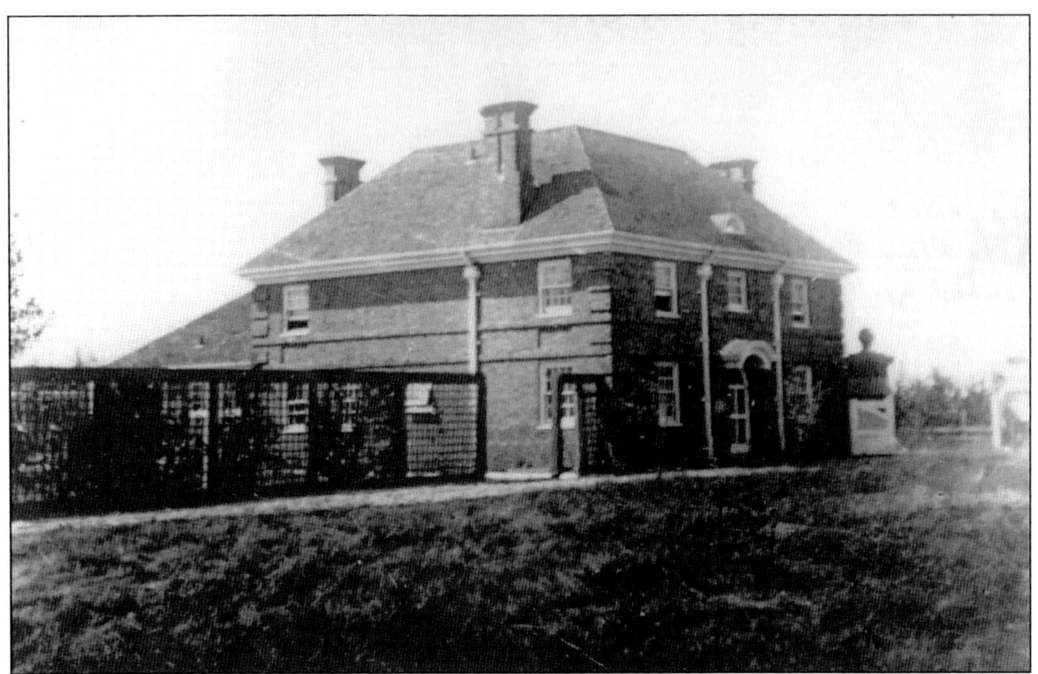

In 1903, construction began on Borie's design of the gatehouse, a two-story redbrick home for use by the head gardener and his family. This 1906 photograph shows the building facing the entrance lane leading to the mansion, with pineapples—the traditional symbol to welcome guests—decorating the entry columns. (APRC.)

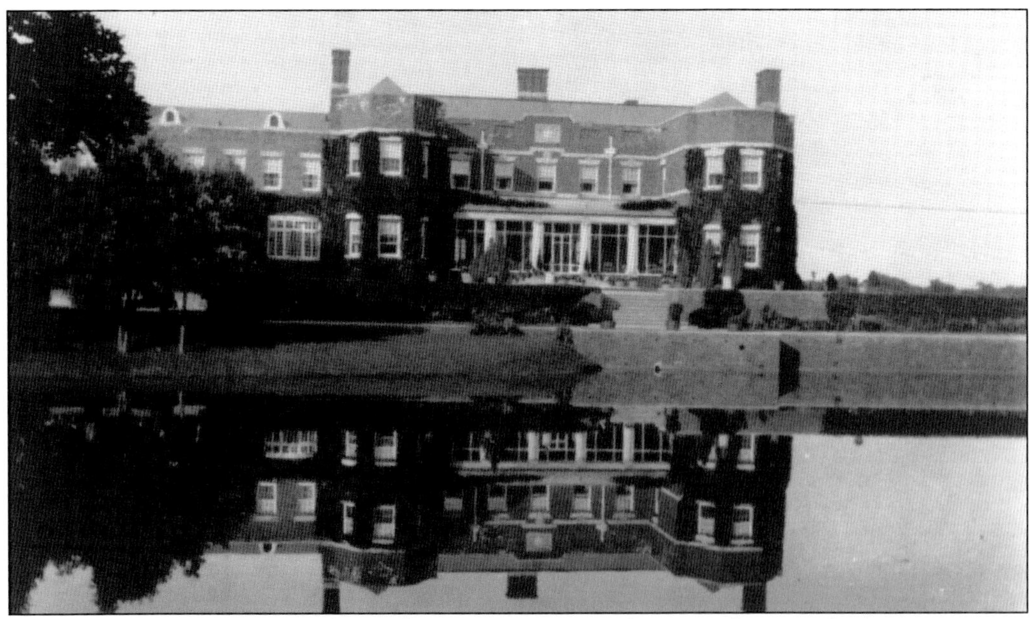

Vines climb up the exterior walls of Allerton's mansion in this 1910 photograph. A parapet wraps around the edges of the roof. After several years of rain and melting ice seeping inside, the parapet had proved problematic. To combat further damage, Allerton commissioned Borie to draw up plans for a redesign of the roof. (APRC.)

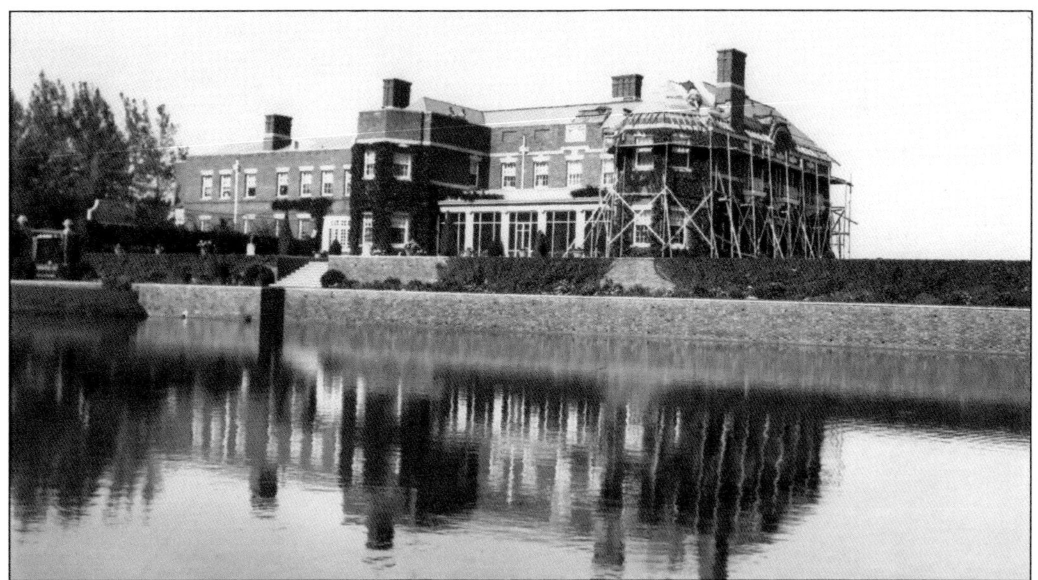

By 1912, the parapet was in the process of being removed, to be replaced by a roof more appropriate for Central Illinois weather. In this photograph, two people stand at the parapet above the conservatory at center. Scaffolding stands at the right. To the left of the far-right chimney, a workman climbs on the new roof. (APRC.)

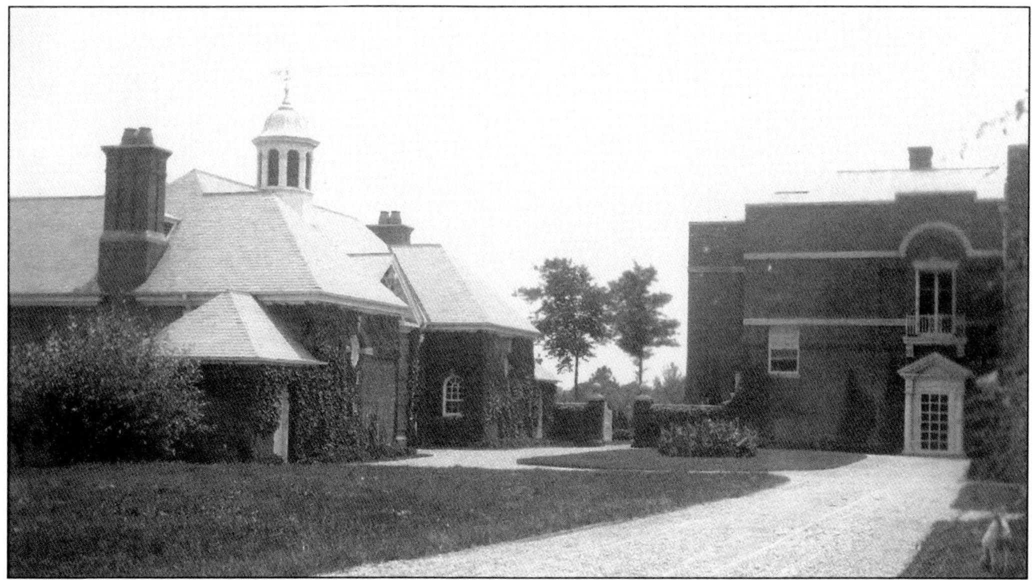

In 1905, the carriage drive approaches the mansion, not yet attached to the stables. A walking path from the entry court leads to a gate for the mansion's back terrace. The first-floor curved stable window was later replaced by a door. The mansion's roof parapet had not yet been replaced. A dog appears at lower right. (APRC.)

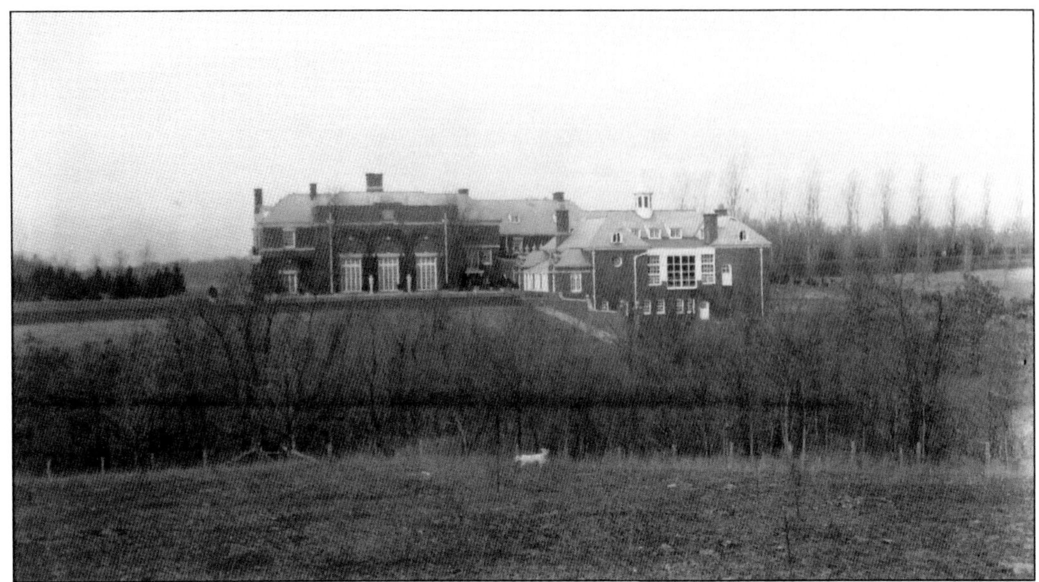

By 1918, all roof work was completed, and additional landscaping had begun. This photograph shows the northeast part of the mansion with a dog running in the foreground near the fence. The gatehouse lies out of frame to the right. Much of the land in the foreground is now occupied by the annex building and parking lot. (APRC.)

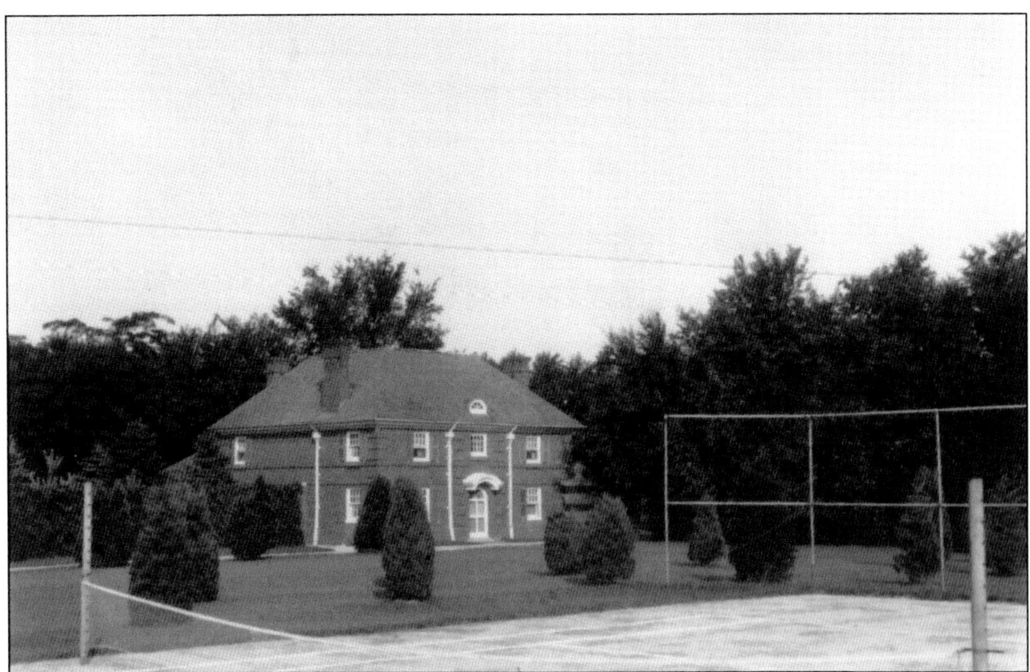

In this 1925 photograph, a tennis court occupies the area in front of the gatehouse. In the 25 years since the house was built, trees had grown tall, and the vines crawling up the fence in 1903 were quite dense. Nowadays, with the tennis court gone, attendees for the music festivals at Allerton Park and Retreat Center fill the lawn. (APRC.)

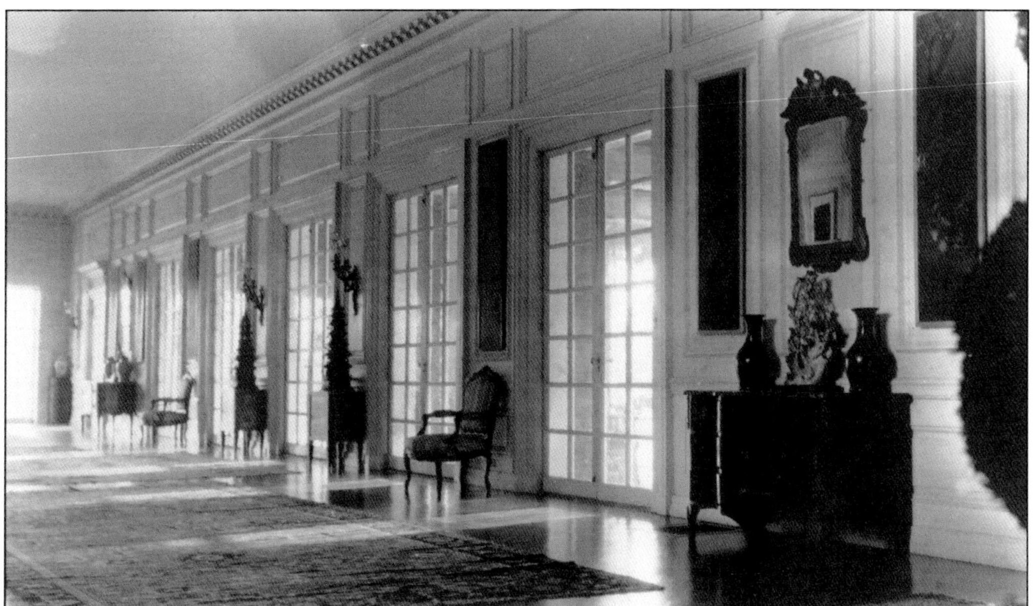

Guests would enter the front door of the mansion directly into this gallery. The gallery measures 20 feet wide, over 90 feet long, and 14 feet in height. The conservatory is past the French doors, between the tables and plants in this 1935 photograph. Beyond the left side of the photograph is the music room. An Iranian rug—still at the mansion—lies in the foreground. (APRC.)

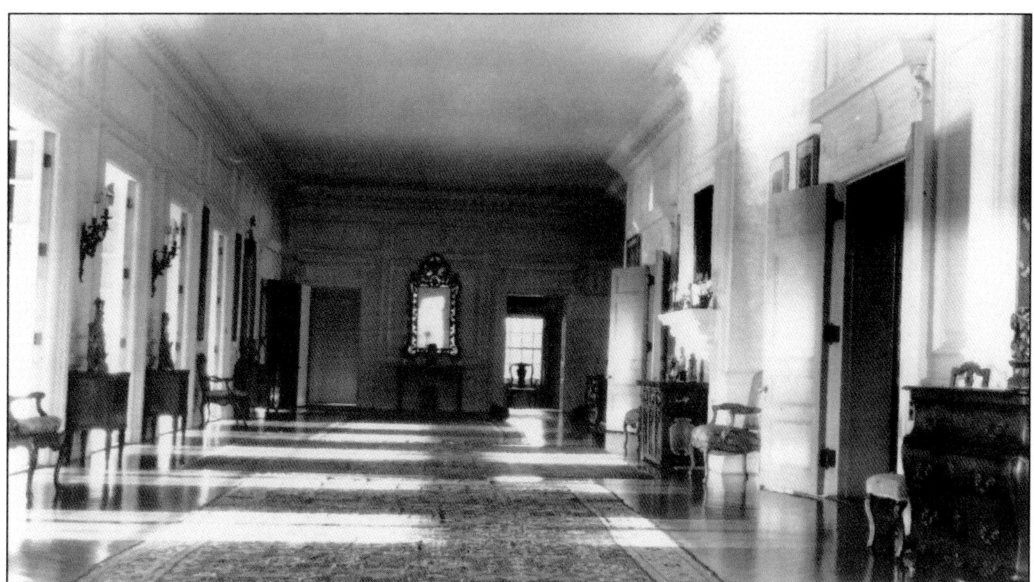

The window in the center background of this photograph is where the original entrance opened into the mansion. After years of dealing with dirt, leaves, rain, and snow finding their way into the gallery, Allerton added a hallway to join the mansion with the stables, and the doorway was moved farther down the hall. The current reception desk, to the right of the mirror, looks upon the hallway. (APRC.)

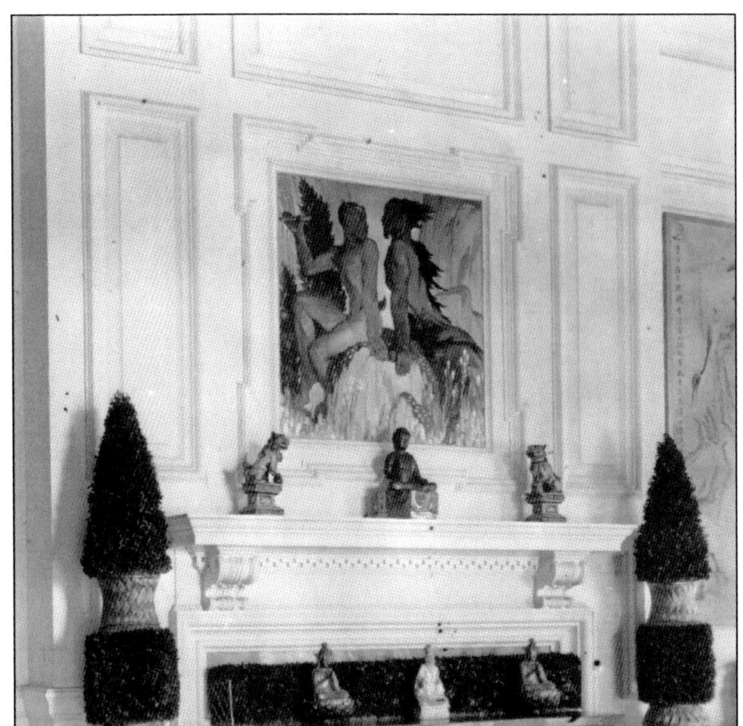

A 1921 painting, *Faun and Satyr*, by Glyn Warren Philpot, hung above the gallery fireplace, showing Allerton as the faun (the character to the left). Satyrs were considered more woman-loving than fauns, and fauns were thought to be more foolish than knowledgeable satyrs. Allerton later brought the painting to Kauai, but it was damaged by a hurricane in the 1980s. Today, Samuel Allerton's portrait hangs above the fireplace. (APRC.)

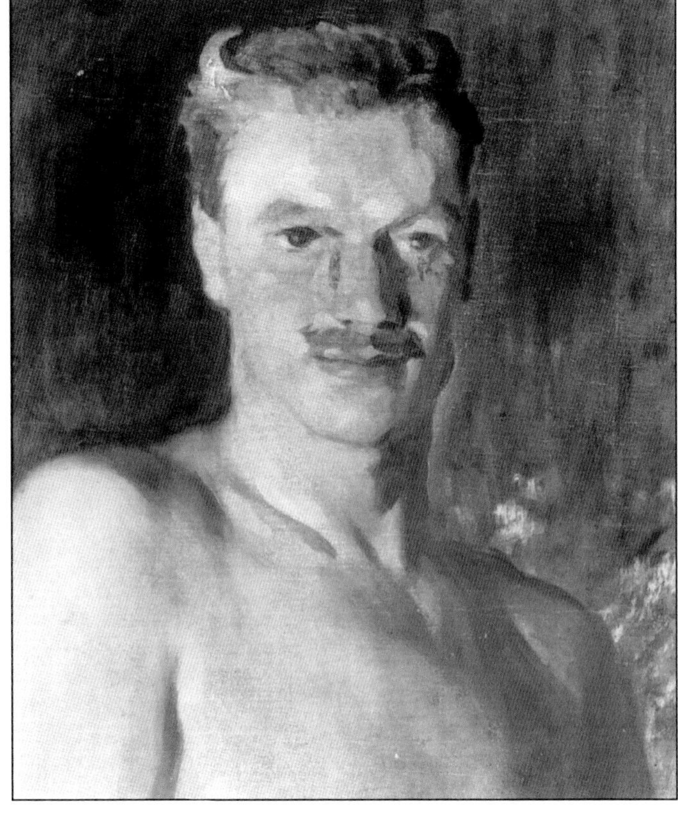

Robert Allerton is again portrayed as a faun by Glyn Warren Philpot in 1913. The faun is a mythological half human–half goat creature from ancient Rome. Often shown with goat's horns and pointed ears, these creatures were symbols of peace and fertility. That same year, Allerton sat for Philpot's *The Man in Black*, a painting that Philpot presented to London's Tate gallery in 1914. (APRC.)

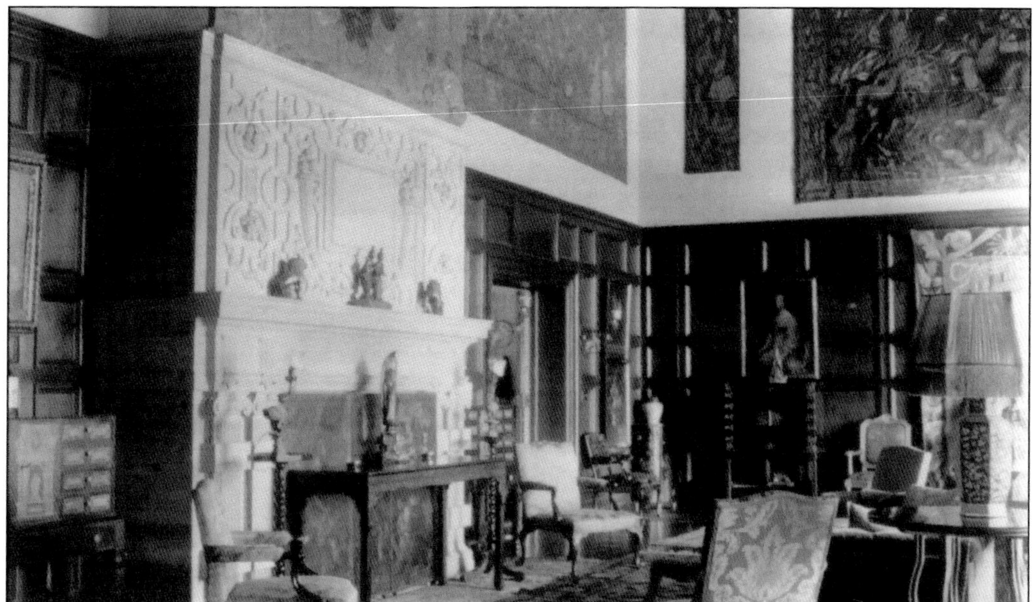

The two-story music room is 50 feet long, 30 feet wide, and reaches 23 feet to the ceiling. The early décor was heavy with tapestries, European furniture, and crimson draperies. The stone mantelpiece measured 10 feet wide and 11 feet high. At one point, Allerton commissioned artist Wilfrid von Glehn to paint a decorative panel over the mantel, but it was never created. (APRC.)

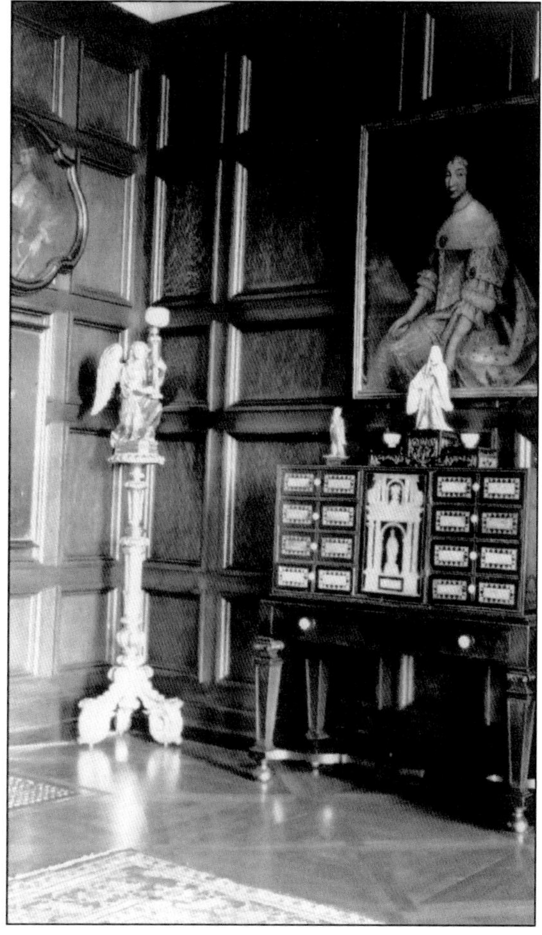

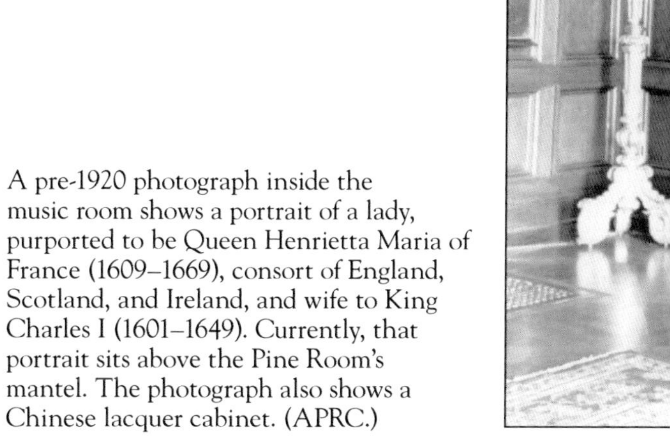

A pre-1920 photograph inside the music room shows a portrait of a lady, purported to be Queen Henrietta Maria of France (1609–1669), consort of England, Scotland, and Ireland, and wife to King Charles I (1601–1649). Currently, that portrait sits above the Pine Room's mantel. The photograph also shows a Chinese lacquer cabinet. (APRC.)

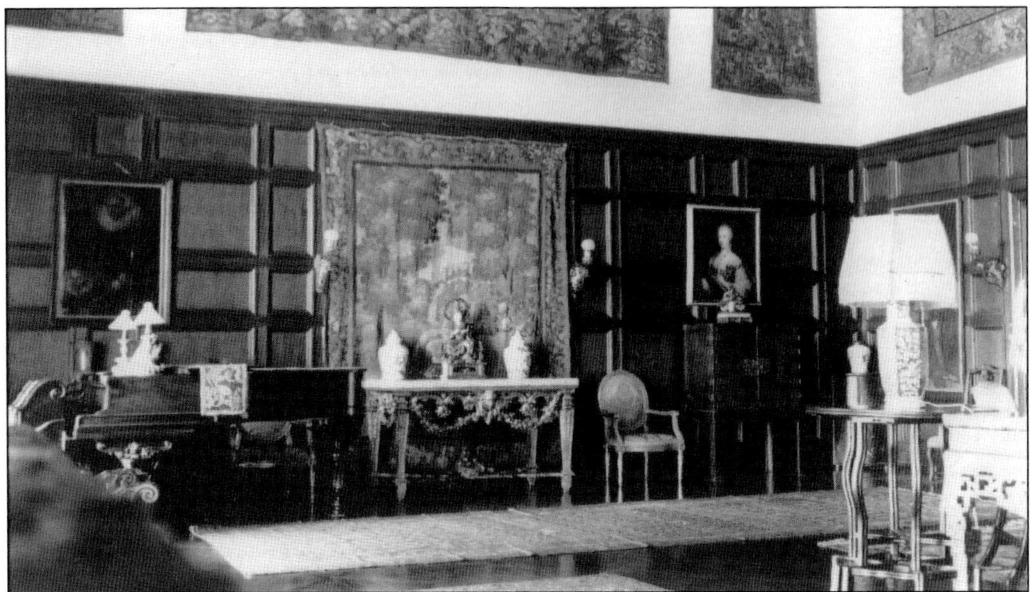

In April 1901, the local newspaper, the *Piatt County Republican*, reported that Allerton had received a new Steinway grand piano for his music room. Soon afterward, he encouraged his composer friends, such as Roger Quilter and others, to stay at the mansion for periods of time and create their music. (APRC.)

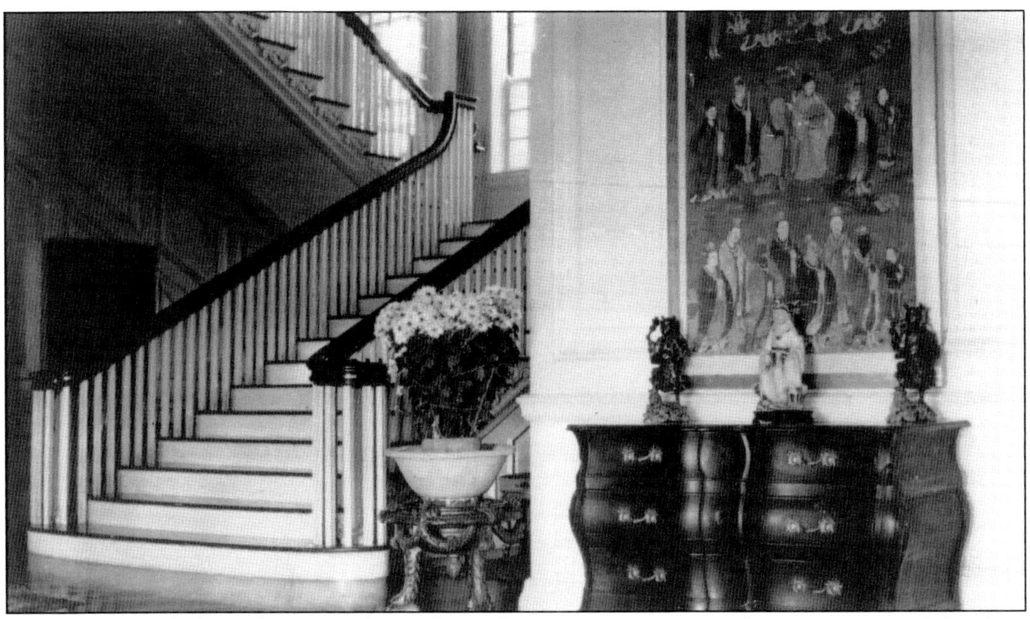

This photograph from the 1920s shows the mahogany stairway near the music room. A landing with French doors gives access to an iron balcony overlooking the back terrace. The placement of the stairway near the front door allowed Allerton and his guests to leave the upstairs bedrooms without disturbing people on the first floor. (APRC.)

Allerton placed a portrait of his father above the mantel in his office, now the Oak Room. The portrait was painted by his close friend, artist Ellen Emmet Rand. To the right of Samuel Allerton's portrait are paintings of Allerton ancestors, possibly by Ammi Phillips, an itinerant portrait painter, now much acclaimed. Robert later donated two of Phillips's paintings of his Allerton ancestors to the Chicago Art Institute. (APRC.)

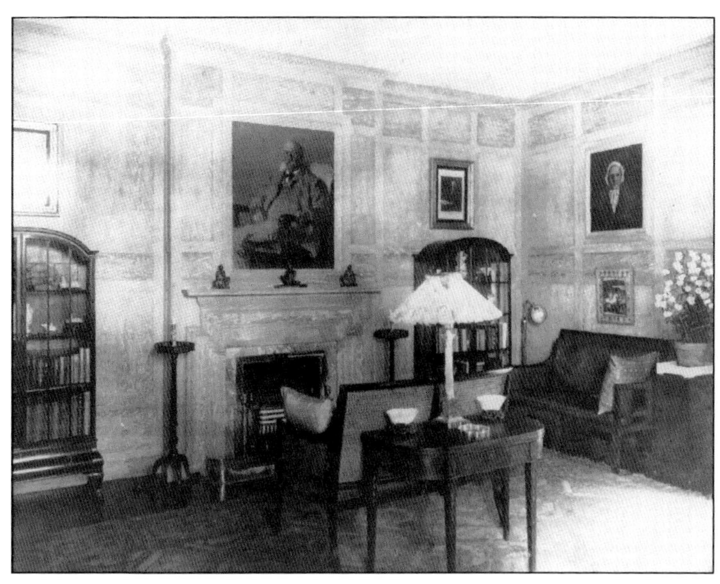

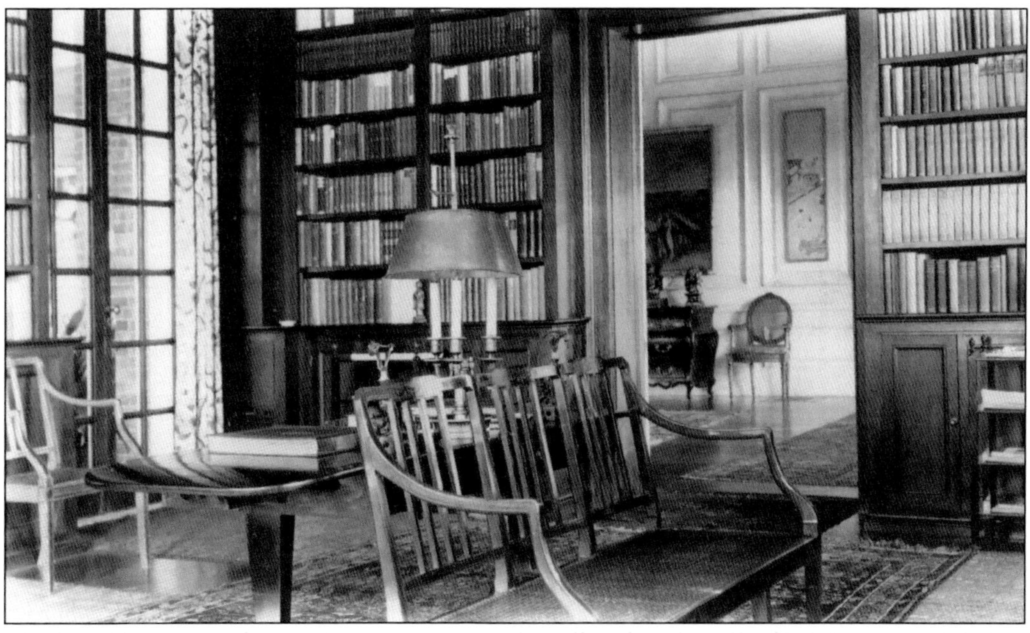

The front library, now the Pine Room, was across the gallery from his office/Oak Room. Bookshelves lined the walls. Eventually, Allerton added bookshelves in the music room, the marble hallway, and what became the current dining area. Allerton had never recovered his hearing from his youth and considered books to be family friends. In the 1940s, he had the room gutted and the shelves removed. (APRC.)

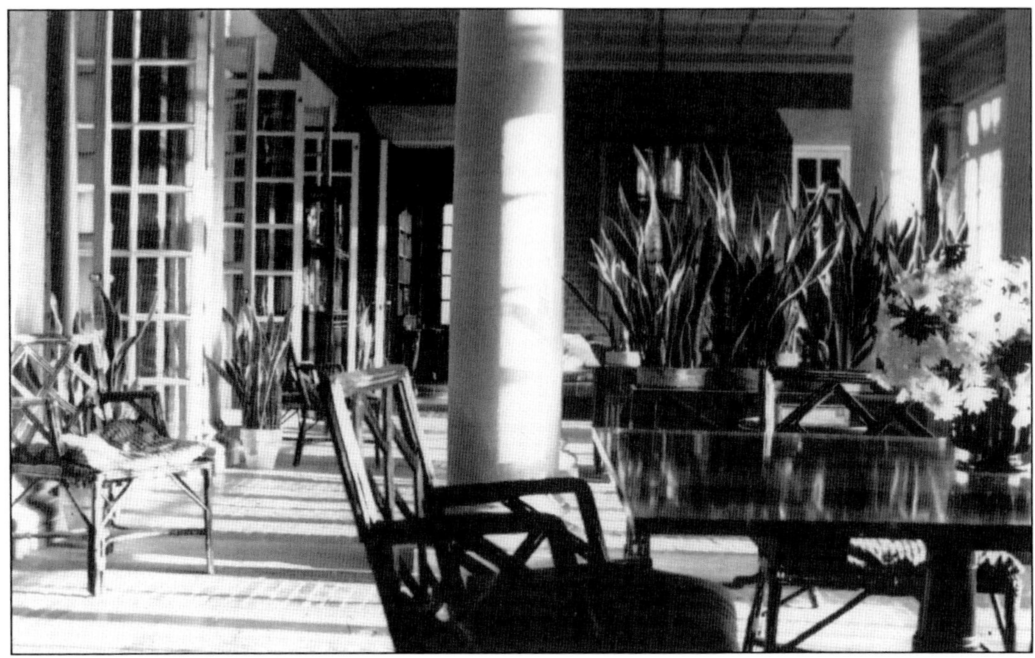

The conservatory was one of Allerton's favorite rooms. However, early on, the glass ceiling made the room unbearable in Illinois summers and winters, forcing him in 1919 to replace the glass with a paneled interior ceiling. The center columns were later removed by the University of Illinois to make it easier to use as a lecture room. (APRC.)

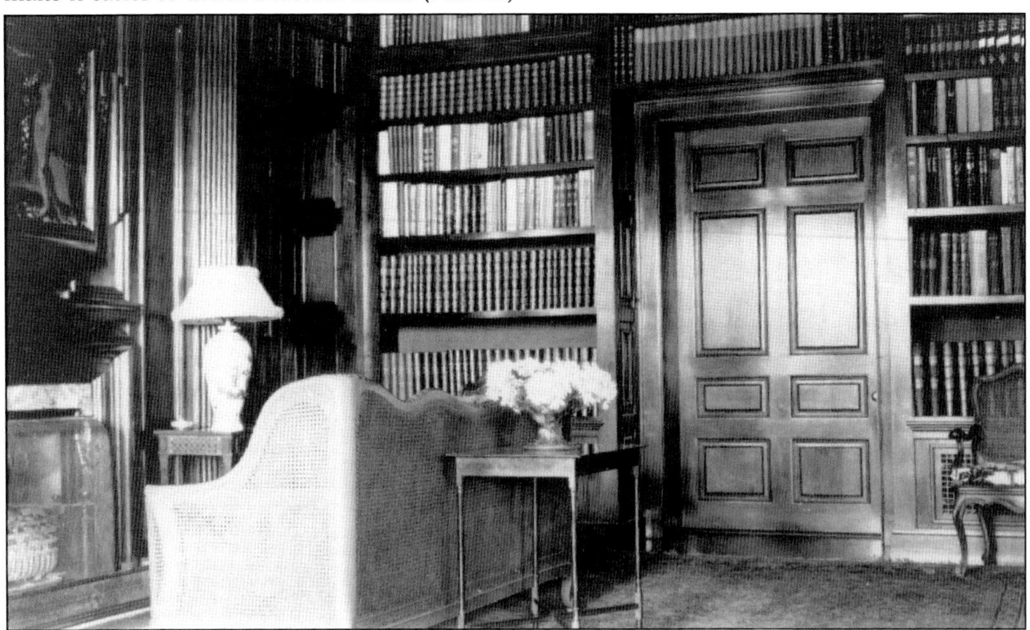

Borie's plan included a dining room near the servants' wing. In 1905, he sketched new plans with more paneling and shelves in the room Robert Allerton named the Butternut Room after the local wood used throughout. Artist Glyn Warren Philpot painted a scene directly onto the panel above the fireplace. Later, the panel painting was removed and taken to Allerton's Kauai estate. (APRC.)

This 1940 photograph of the Butternut Room shows a slight change in furniture. When dining there, Allerton could press a floor button to summon his butler. A rack capable of storing almost 300 bottles of wine and brandy stood in the cellar below. During Prohibition, Allerton moved his bottles to a crawl space under the music room, forgetting about them until years later. (APRC.)

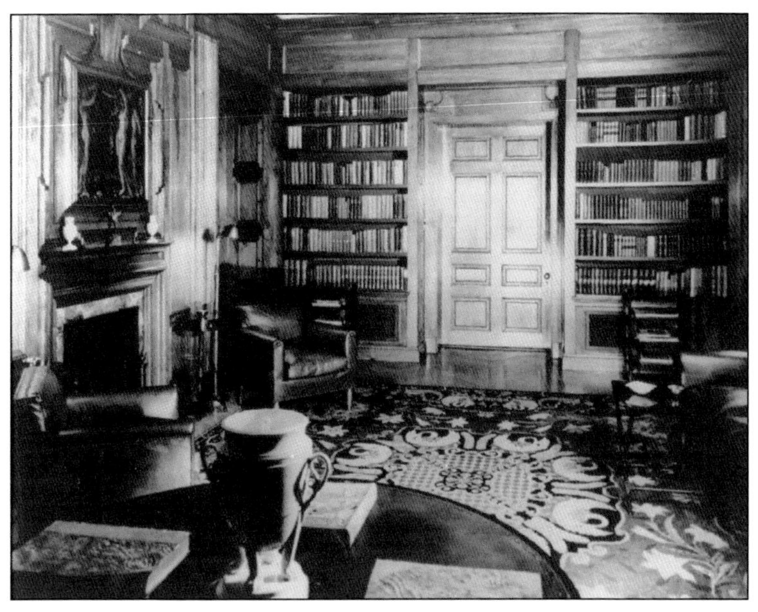

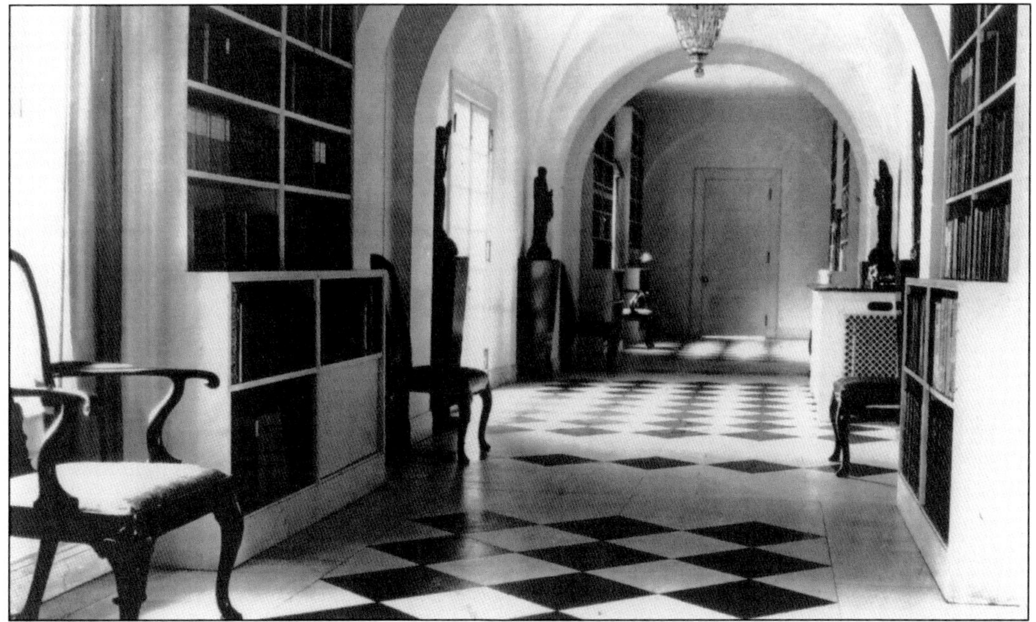

To avoid weather and dirt making its way into the gallery, Allerton commissioned Borie in 1916 to add the marble hallway between the house and the stable. The architect moved the courtyard door to a position midway down the new hallway. More bookcases line the walls in this view toward the door to the stables. (APRC.)

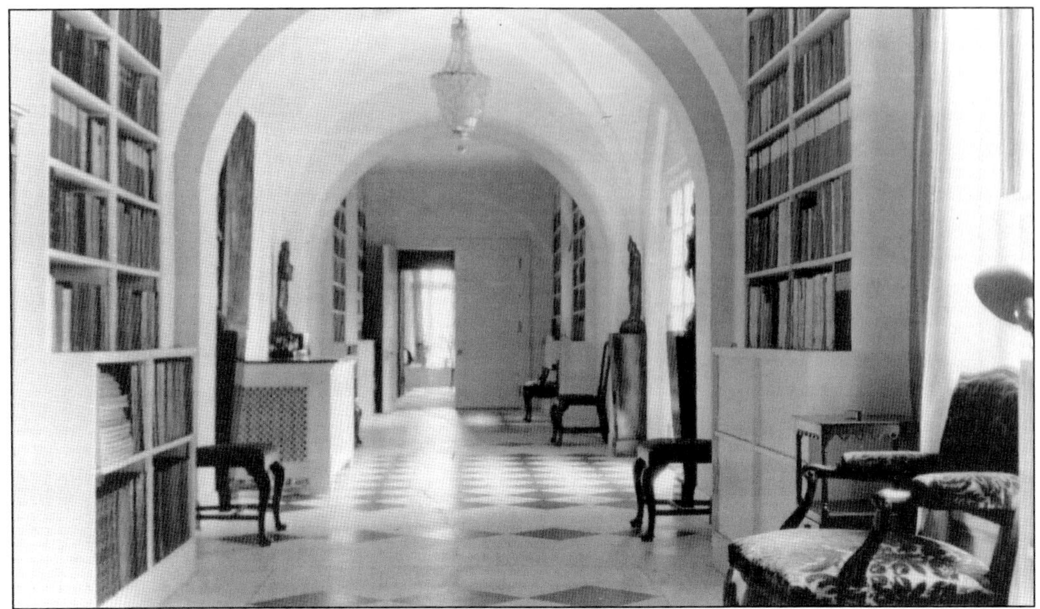

The new hallway leads toward doors where the current reception desk is now. Allerton kept part of his porcelain collection from his world travels in the room beyond the doors. Although it was called the breakfast room, Allerton ate breakfast in his own bedroom, as he preferred to use the breakfast room as a winter dining room or for informal meals. It is now an office. (APRC.)

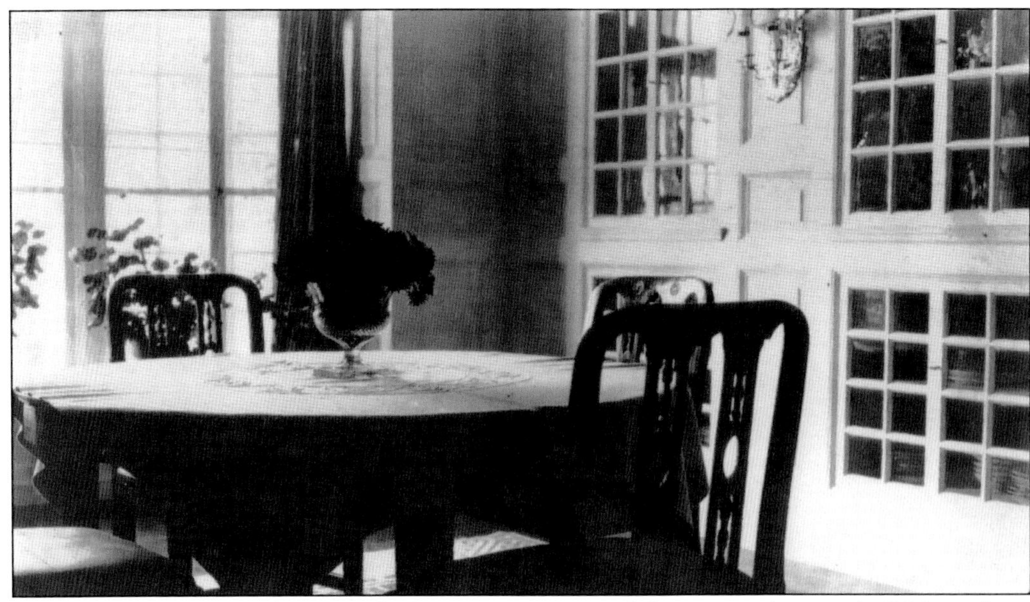

The breakfast room was between the Butternut Room and the servants' wing. A 1904 article in *House Beautiful* about Allerton's mansion mentioned the floor-to-ceiling paneling of white woodwork and built-in china cupboards lining one side of the room. During the room's 1937 remodeling, the fireplace was removed, a closet added, and the room was painted Wedgwood blue. (APRC.)

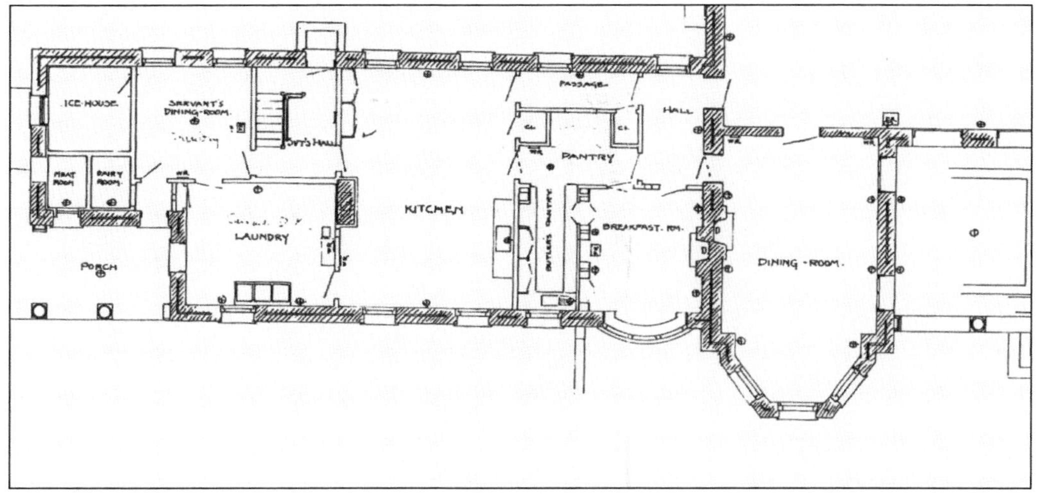


Allerton occasionally commissioned architect Joseph Corson Llewellyn for additional building projects. This excerpt is from Llewellyn's "Plan of Heating System" from August 18, 1916, showing the servants' wing past the dining room, now the Butternut Room. It includes a pantry, the kitchen, the servants' dining room, and a milk room. (UI.)

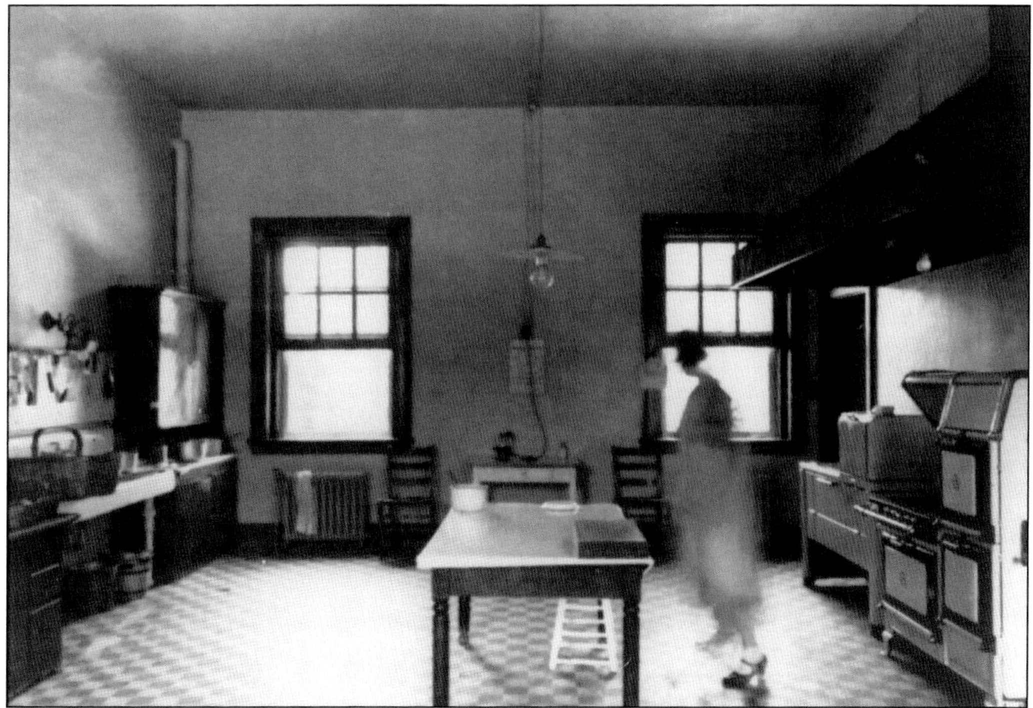

In this photograph of the mansion's 1920 kitchen, a woman moves across the room. It might be Florence Fry, who came from England to be the cook. Other English staff included butler Thomas Gollop, his sister laundress Emily Gollop, his other sister Edith Cackett, and her husband, Arthur Cackett, who became housekeeper and assistant butler. Edith's nephew Edward Page joined the staff as the houseboy. (APRC.)

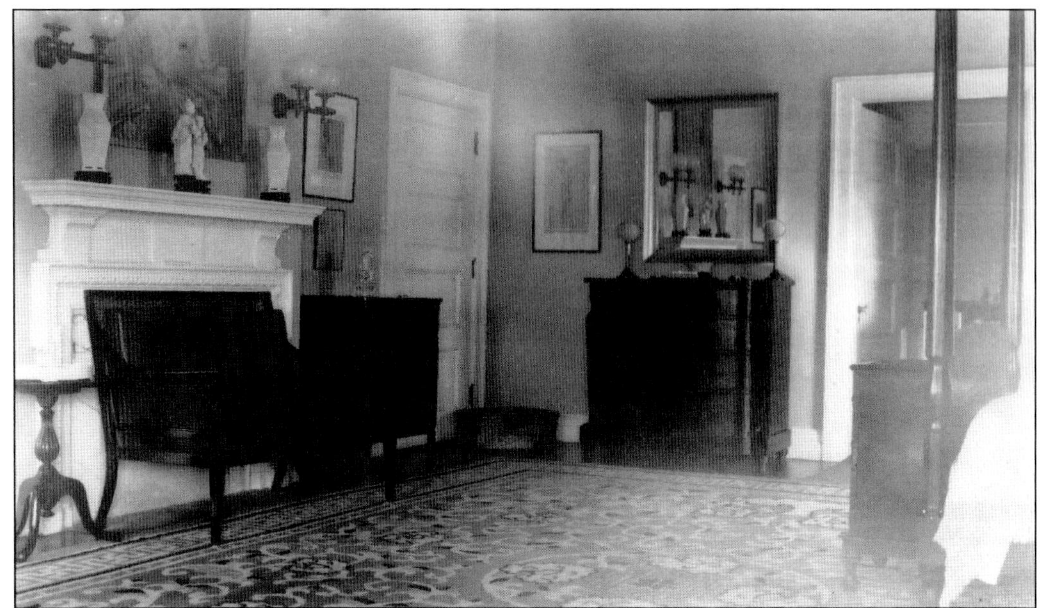

Several upstairs bedrooms were available for family and friends. Three rooms faced the pond and meadow, with one bedroom facing the back of the house. Across from the stairs lay the Blue Bedroom with private bathroom, where Allerton's parents always stayed. Anna Rathbone, Allerton's godmother and a friend to his mother and stepmother, appears in the painting hanging above the mantel. (APRC.)

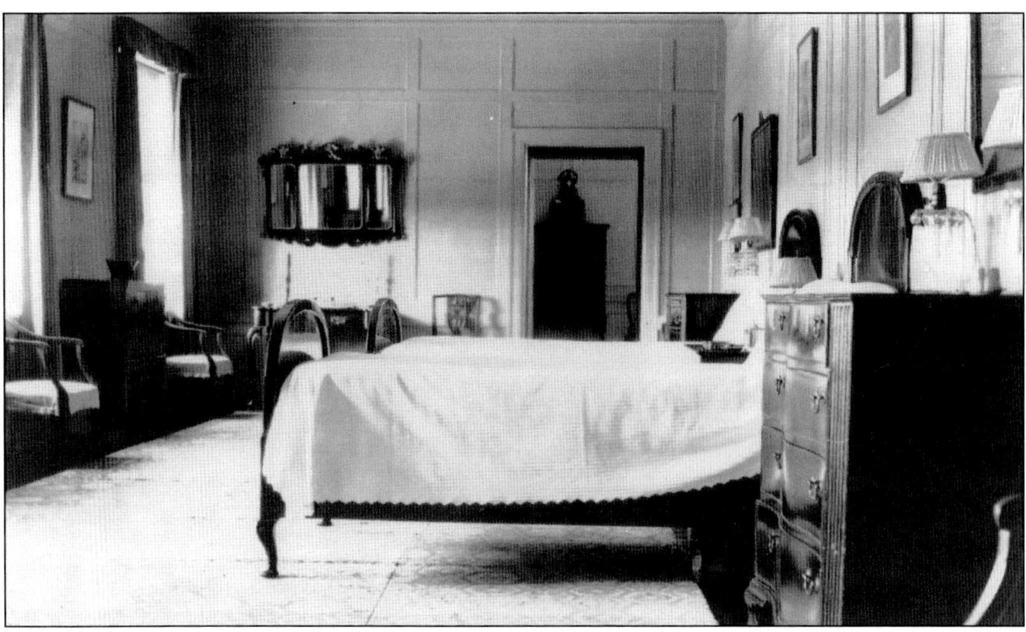

Initially, two guest bedrooms that faced each other above the conservatory were reached via the long upstairs hallway and a small foyer. But guests with children found it preferable to be in the same room with their offspring. In 1916, Allerton hired architect Joseph Corson Llewellyn to connect the two rooms into one large room, as seen in this photograph, with a private bathroom. (APRC.)

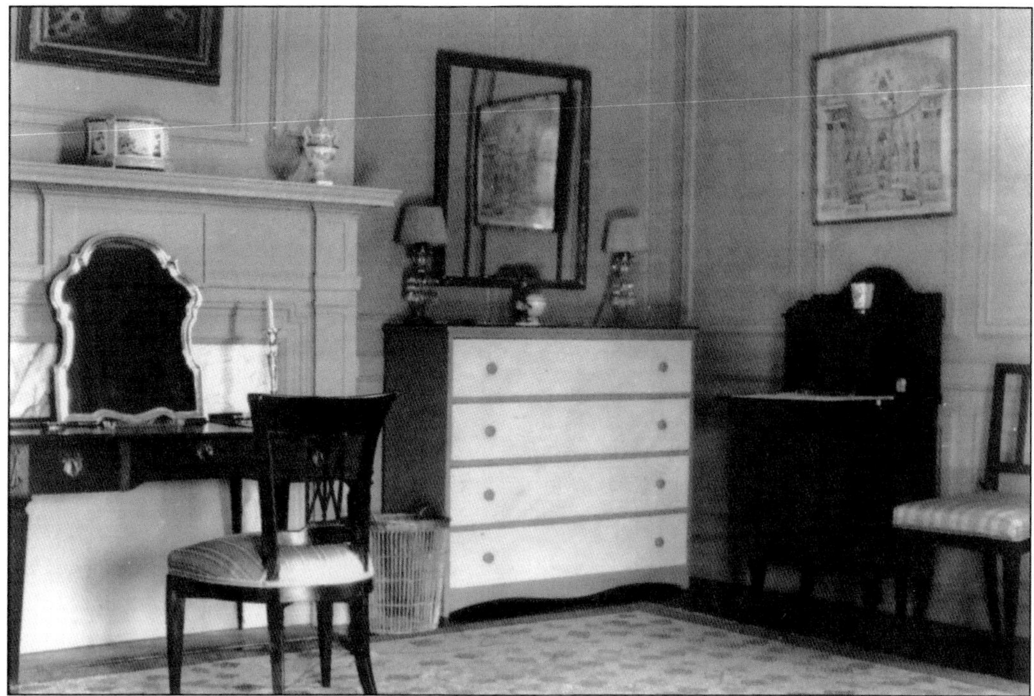

The southeast guest bedroom sits above the office and overlooks the music room terrace. Although smaller than the other bedrooms, it was painted a light cream color to make it seem larger. John Borie revised the fireplace, along with paneling and molding, in 1905. In the 1920s, this became the room for the man Allerton called his adopted son, John Gregg. (APRC.)

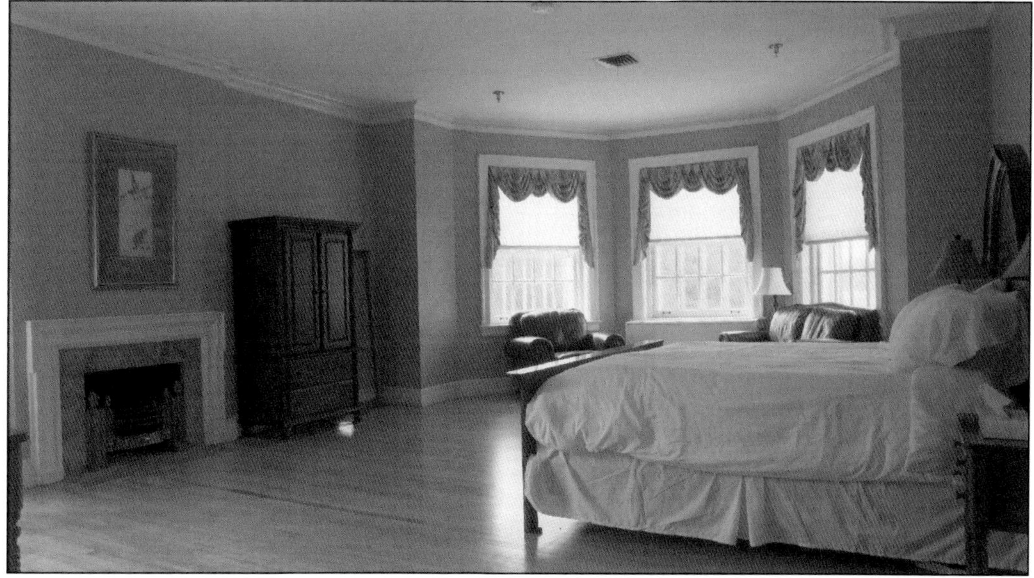

From his bedroom windows, Allerton enjoyed three possible views of his estate: toward the Sangamon River, across the pond to the meadow, or past the house toward the brick wall garden. A chest of drawers built into the passageway to his private bathroom is original, as are the German silver bathroom fixtures. In June 1901, a severe storm blew out Allerton's bedroom windows and those of the library below. (MH.)

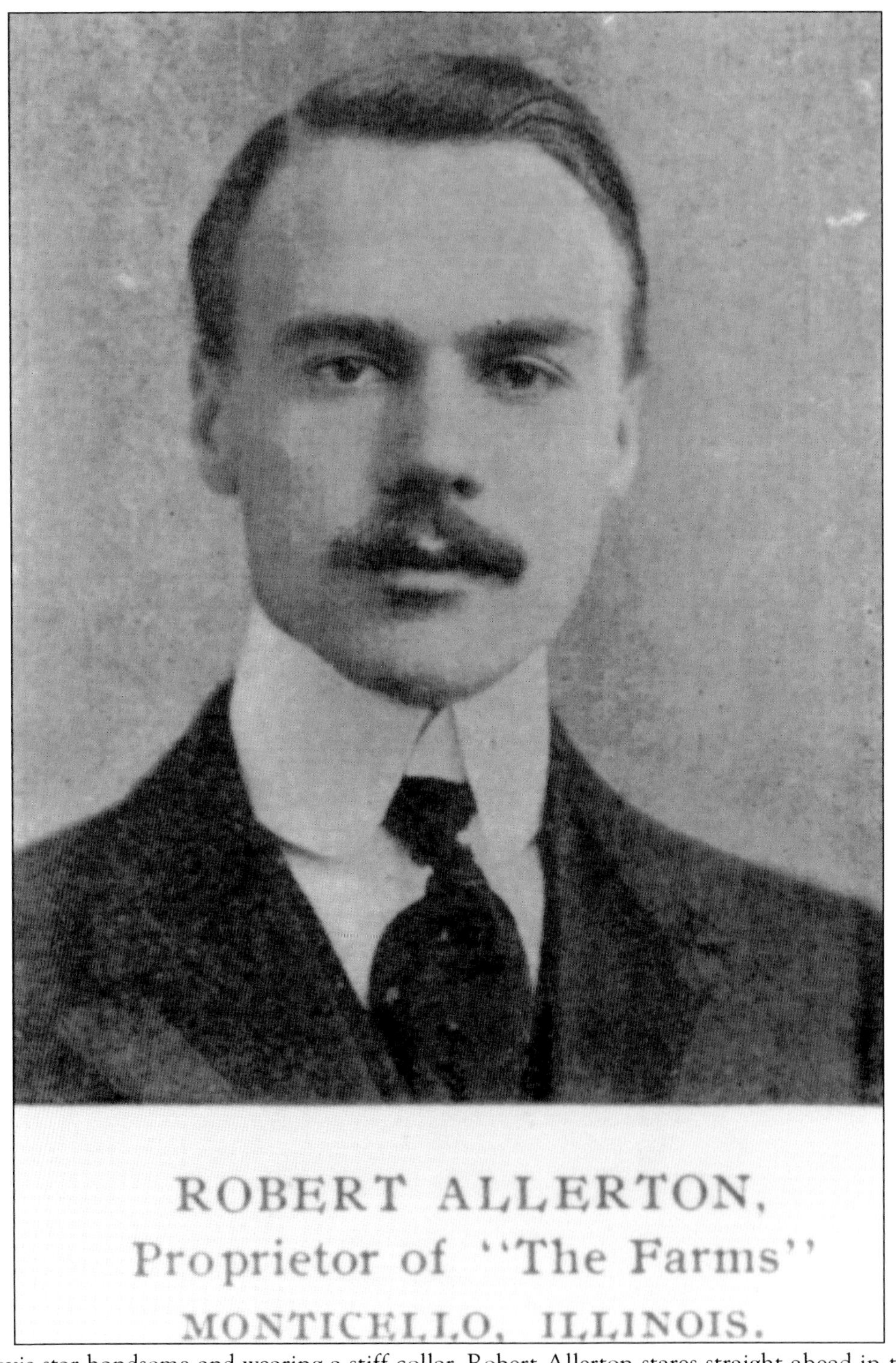


Movie-star handsome and wearing a stiff collar, Robert Allerton stares straight ahead in this photograph. He is listed as the proprietor of the land that the Allerton family referred to as the Farms. In time, the Piatt County property grew to over 12,000 acres, worked by a number of tenant farmers. (APRC.)

# *Three*

# Relationships 1901–1921

As the mansion neared completion, Robert Allerton's focus turned to his personal life. Through friends made in Paris, he met a young artist named Ellen Emmet. Soon they were corresponding, and in 1901, Allerton asked her to come to Lake Geneva to paint his father's portrait. Afterward, she visited him at the Farms to paint his portrait as well, for which she was paid $500. During that year, he wrote to her several times each month. In one letter, he wrote, "I keep thinking of you so much. I have to. I wonder what you are up to. . . . How I wish I was with you." But Emmet ended up marrying another man, no matter how attracted she may have been to Allerton.

His family's Chicago ties stayed part of Allerton's life; thus, the *Chicago Tribune's* top society reporter continued to monitor the Allertons. "Madame X" peppered articles with comments about his home, property, good looks, summer parties, and visitors. His many guestbooks were filled with signatures, photographs, sketches, and poems.

Allerton once entertained his staff and guests with a performance by famed flamenco dancer La Estrellita (Stella Hurtig from Cincinnati). He encouraged his artist, writer, and musician friends to stay with him as long as they wished and use his mansion as a studio. One English painter, Glyn Warren Philpot, visited twice—in 1913 and 1921. It was during his 1913 visit that Philpot wrote his sister about his infatuation for Allerton, apparently unfulfilled.

Allerton followed his parents' philanthropic bent. Early on, as a treat for the local residents, Samuel Allerton had planted 5,000 fruit trees along what today is Allerton Road. Additionally, he organized donations for a Chicago area boy's school and helped fund Monticello's library. Robert's own largesse included funds toward Monticello's new courthouse, St. Philomena Church, Forest Preserve Park, Monticello Community House, Willow Branch Township library, the Red Cross, a French hospital during World War I, the profits from his crops for 1917, and acreage for an old people's home and sanitarium. Later, his attention turned to museums.

Ellen Gertrude Emmet was an artist whom Allerton met around 1900, soon after she returned from studies in Paris under Frederick MacMonnies. Emmet wrote her sister about attending an opera with friends, including Borie and the very deaf son of a rich Chicago pork packer. She mentioned his nice expression and that he was "very well made" and "extremely nice . . . you would find him attractive just as I do." (RR.)

Ellen Emmet sits on horseback in Monticello in 1902 while men work on Allerton's mansion roof. An acclaimed portrait artist and illustrator, Emmet painted over 500 works, including two portraits of Pres. Franklin D. Roosevelt. Upon her return from Europe, she set up a studio in New York City's Washington Square. Occasionally, Eleanor Roosevelt dropped in to visit. (APRC.)

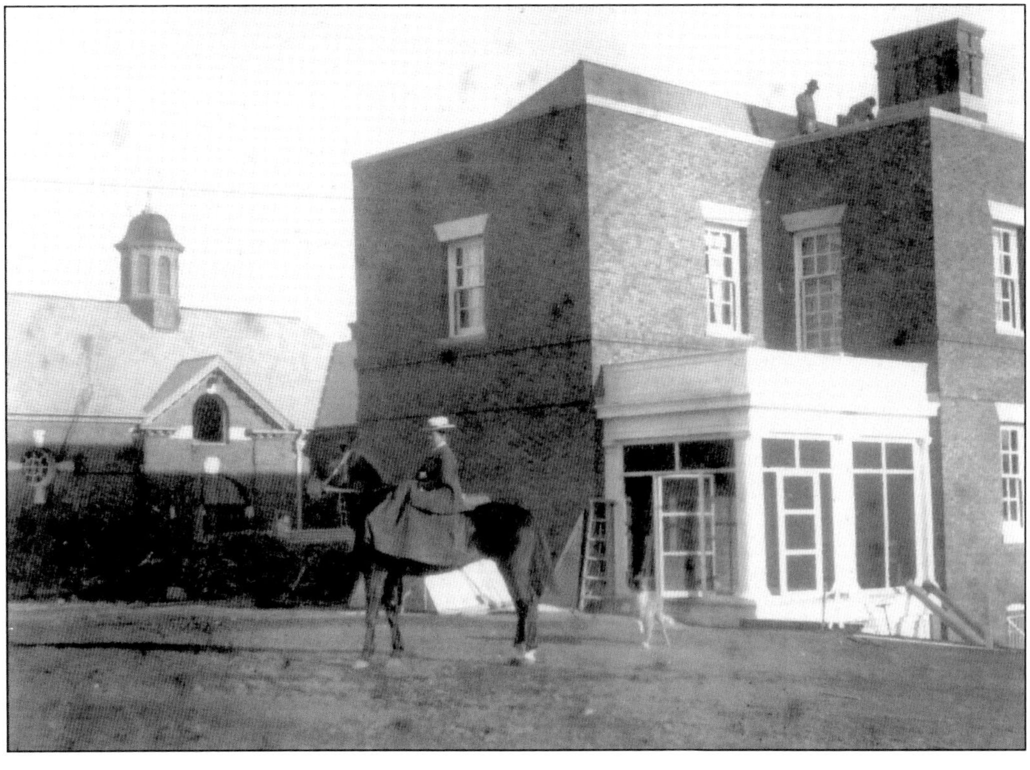

While in Lake Geneva in 1901, Ellen Emmet painted Samuel Allerton's portrait, now hanging above the mansion's gallery fireplace. Her work garnered praise from artists such as John Singer Sargent and Frederick MacMonnies. Letters later flew between her sisters and Henry James, her mother's cousin, discussing whether she would marry Robert Allerton. (MH.)

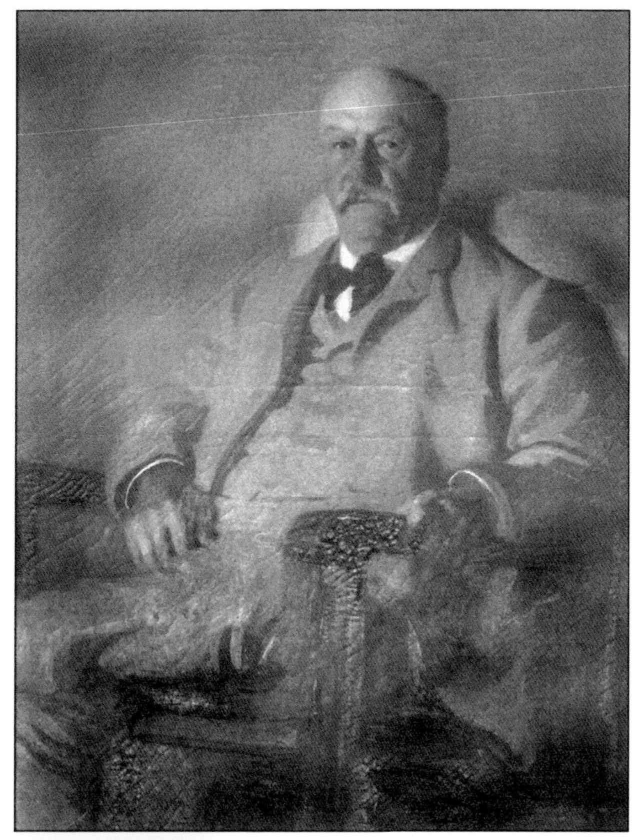

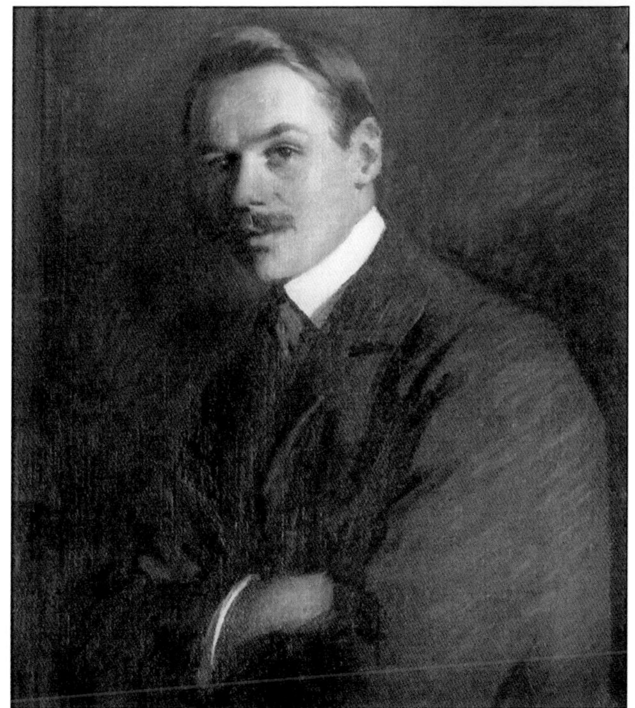

Robert Allerton's portrait, painted by Ellen Emmet, now hangs in the Butternut Room. He visited her in July 1901 in New York while she painted a portrait of Borie's sister (Emily Ryerson, later a *Titanic* survivor). Allerton wrote often, wishing "you were here or I where you are," sending her his love, apparently jealous whenever Borie was in New York, because "you never write when he is there." (MH.)

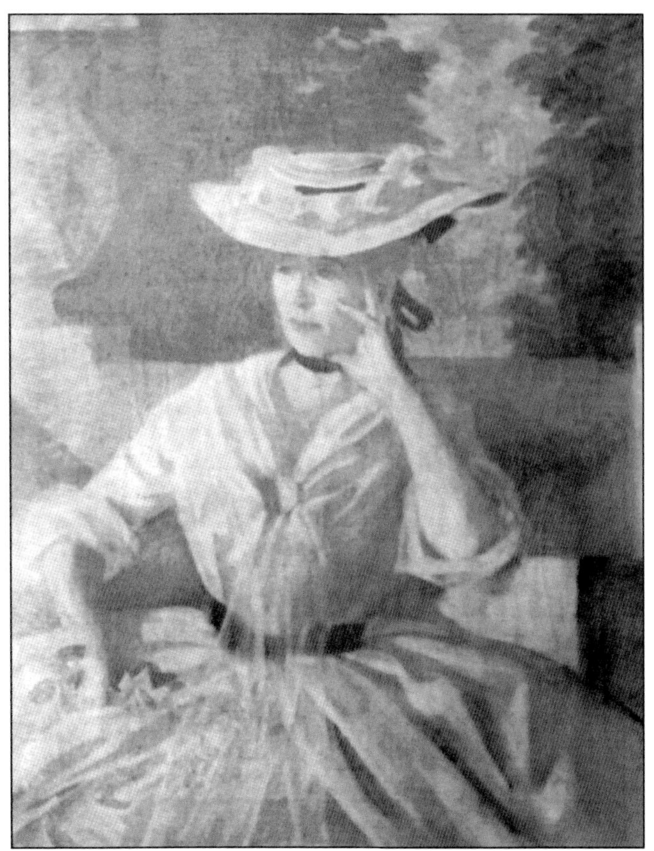

Ellen Emmet also painted a portrait of Anna Rathbone, Robert Allerton's godmother and best friend to his mother and stepmother. With the portrait's pose and hat, Rathbone bears a striking resemblance to Emmet's undated portrait of fellow artist Mary Foote, which can be seen at the Ellen Emmet Gallery at the University of Connecticut's William Benton Museum of Art. The Rathbone painting currently hangs in the Oak Room. (APRC.)

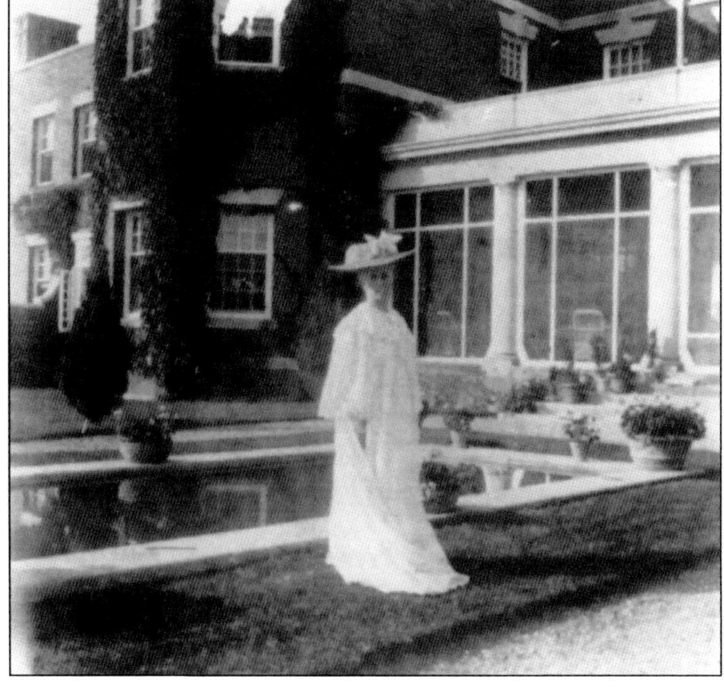

After Allerton was born, his godmother Anna Rathbone carried him up the church aisle for his baptism because his mother was too ill to attend. This 1910 photograph shows Rathbone on the conservatory terrace next to Allerton's pool, one of the few in Illinois at that time. *Chicago Tribune* society columnists, in writing about his summer parties, mentioned his pool. (APRC.)

THE FARMS
MONTICELLO, PIATT COUNTY
ILLINOIS

In June 1901, Allerton wrote to Ellen Emmet, excited to describe the previous night's thunderstorm: "That the Farms is standing to day is a miracle . . . the kitchen wing was struck by lightning, tearing the roof all to pieces . . . with great balls of fire rolling across the front of the house. . . . Such a blowing of wind and then a solid wall of water and hail. Really a magnificent sight." (AO.)

In an August 1901 letter, Allerton wrote to Emmet, "What I would not give to start off for a ride this afternoon with you. . . . I sort of expect Aunt Lois and Dad for Sunday but they are very indefinite. I hate to have any woman here after you. You make them all seem such small potatoes. Worlds of love, yours affectionately, Robert." (AO.)

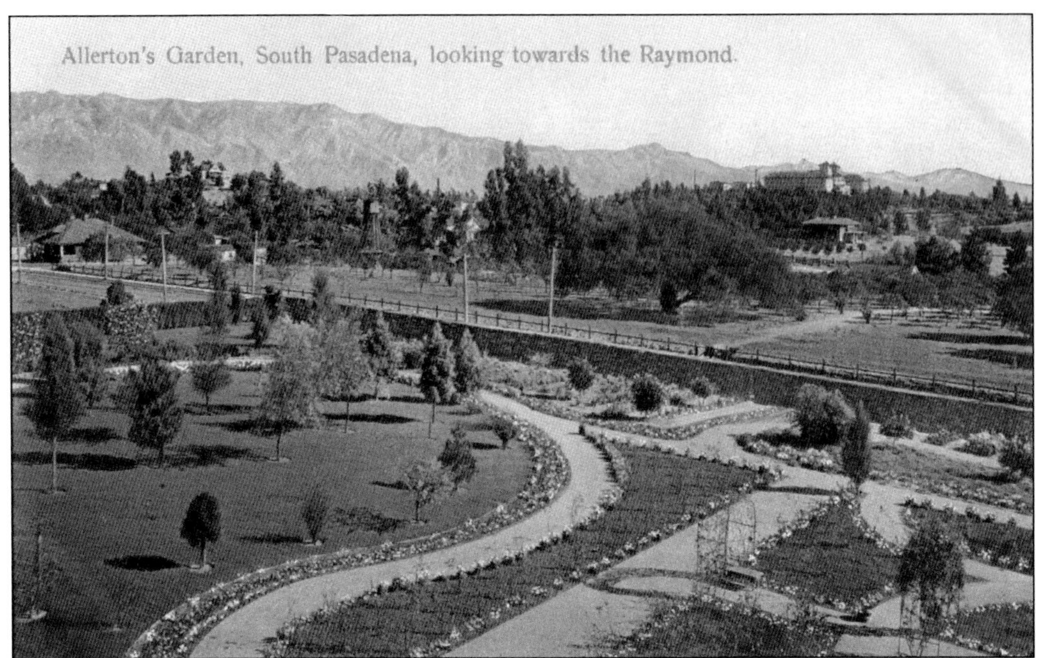


This 1910 postcard shows gardens filling the California property Samuel Allerton purchased in Pasadena around 1903 that may have guided Robert while creating his own gardens in Monticello. Robert's sister Kate Johnstone; her husband, Hugo; and two sons, Allerton and Vanderburgh Johnstone, also lived near her father and stepmother in Pasadena. (AO.)

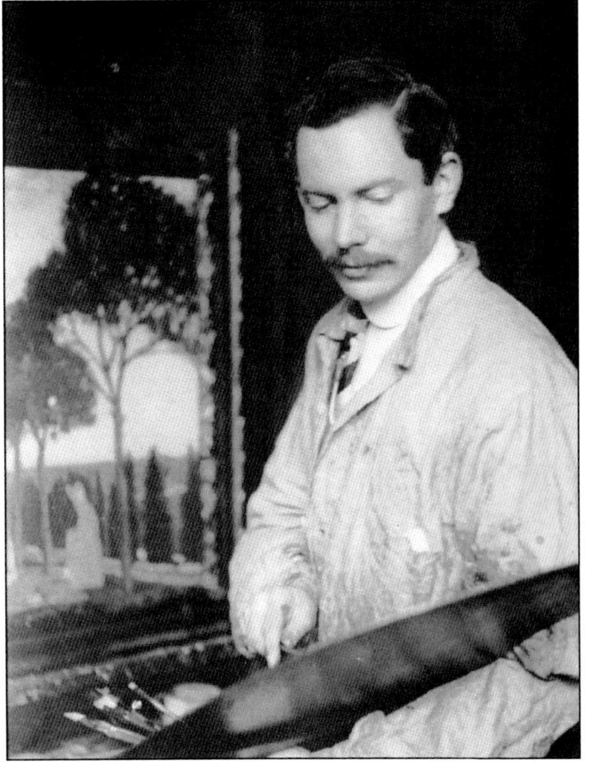

By the time of this 1906 photograph, Allerton's best friend, 33-year-old Frederic Clay Bartlett, had an art studio in Chicago's Fine Arts Building on Michigan Avenue. He helped create a mural for the city's Second Presbyterian Church, as well as a stained-glass frieze on the campus of the University of Chicago, and paintings covering 50 ceiling panels at the University Club. (APRC.)

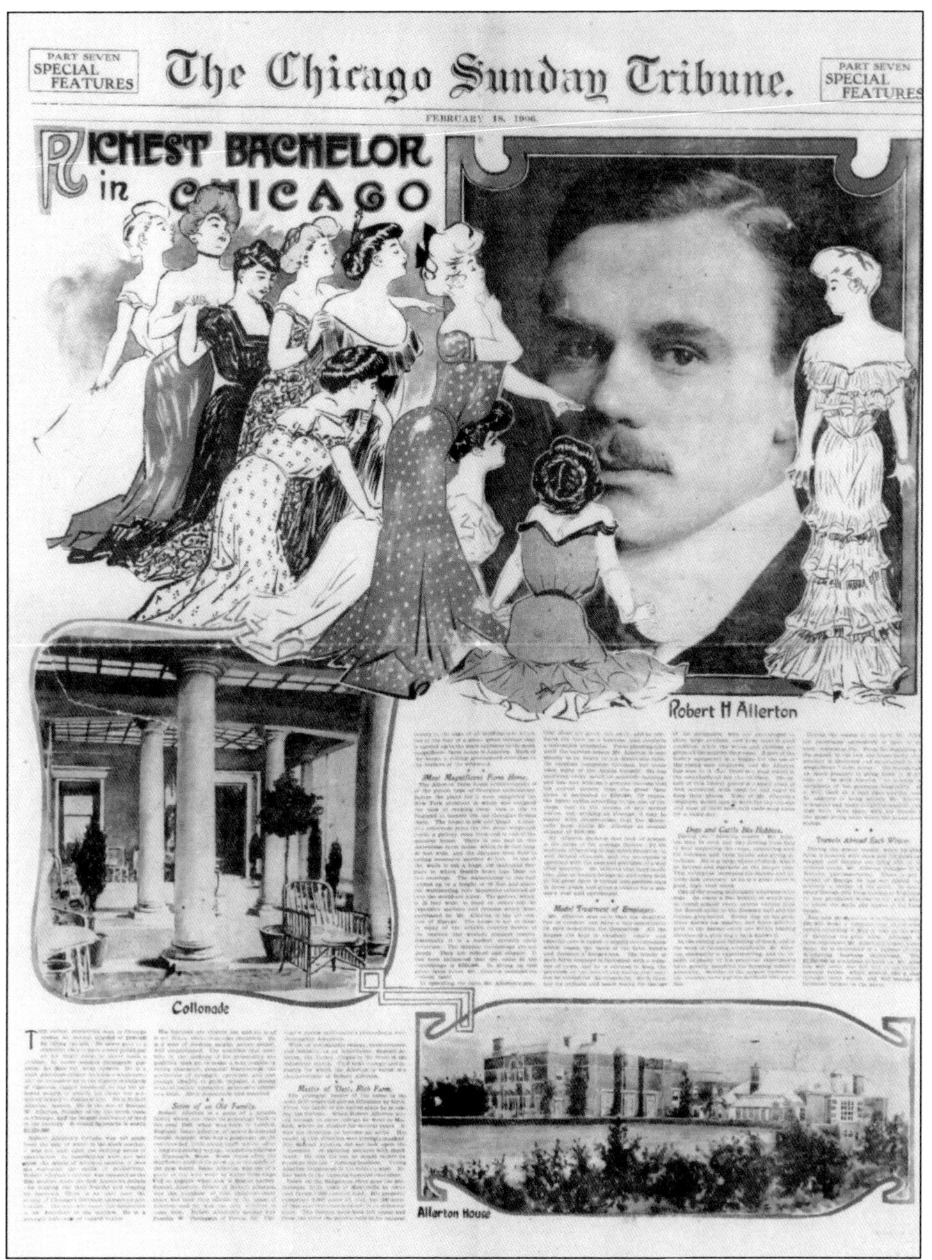

PART SEVEN SPECIAL FEATURES

The Chicago Sunday Tribune.

PART SEVEN SPECIAL FEATURES

FEBRUARY 18, 1906

RICHEST BACHELOR in CHICAGO

Robert H Allerton

Collonade

Allerton House

A *Chicago Sunday Tribune* article on February 18, 1906, gushed over Allerton, noting, "The richest unmarried man in Chicago makes an annual stipend of $100,000. . . . He measures up to the highest standards of rigorous, rugged manhood. . . . His features are cleanly cut and his head is set firmly above muscular shoulders. He is a man of medium height, active, robust, well proportioned . . . the gentleness of strength, optimism, and just enough ideality to guide impulse, a strong sense of justice, humanity, generosity almost to a fault." The article noted his "Most Magnificent Farm Home," his "nucleus to build on" of $2,250,000, that he traveled abroad every winter, and referred to his future inheritance of over 70 farms across three states. Throughout the article, the society columnist reiterated Allerton's annual income of $100,000. Clearly, the writer was doing his or her best to help Samuel Allerton find a wife for his son. (UI/CT.)

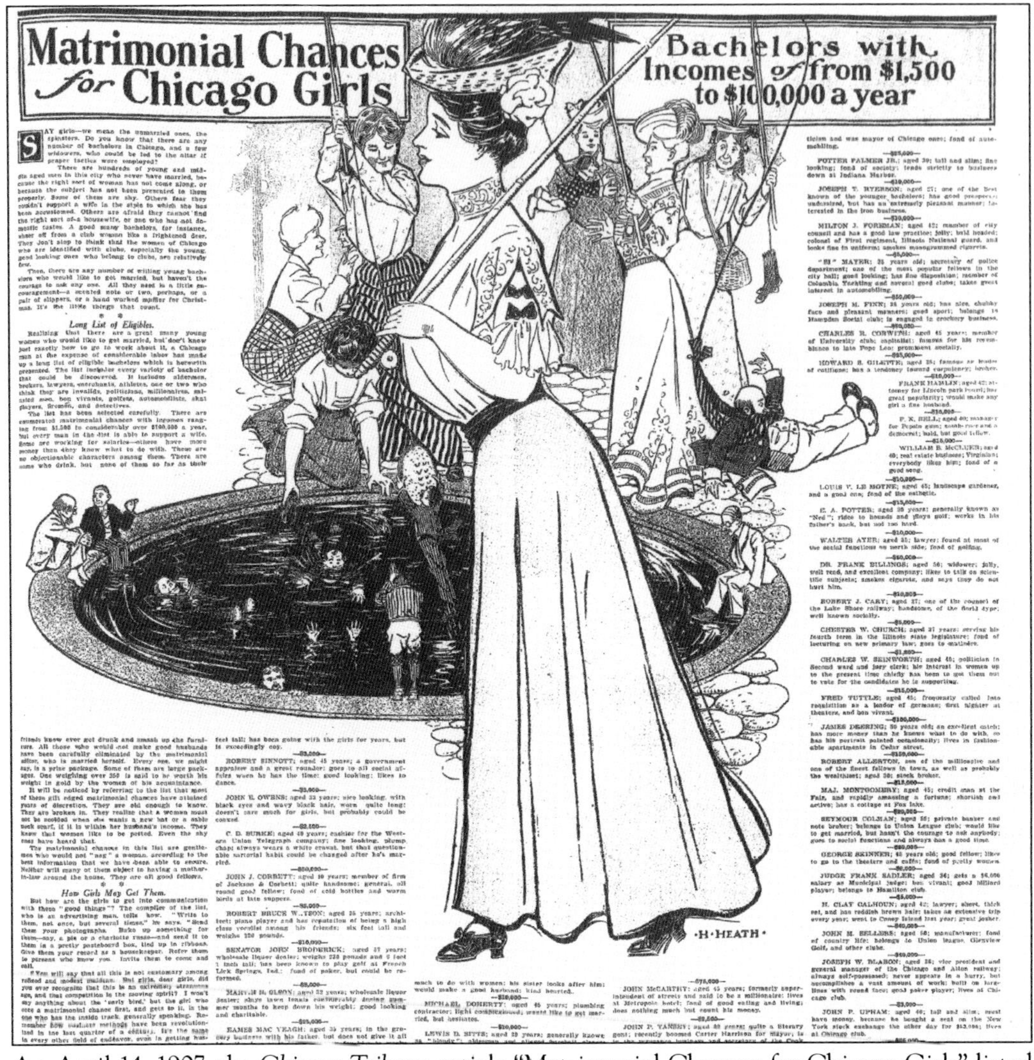

# Matrimonial Chances for Chicago Girls

## Bachelors with Incomes of from $1,500 to $100,000 a year

SAY girls—we mean the unmarried ones, the spinsters. Do you know that there are any number of bachelors in Chicago, and a few widowers, who could be led to the altar if proper tactics were employed?

There are hundreds of young and middle aged men in this city who never have married, because the right sort of woman has not come along, or because the subject has not been presented to them properly. Some of them are shy. Others fear they couldn't support a wife in the style to which she has been accustomed. Others are afraid they cannot find the right sort of a housewife, or one who has not domestic tastes. A good many bachelors, for instance, sheer off from a club woman like a frightened deer. They don't stop to think that the women of Chicago who are identified with clubs, especially the young, good looking ones who belong to clubs, are relatively few.

Then, there are any number of willing young bachelors who would like to get married, but haven't the courage to ask any one. All they need is a little encouragement—a scented note or two, perhaps, or a pair of slippers, or a hand worked muffler for Christmas. It's the little things that count.

*Long List of Eligibles.*

Realizing that there are a great many young women who would like to get married, but don't know just exactly how to go to work about it, a Chicago man at the expense of considerable labor has made up a long list of eligible bachelors which is herewith presented. The list includes every variety of bachelor that could be discovered. It includes aldermen, brokers, lawyers, merchants, athletes, one or two who think they are invalids, politicians, millionaires, salaried men, bon vivants, golfers, automobilists, skat players, firemen, and detectives.

The list has been selected carefully. There are enumerated matrimonial chances with incomes ranging from $1,500 to considerably over $100,000 a year, but every man in the list is able to support a wife. Some are working for salaries—others have more money than they know what to do with. There are no objectionable characters among them. There are some who drink, but none of them so far as their friends know ever got drunk and smash up the furniture. All those who would not make good husbands have been carefully eliminated by the matrimonial editor, who is married herself. Every one, we might say, is a prize package. Some of them are large packages. One weighing over 250 is said to be worth his weight in gold by the women of his acquaintance.

It will be noticed by referring to the list that most of these gilt edged matrimonial chances have attained years of discretion. They are old enough to know. They are broken in. They realize that a woman must not be scolded when she wants a new hat or a sable neck scarf, if it is within her husband's income. They know that women like to be petted. Even the shy ones have heard that.

The matrimonial chances in this list are gentlemen who would not "nag" a woman, according to the best information that we have been able to secure. Neither will many of them object to having a mother-in-law around the house. They are all good fellows.

*How Girls May Get Them.*

But how are the girls to get into communication with these "good things"? The compiler of the list, who is an advertising man, tells how. "Write to them, not once, but several times," he says. "Send them your photographs. Bake up something for them—say, a pie or a charlotte russe—and send it to them in a pretty pasteboard box, tied up in ribbons. Give them your record as a housekeeper. Refer them to persons who know you. Invite them to come and call.

"You will say that all this is not customary among refined and modest maidens. But girls, dear girls, did you ever recognize that this is an extremely strenuous age, and that competition is the moving spirit? I won't say anything about the 'early bird,' but the girl who sees a matrimonial chance first, and gets to it, is the one who has the inside track, generally speaking. Remember how business methods have been revolutionized in the last quarter of a century. It's the same in every other field of endeavor, even in getting hus-

feet tall; has been going with the girls for years, but is exceedingly coy.

—$3,000—

ROBERT SINNOTT; aged 45 years; a government appraiser and a great rounder; goes to all social affairs when he has the time; good looking; likes to dance.

—$5,000—

JOHN H. OWENS; aged 33 years; nice looking, with black eyes and wavy black hair, worn quite long; doesn't care much for girls, but probably could be coaxed.

—$2,500—

C. D. BURKE; aged 40 years; cashier for the Western Union Telegraph company; fine looking, plump chap; always wears a white cravat, but that questionable sartorial habit could be changed after he's married.

—$50,000—

JOHN J. CORBETT; aged 40 years; member of firm of Jackson & Corbett; quite handsome; general, all round good fellow; fond of cold bottles and warm birds at late suppers.

—$5,000—

ROBERT BRUCE W..TSON; aged 35 years; architect; piano player and has reputation of being a high class vocalist among his friends; six feet tall and weighs 120 pounds.

—$10,000—

SENATOR JOHN BRODERICK; aged 47 years; wholesale liquor dealer; weighs 220 pounds and 6 feet 1 inch tall; has been known to play golf at French Lick Springs, Ind.; fond of poker, but could be reformed.

—$8,000—

MARTIN H. OLSON; aged 32 years; wholesale liquor dealer; plays lawn tennis continually during summer months to keep down his weight; good looking and charitable.

—$25,000—

EAMES MAC VEAGH; aged 35 years; in the grocery business with his father, but does not give it all

much to do with women; his sister looks after him; would make a good husband; kind hearted.

—$18,000—

MICHAEL DOHERTY; aged 45 years; plumbing contractor; light complexioned; wants to get married, but hesitates.

—$10,000—

LEWIS D. SITTS; aged 33 years; generally known as "bloody"; alderman

—$75,000—

JOHN McCARTHY; aged 45 years; formerly superintendent of streets and said to be a millionaire; lives at Metropole hotel; fond of good eating and living; does nothing much but count his money.

—$3,000—

JOHN P. TANSEY; aged 38 years; quite a literary gent; recently boomed Carter Harrison for mayor; is

ticism and was mayor of Chicago once; fond of automobiling.

—$25,000—

POTTER PALMER JR.; aged 30; tall and slim; fine looking; fond of society; tends strictly to business down at Indiana Harbor.

—$10,000—

JOSEPH T. RYERSON; aged 27; one of the best known of the younger bachelors; has good prospects; undersized, but has an extremely pleasant manner; interested in the iron business.

—$10,000—

MILTON J. FOREMAN; aged 42; member of city council and has a good law practice; jolly; bald headed; colonel of First regiment, Illinois National guard, and looks fine in uniform; smokes monogrammed cigarets.

—$5,000—

"BI" MAYER; 35 years old; secretary of police department; one of the most popular fellows in the city hall; good looking; has fine disposition; member of Columbia Yachting and several good clubs; takes great interest in automobiling.

—$50,000—

JOSEPH M. FINN; 35 years old; has nice, chubby face and pleasant manners; good sport; belongs to Hampden Social club; is engaged in crockery business.

—$60,000—

CHARLES R. CORWITH; aged 45 years; member of University club; capitalist; famous for his resemblance to late Pope Leo; prominent socially.

—$25,000—

HOWARD S. GILLETT; aged 35; famous as leader of cotillions; has a tendency toward corpulency; broker.

—$25,000—

FRANK HAMLIN; aged 42; attorney for Lincoln park board; has great popularity; would make any girl a fine husband.

—$20,000—

P. K. BELL; aged 40; manager for People gas; democrat; bald, but good fellow.

—$10,000—

WILLIAM B. McCLUER; aged 40; real estate business; Virginian; everybody likes him; fond of a good song.

LOUIS V. LE MOYNE; aged 45; landscape gardener, and a good one; fond of the esthetic.

—$15,000—

E. A. POTTER; aged 38 years; generally known as "Ned"; rides to hounds and plays golf; works in his father's bank, but not too hard.

—$10,000—

WALTER AYER; aged 35; lawyer; found at most of the social functions on north side; fond of golfing.

—$40,000—

DR. FRANK BILLINGS; aged 56; widower; jolly, well read, and excellent company; likes to talk on scientific subjects; smokes cigarets, and says they do not hurt him.

—$10,000—

ROBERT J. CARY; aged 37; one of the counsel of the Lake Shore railway; handsome, of the Gorld type; well known socially.

—$5,000—

CHESTER W. CHURCH; aged 37 years; serving his fourth term in the Illinois state legislature; fond of lecturing on new primary law; goes to matinées.

—$1,800—

CHARLES W. SKINWORTH; aged 45; politician in Second ward and jury clerk; his interest in women up to the present time chiefly has been to get them out to vote for the candidates he is supporting.

—$15,000—

FRED TUTTLE; aged 45; frequently called into requisition as a leader of germans; first nighter at theaters, and bon vivant.

—$100,000—

JAMES DEERING; 50 years old; an excellent catch; has more money than he knows what to do with, so has his portrait painted occasionally; lives in fashionable apartments in Cedar street.

ROBERT ALLERTON, son of the millionaire and one of the finest fellows in town, as well as probably the wealthiest; aged 30; stock broker.

—$12,000—

MAJ. MONTGOMERY; aged 45; credit man at the Fair, and rapidly amassing a fortune; and active; has a cottage at Fox lake.

—$20,000—

SEYMOUR COLMAN; aged 55; private banker and note broker; belongs to Union League club; would like to get married, but hasn't the courage to ask anybody; goes to social functions and always has a good time.

—$20,000—

GEORGE SKINNER; 45 years old; good fellow; likes to go to the theaters and cafés; fond of pretty women.

—$6,000—

JUDGE FRANK SADLER; aged 34; gets a $6,000 salary as Municipal judge; bon vivant; good billiard player; belongs to Hamilton club.

—$5,000—

H. CLAY CALHOUN; aged 42; lawyer; short, thick set, and has reddish brown hair; takes an extensive trip every year; went to Coney Island last year; great joker.

—$40,000—

JOHN H. SELLERS; aged 50; manufacturer; fond of country life; belongs to Union league, Glenview Golf, and other clubs.

—$40,000—

JOSEPH W. McABON; aged 38; vice president and general manager of the Chicago and Alton railway; always self-possessed; never appears in a hurry, but accomplishes a vast amount of work; lines with round face; good poker player; lives at Chicago club.

—$3,000—

JOHN P. UPHAM; aged 40; tall and slim; must have money, because he bought a seat on the New York stock exchange the other day for $53,000; lives at Chicago club.



An April 14, 1907, the *Chicago Tribune* article "Matrimonial Chances for Chicago Girls" listed over 80 carefully chosen Chicago bachelors, including Robert Allerton. "Some are working for salaries. . . . There are no objectionable characters among them. . . . Some of them are large packages. One weighing over 250 is said to be worth his weight in gold. . . . They are broken in." Allerton was referred to as "son of the millionaire and one of the finest fellows in town, as well as probably the wealthiest, aged 30; stock broker," with an annual income of $150,000. One young man, with a $5,000 annual income, was summarized as "doesn't care much for girls, but probably could be coaxed." Another, with a $100,000 income, had "more money than he knows what to do with, so has his portrait painted occasionally." A lawyer with an income of $5,000 per year "takes an extensive trip every year; went to Coney Island last year." Overall, Allerton appeared to be the columnist's choice. (CT.)

During the late 1890s and early 1900s, costume parties were the rage in high society. Allerton once attended a party wearing a pale-blue Bavarian officer's uniform. While traveling, he liked to purchase clothing and headwear from various countries to add to his costume closet, which included, among other items, togas, kimonos, a harem girl outfit, and multiple pieces of headgear. (APRC.)

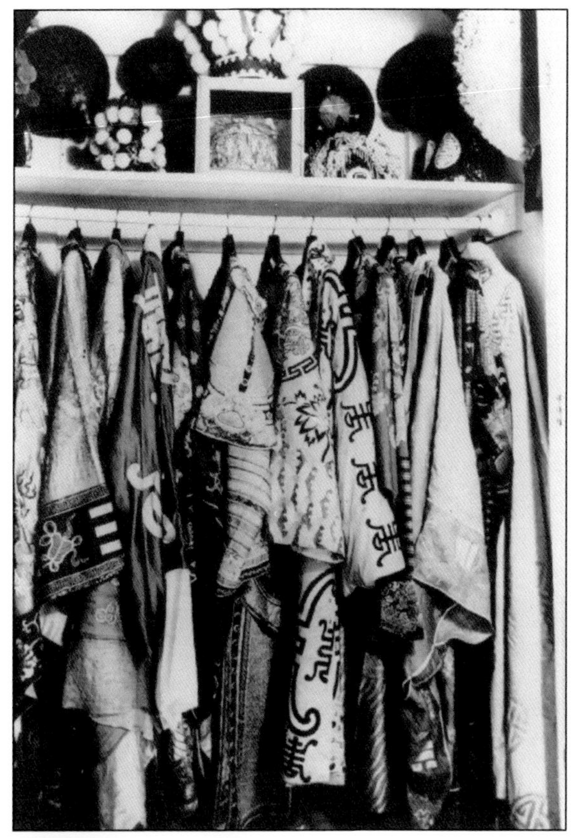

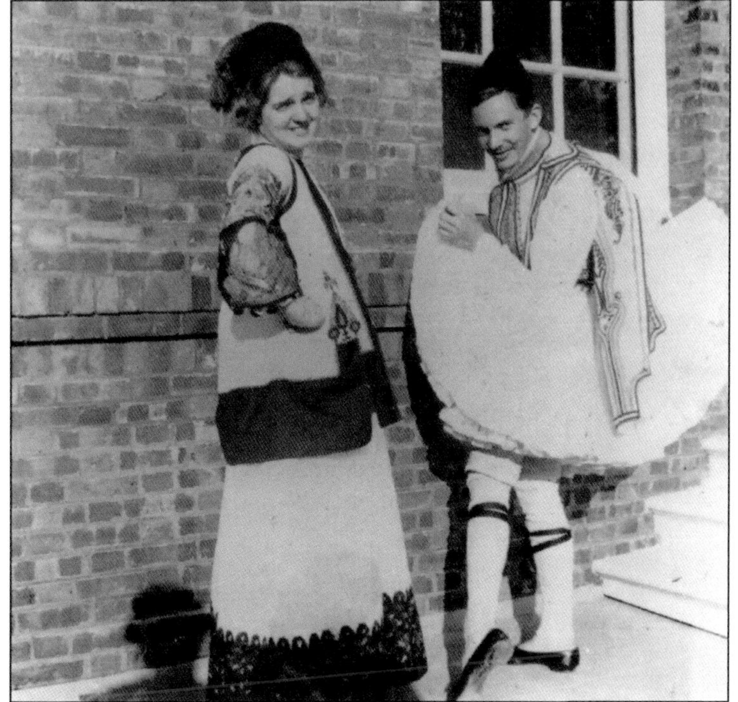

Allerton's guests enjoyed relaxing at the Farms. In those days, the well-off dressed up for dinner, with women in their corsets and jewelry, while men wore their starched shirts and high collars. To make his visitors more comfortable, Allerton would suggest they choose a costume to wear during dinner. Two unidentified guests pose on the laundry porch roof. Two of his kimonos hang framed in the mansion's hallway today. (APRC.)

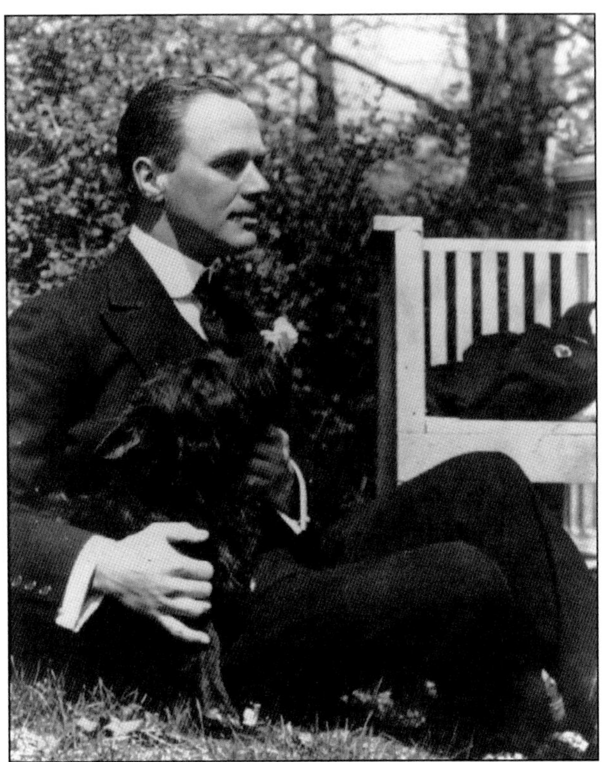

An Allerton friend, Russell Hewlett, was also acquainted with Ellen Emmet (nicknamed "Bay") and her family, which included her aunt and artist cousins. In 1905, correspondence about Allerton, seen here in a 1915 photograph, floated between Emmet's relatives. Her aunt wrote, "It is plain from Russell's letter that Robert Allerton is not to marry Bay this time." The conjecture was that Emmet's mother was not in favor of it. (APRC.)

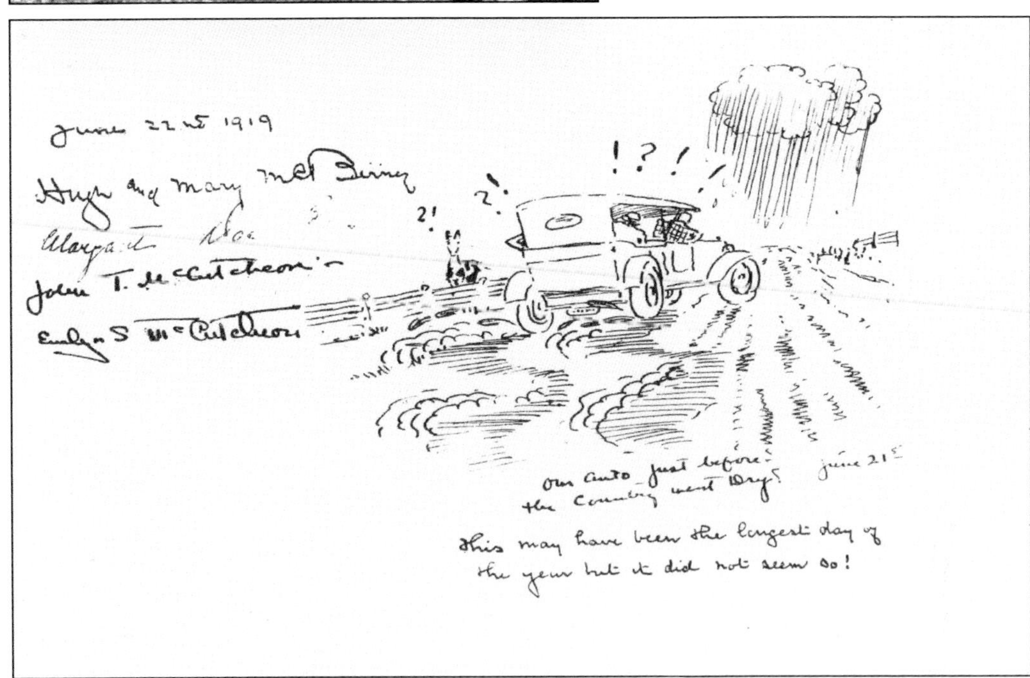


In Allerton's guest book in 1919, John T. McCutcheon referred to Prohibition taking effect soon: "June 21st. Our auto just before the country went dry. This may have been the longest day of the year but it did not seem so." Other signers included Chicago manufacturer Hugh McBirney and his wife, Mary; Margaret Day Blake; and McCutcheon's wife, Evelyn Shaw McCutcheon. (APRC.)

English composer Roger Quilter came into Robert Allerton's life around 1910, having met through Ellen Emmet's cousin Jane Emmet von Glehn, wife to artist Wilfrid von Glehn. Soon, Quilter and Allerton grew close. Quilter initially agreed with Allerton's suggestion to come to the Farms and compose there, but being perpetually ill, he worried about being away. (TM.)

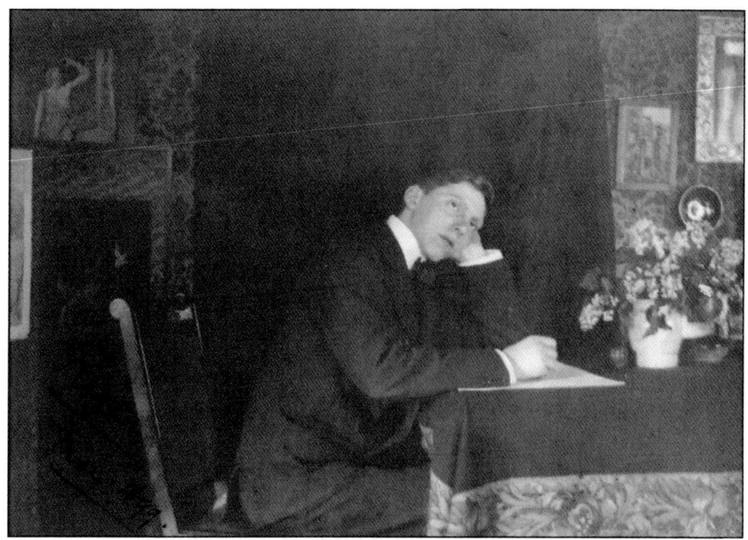

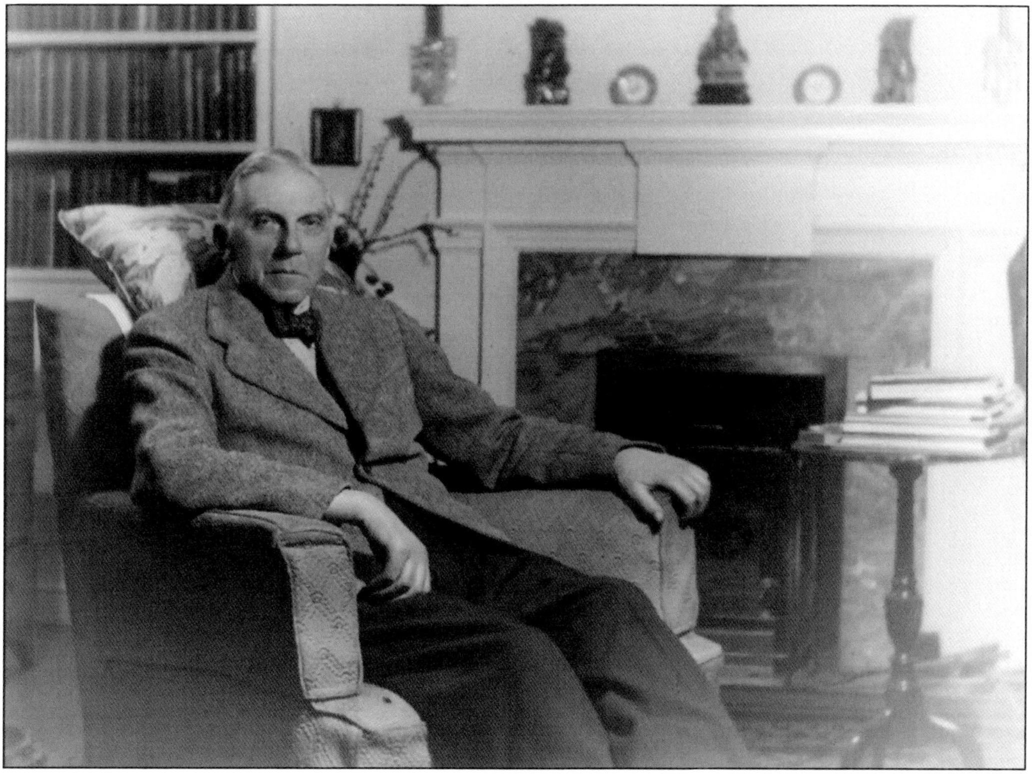

Offering various excuses, Roger Quilter decided against visiting Monticello, disappointing Allerton. In 1911 from Munich, Robert Allerton wrote to him, "I do so love you Roger every body that knows you must but no one can as much as I." According to an acquaintance of Quilter's, Allerton's relationship with him "was very important and the only homosexual one that Quilter admitted." (VL.)

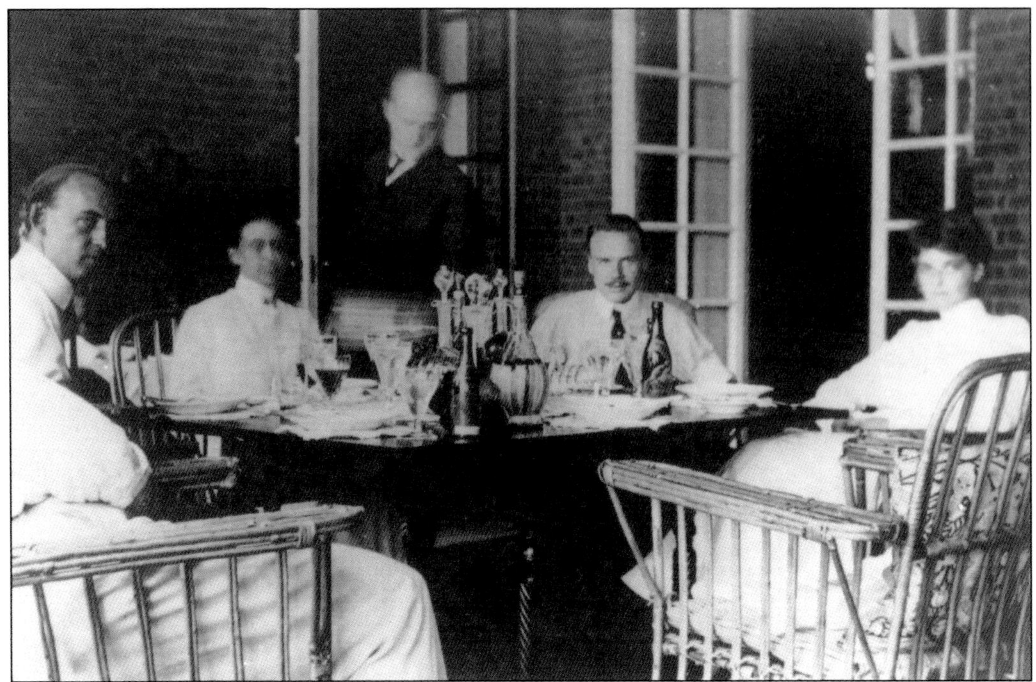

In 1911, Robert Allerton learned that Ellen Emmet was married—a "dark day," according to his chauffeur. It was later said that Allerton preferred to avoid marriage, not wishing to burden anyone with a near-deaf husband. Meanwhile, Emmet continued their friendship. This photograph from 1913 shows, from left to right, unidentified, Glyn Philpot, butler Ranholt Richards, and Allerton. Ellen Emmet is presumed to be the woman. (APRC.)

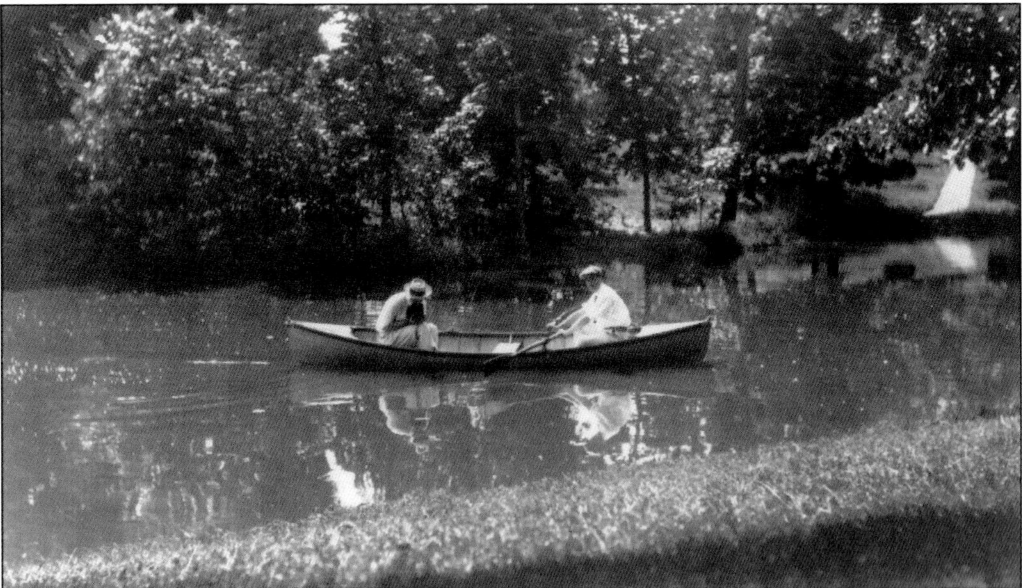

Robert Allerton's guests had the run of the estate, from horseback riding (sometimes *au naturel*, as one employee noted), to hiking, fishing, or playing tennis. This 1920 photograph shows two guests canoeing on the reflecting pond. Toward the right, the path following the other side of the pond to the greenhouses is visible. (APRC.)

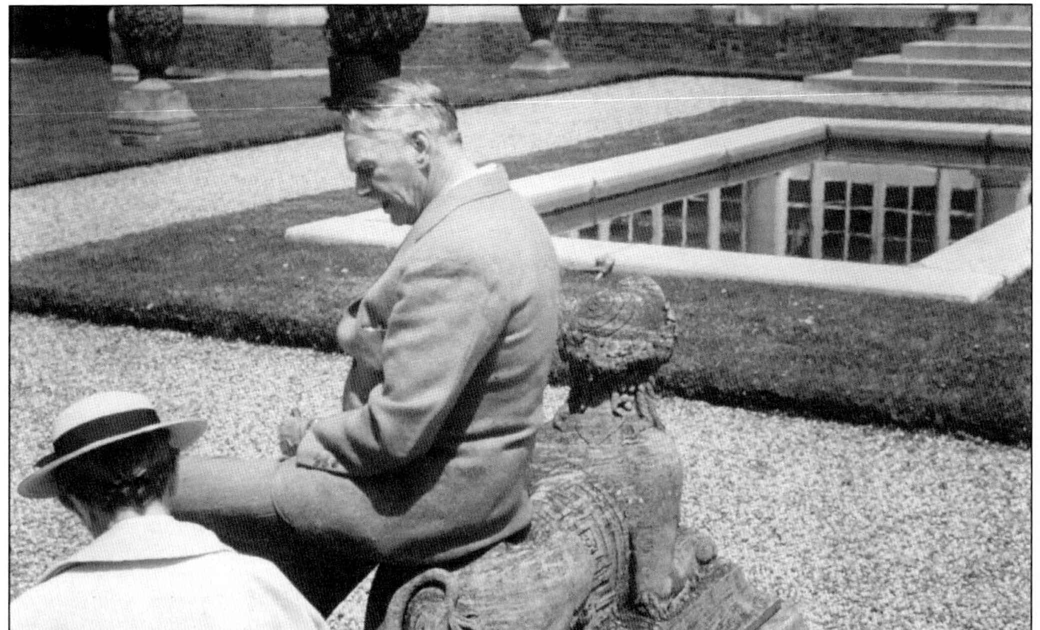

Col. George and Mary Langhorne, good donors to the Art Institute, visited Robert Allerton on many occasions. During his Army service, Langhorne's squadron, among whom was George Patton, pursued revolutionary and guerrilla leader Pancho Villa. Langhorne's circle of friends and family included his cousin Viscountess Nancy Langhorne Astor of England, Allerton's friend and composer John Alden Carpenter, and Carpenter's wife. (APRC.)

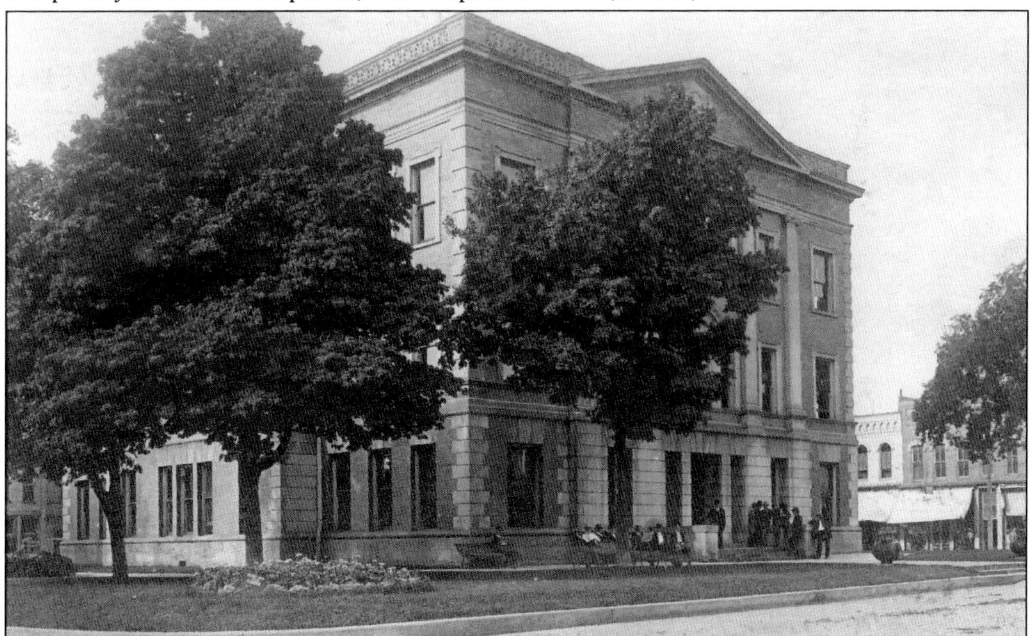

While struggling to make his farmland profitable, Allerton still managed to help the city of Monticello. When a new county courthouse was being built in 1903, a number of prominent citizens pledged $200 toward its construction. Allerton donated $500, a value of $15,000 in 2020. Architect Joseph Royer of Urbana completed the construction of the building in 1904. (APL.)

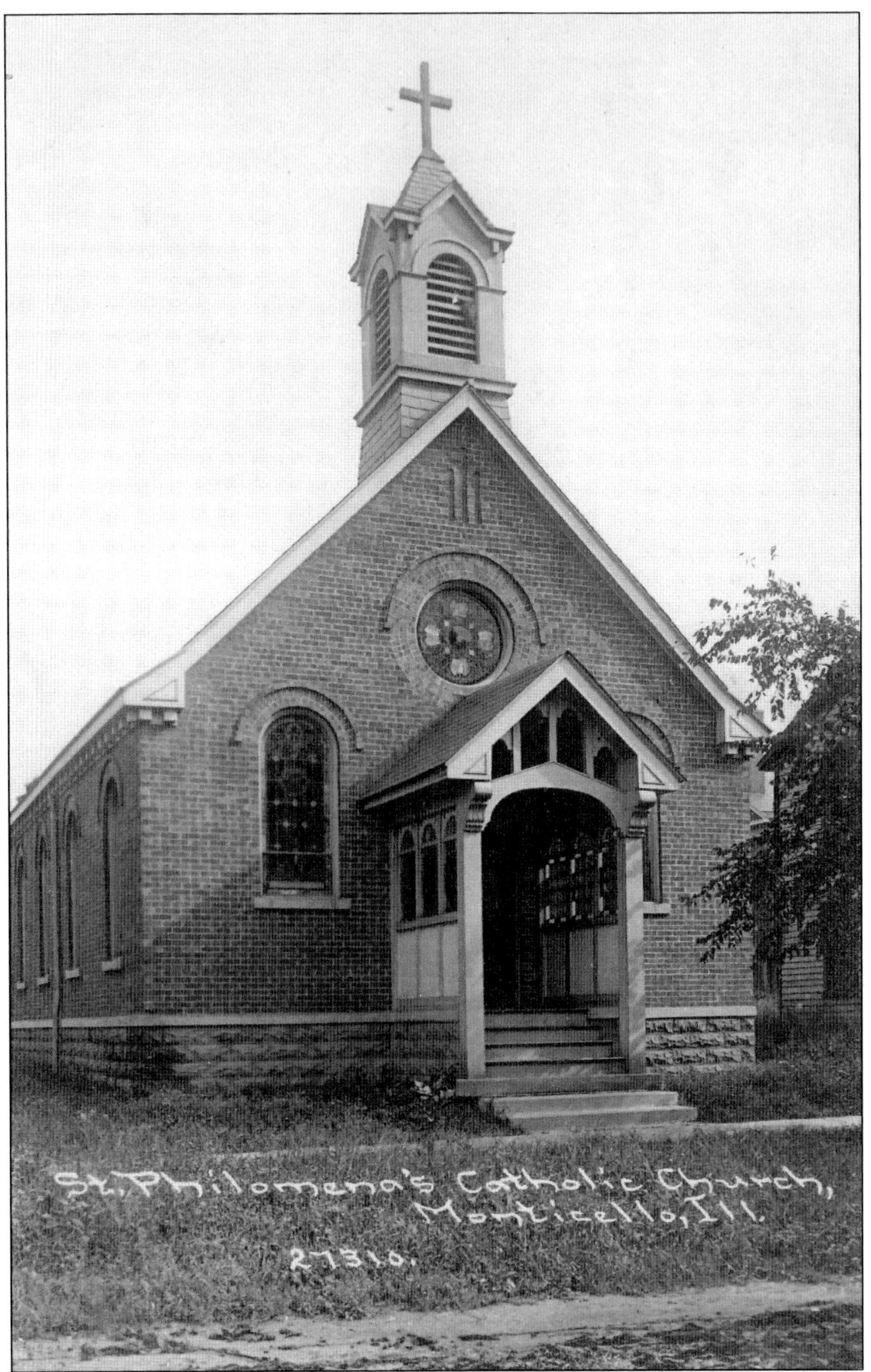


In 1906, Monticello's wooden Catholic church, St. Philomena, was replaced by a new brick building at the corner of State and Lafayette Streets. To honor his friendship with the priest, Father Selva, Allerton donated funds to decorate the church. Later, he purchased a brick home for Monticello's various clubs to use as a community house. He later sold the house and gave the proceeds to Monticello's library. (APL.)

# *Four*

# The Gardens 1900–1920s

Robert Allerton's first landscaping efforts centered on the terraces around his mansion. Between the conservatory and reflecting pond lay a swimming pool, an unusual feature for homes of most of his friends and acquaintances. The music terrace lay behind the mansion, and the bowling terrace led down from the mansion to the Sangamon River.

Guests could walk along the "Avenue of the Formal Gardens" to the rose terrace, then enter the brick wall garden with its eight-foot-diameter "dipping" pool, originally installed for the gardeners to refresh themselves. In the east wall of the brick wall garden, an arched doorway led to the gatehouse for many years, while to the west, more gardens lay past iron gates designed by John Borie and marked with an "A" for Allerton.

The current visitor center, greenhouses, and the square parterre garden were all created in 1902. Surrounded by low hedges, the square parterre was enhanced with sculpture. In 1908, Allerton created the triangle parterre garden, a gravel path lined first with junipers and later arborvitae. Four seasonal gardens lay beyond the junipers. Further beyond those gardens, enclosed by concrete walls, lay the Chinese parterre garden. From there, guests could stroll to the "Avenue of the Chinese Musicians" with sculpture lining its gravel pathway.

By the end of his landscaping efforts, Allerton had created 14 gardens with sculpture in all of them. As his collection grew and his tastes changed, many pieces were moved to a different location. The shepherd and shepherdess that once graced the square parterre garden were replaced by Diana and an ephebe (Diana's male companion), each with a dog at their feet. At different times, the shepherd and shepherdess also stood in front of the gatehouse and the "House in the Woods."

The triangle parterre's Assyrian lion sculptures, only one set of which is original, have flat backs and are carved only on the front, which was normal for pieces functioning as ornaments. This meant they were probably decorations against a wall. The other set was reproduced by Allerton's favorite stone carver, Charles Laing.

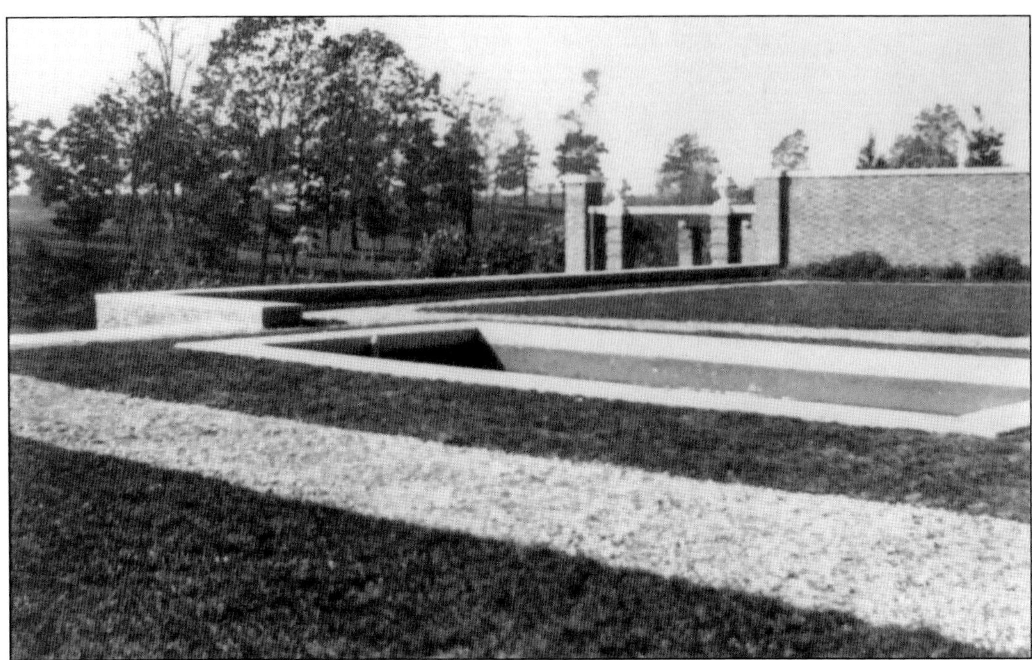

In 1901, the conservatory (upper) terrace's pool and the pergola near the pond had just been built. The sphinxes were not yet placed in the positions where they sit today. Twice weekly, the farm manager hauled fresh well water by horse and wagon to the swimming pool because Robert Allerton liked his water to be cold. These days, the pool is filled with koi. (APRC.)

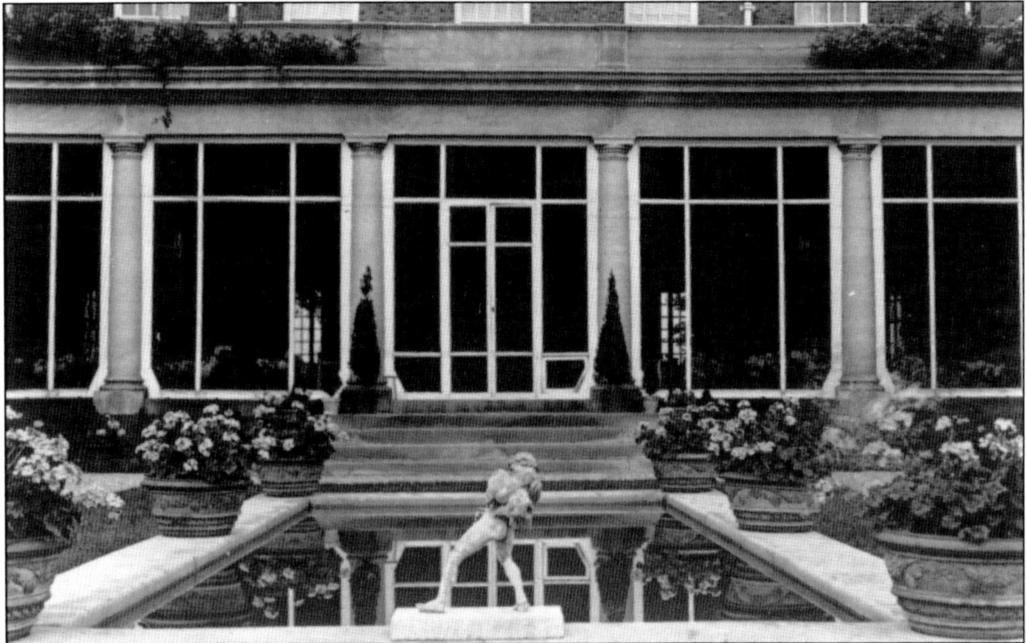

The area around the screened-in conservatory, with the pool flanked by geraniums, is seen here in the 1920s. The statue in the foreground may be of Dionysus, the Olympian god of wine, vegetation, pleasure, and festivity. *House Beautiful* magazine included an article in April 1904 about Allerton's mansion, lauding it for its "consistent good taste and beauty." (APRC.)

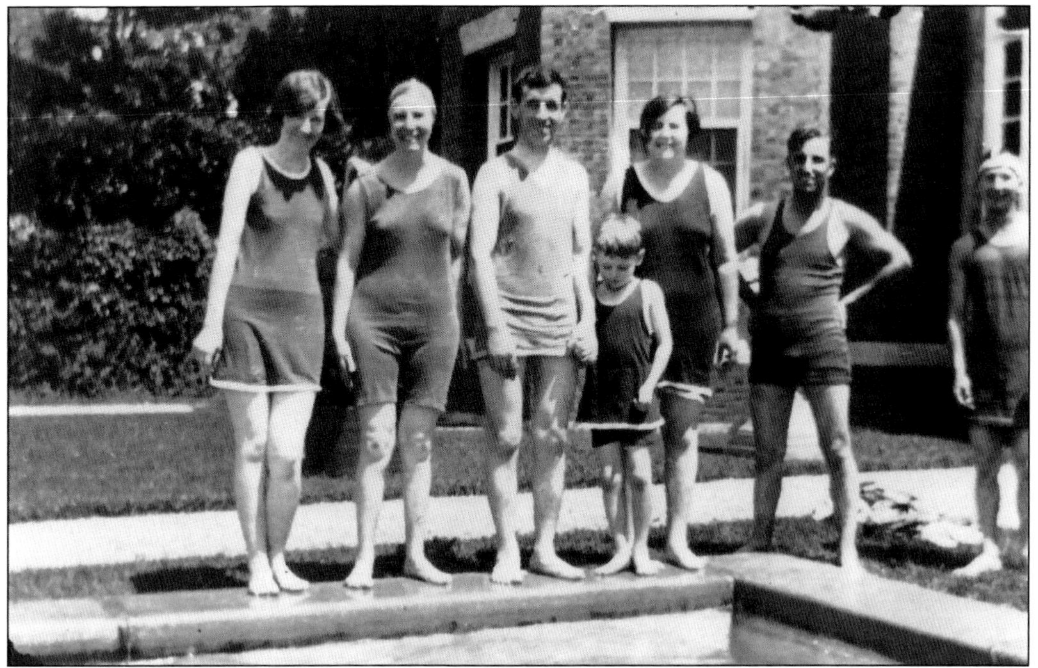

Allerton's employees enjoyed the pool when he was not using it. Posing from left to right in this 1924 photograph are Nell Fairbairn, Florence Fry, Arthur Cackett (assistant butler and occasional chauffeur), young Cyril Cackett, Emily Gollop, Elmer Priebe, and unidentified. Cyril Cackett recalled that Allerton would play games with him from 6:00 to 7:00 every evening during "Cyril's Hour." (APRC.)

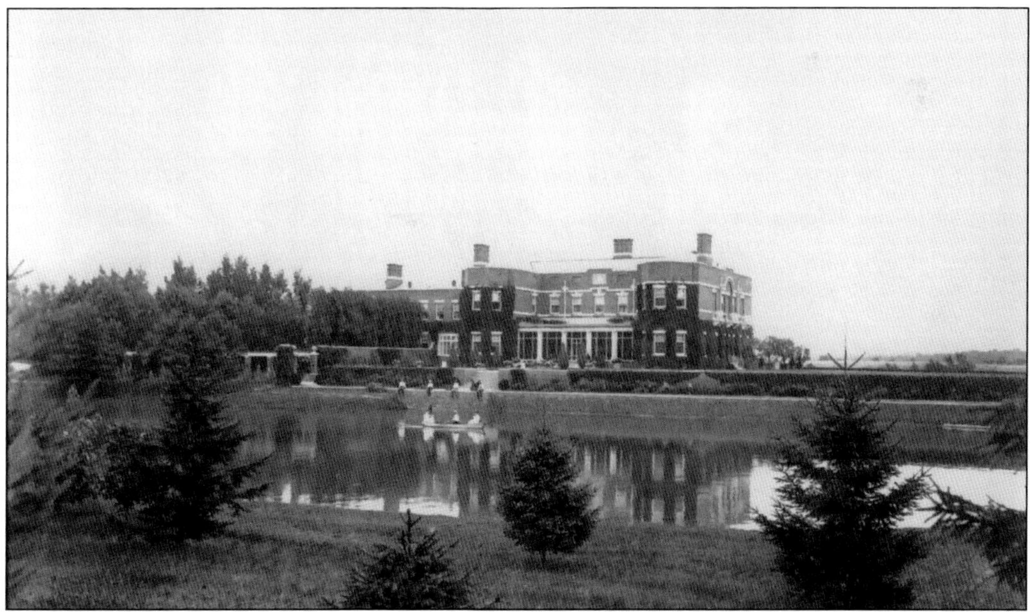

Allerton's employees also enjoyed boating parties and fishing on the reflecting pond. This 1909 photograph shows the mansion before the parapet had been removed. From left to right, Waneta Ashby, Albert Priebe, and Emma Ashby sit in the boat and James Shield, James Louis, John Aldt, and A. McNaughton stand near the wall. (APRC.)

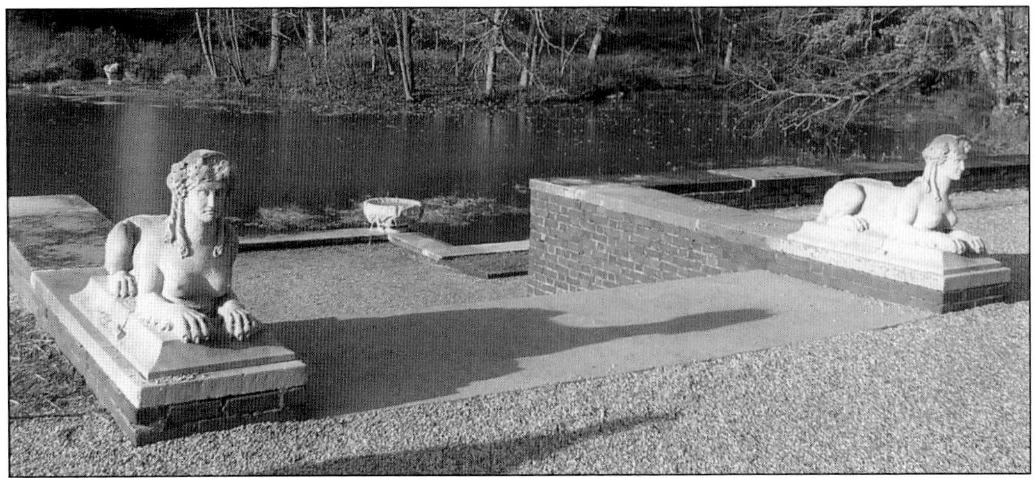

Designed by John Borie, two limestone sphinxes stare toward the conservatory. At the time, anything related to Egypt was popular. According to Allerton's wishes, the two sculptures were placed facing the house rather than away because he preferred seeing the female faces, not the creatures' rear ends. (MH.)

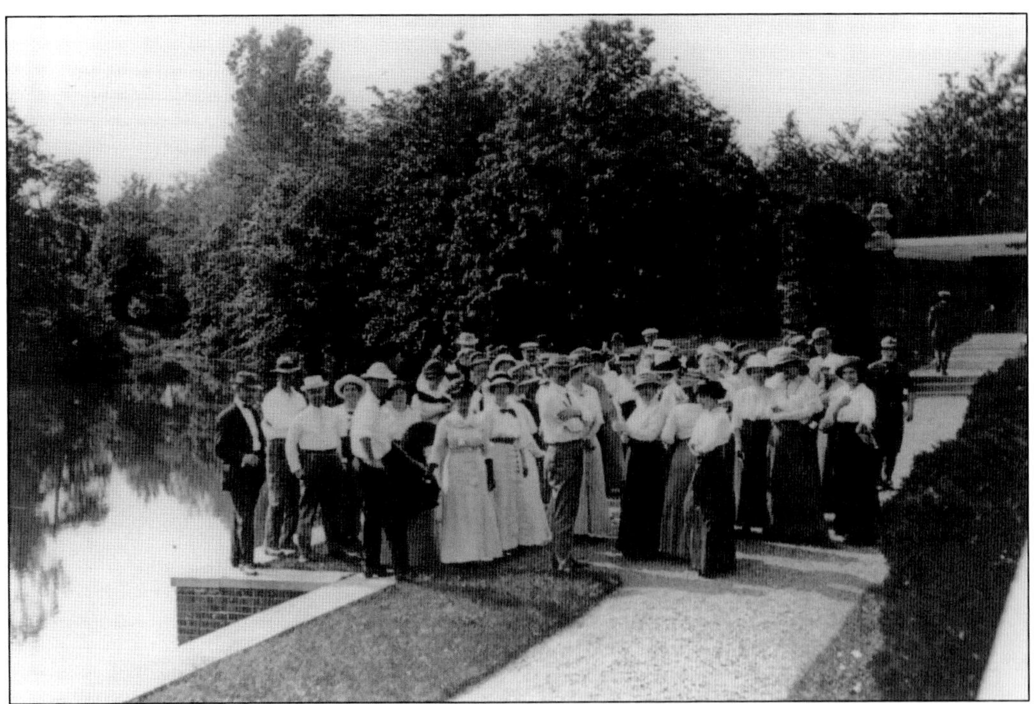

In this 1915 photograph, the University of Illinois Hikers' Club, founded sometime after 1909 by Prof. William Abbott Oldfather, enjoy the Farms. Several of them cluster on the lower terrace by the reflecting pond. Visible at far right is the pergola, which had been damaged severely by lightning during the 1901 storm referred to in a letter Allerton wrote to Ellen Emmet. (APRC.)

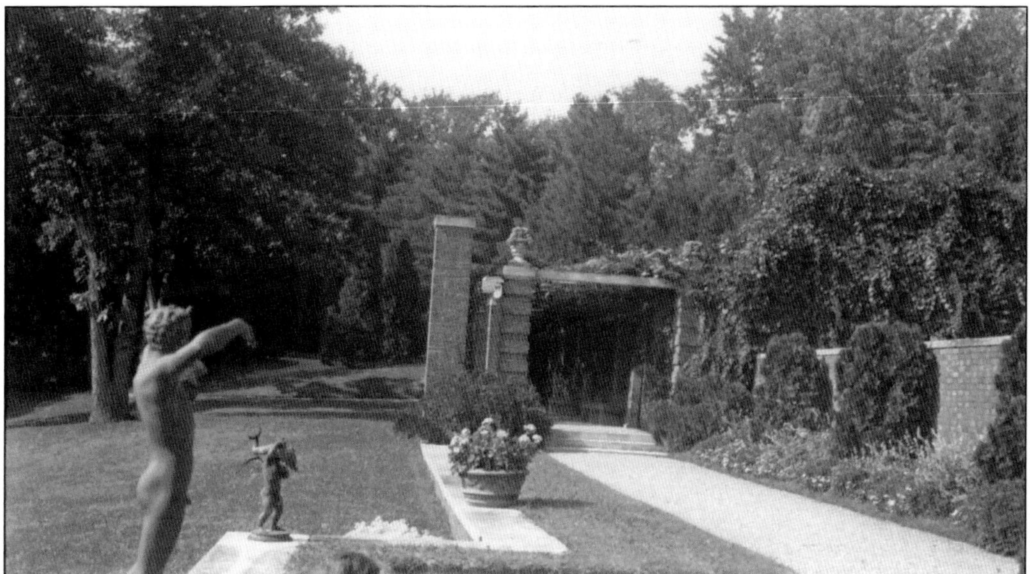

The statues of young Sophocles and a cherub with a dolphin stand by the pool in 1920. Flowers fill a terra-cotta pot. The vine-covered pergola with stone fruit baskets, designed by John Borie, shelters stone benches. The young Sophocles piece was sent to Allerton's Kauai estate in the 1940s. (APRC.)

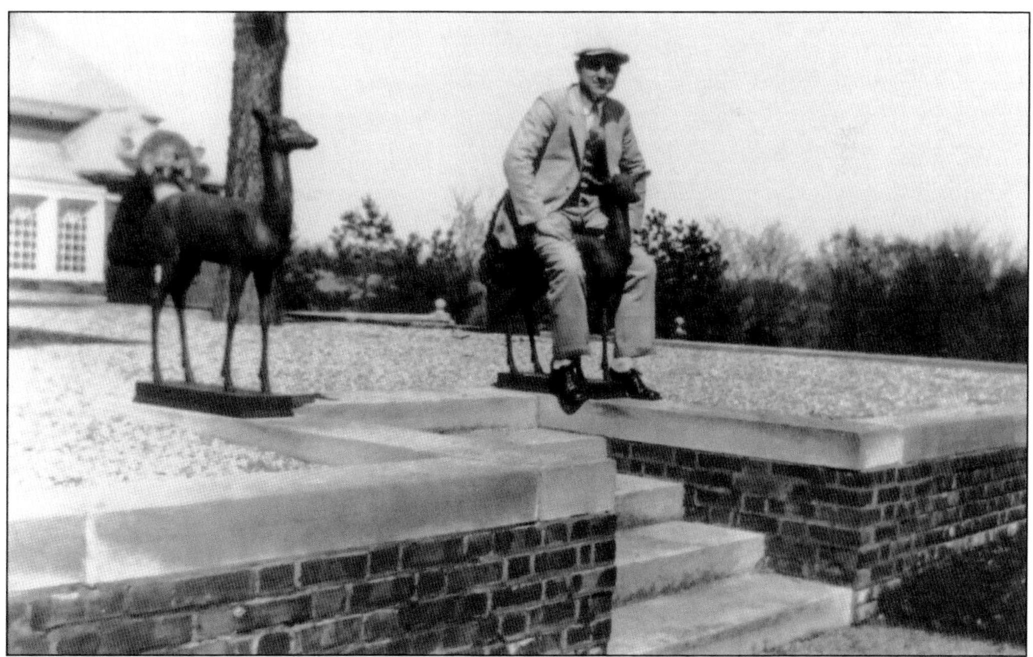

This 1935 photograph was taken outside of the Oak Room. Two bronze Herculaneum gazelles, which Allerton called "deer," gaze forward toward the river, with Elmer Priebe sitting on one of them. The gazelles were based on designs from Herculaneum, an ancient town buried by the eruption of Mount Vesuvius in 79 A.D. The National Museum of Naples owns an original. (APRC.)

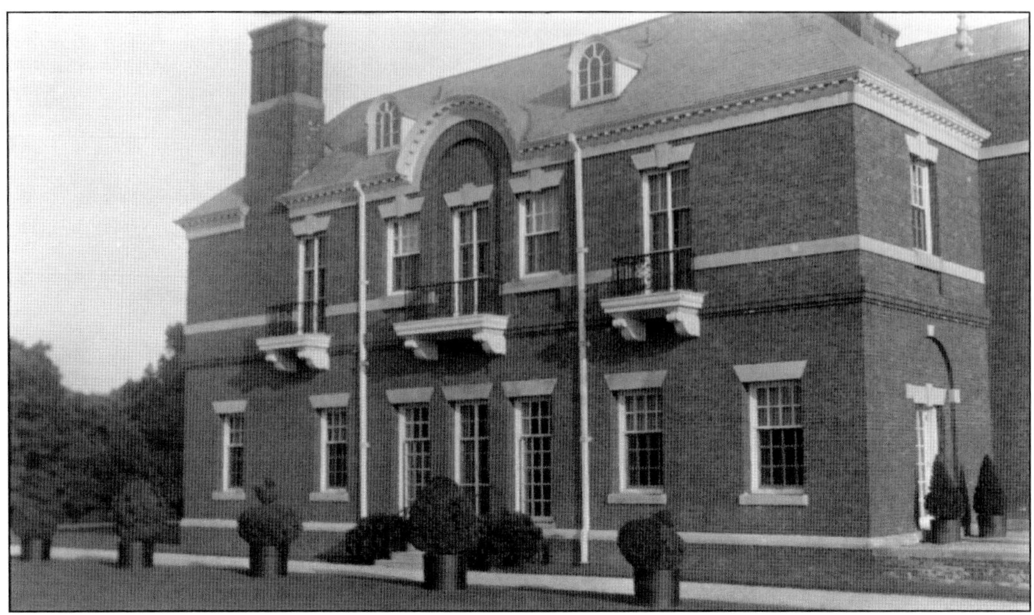

Seven tubs of topiary, one clipped in a bird shape, stand along the grass terrace at the southeast side of the mansion in 1915. By then, the roof's parapet had been replaced. The second floor's leftmost window and balcony were Allerton's bedroom. His plan after commissioning the *Sun Singer* was to place it on the terrace, but when a taller version arrived, he realized it needed a different location. (APRC.)

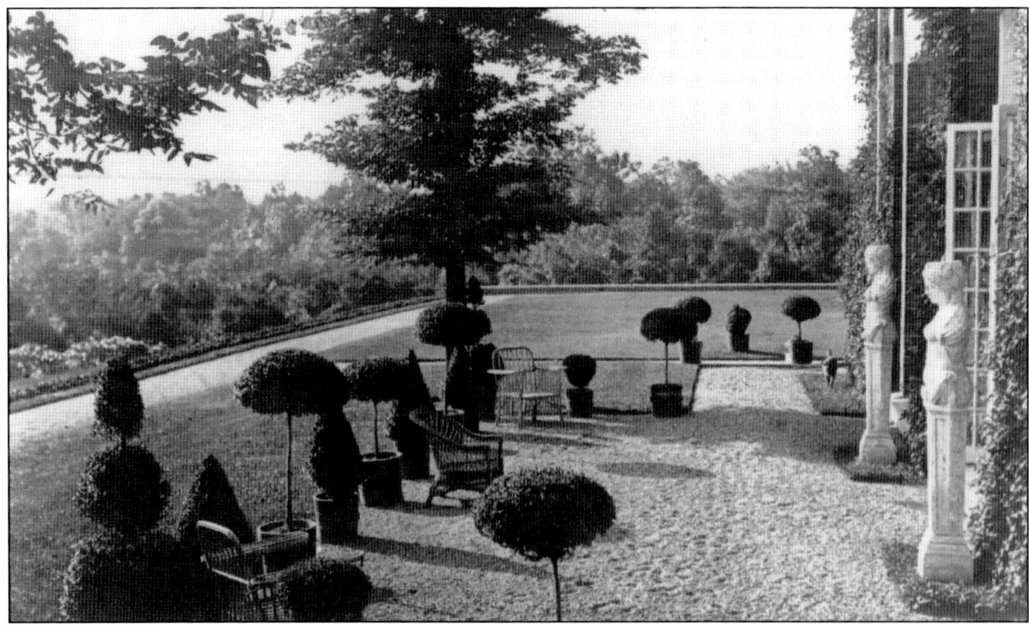

This 1915 photograph shows the music terrace with the Sangamon River beyond the tree line at center. A dog approaches the first of two caryatid sculptures that stand with their backs against the mansion. While traveling in Rome, Allerton had purchased the armless female nude sculptures, supposedly originals, but more probably copies, from the pope's villa. (APRC.)

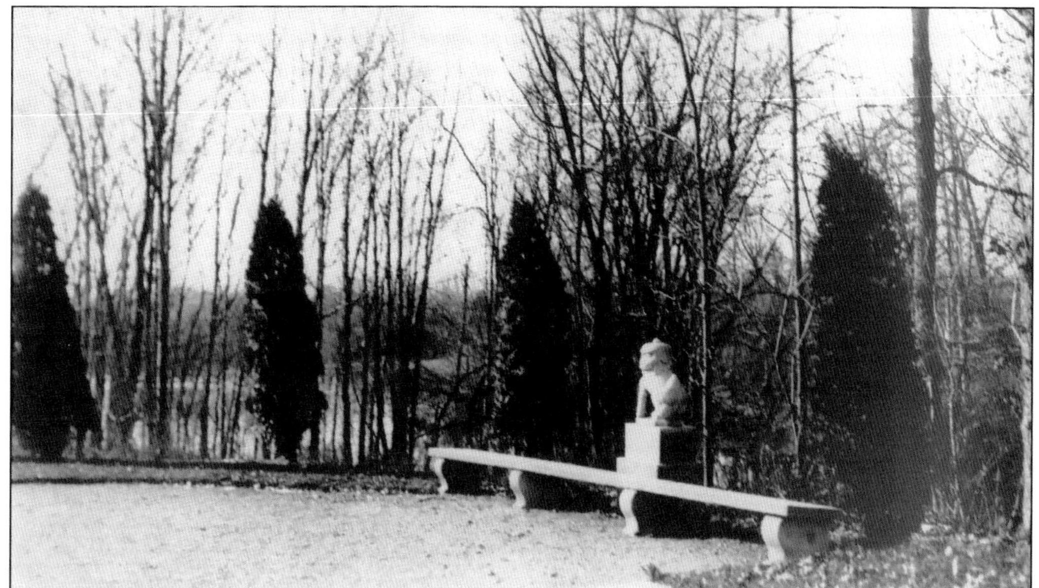

Guests walking along the Avenue of the Formal Gardens from the mansion toward the brick wall garden in 1915 would encounter two fu dogs on pedestals facing each other behind stone benches. This photograph shows one with the reflecting pond beyond. The *Primitive Man* sculptures later took positions on higher pedestals behind the benches. (APRC.)

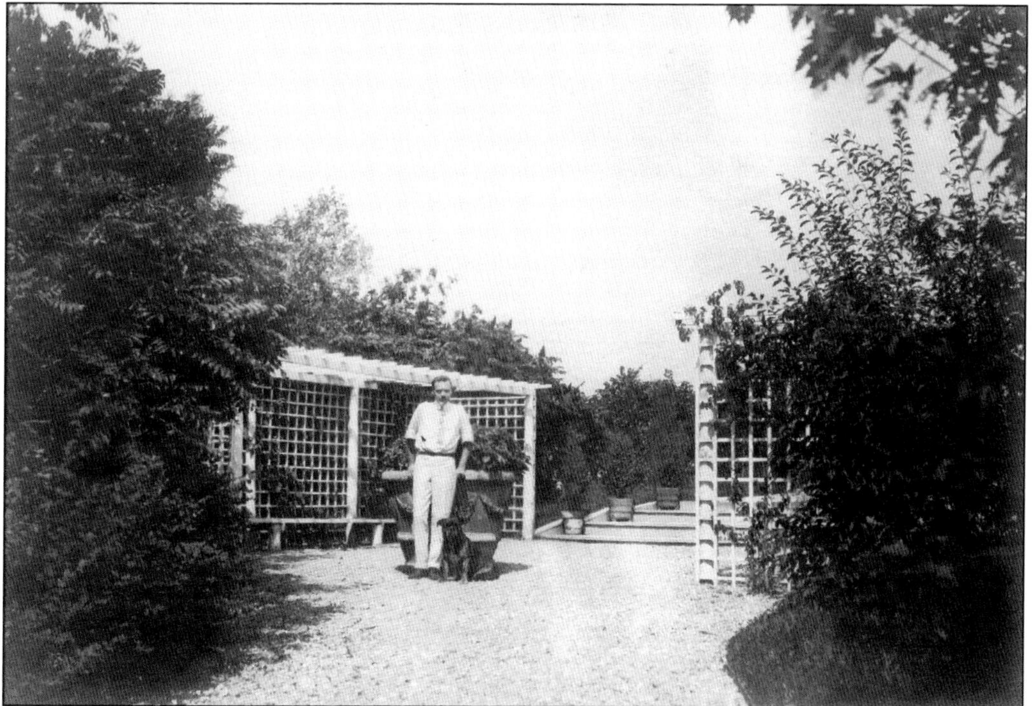

Until 1910, lattice arbors and benches stood on the Avenue of the Formal Gardens, midway between the mansion and the brick wall garden. Steps lead up to the path, which continues behind Robert Allerton and his dog. The *Primitive Man* sculptures stand there now. Guests caught in rainstorms could find umbrellas, capes, and low-heeled shoes hidden in shelters around the estate. (BH.)

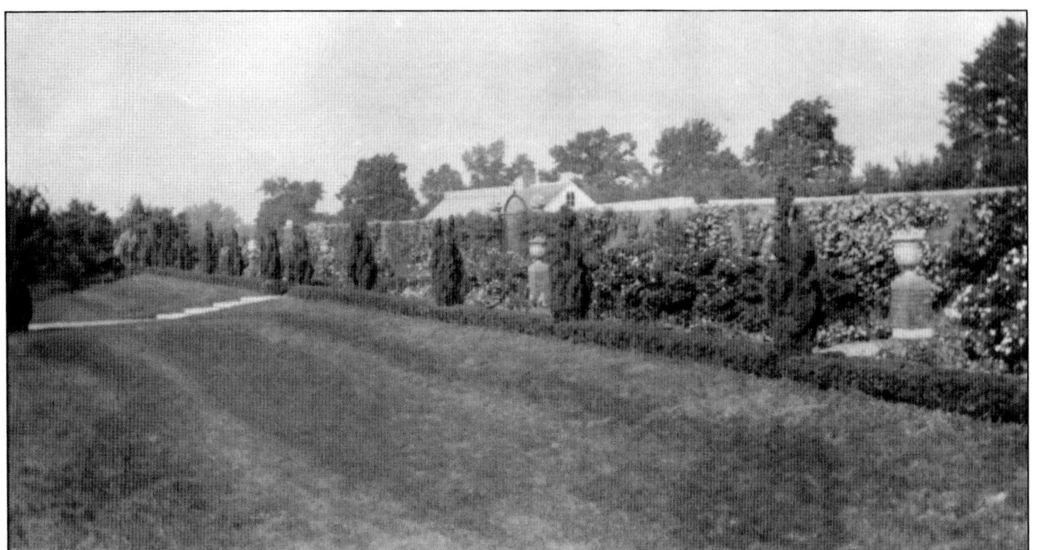

The rose terrace appears in the foreground of this 1908 photograph. Terra-cotta urns sit on columns. Borie's black-painted iron gates flanked by his stone fruit baskets stand in the center and lead to the brick wall garden. Built in 1902, the greenhouses and current visitor center are barely visible beyond the top of the gates. (APRC.)

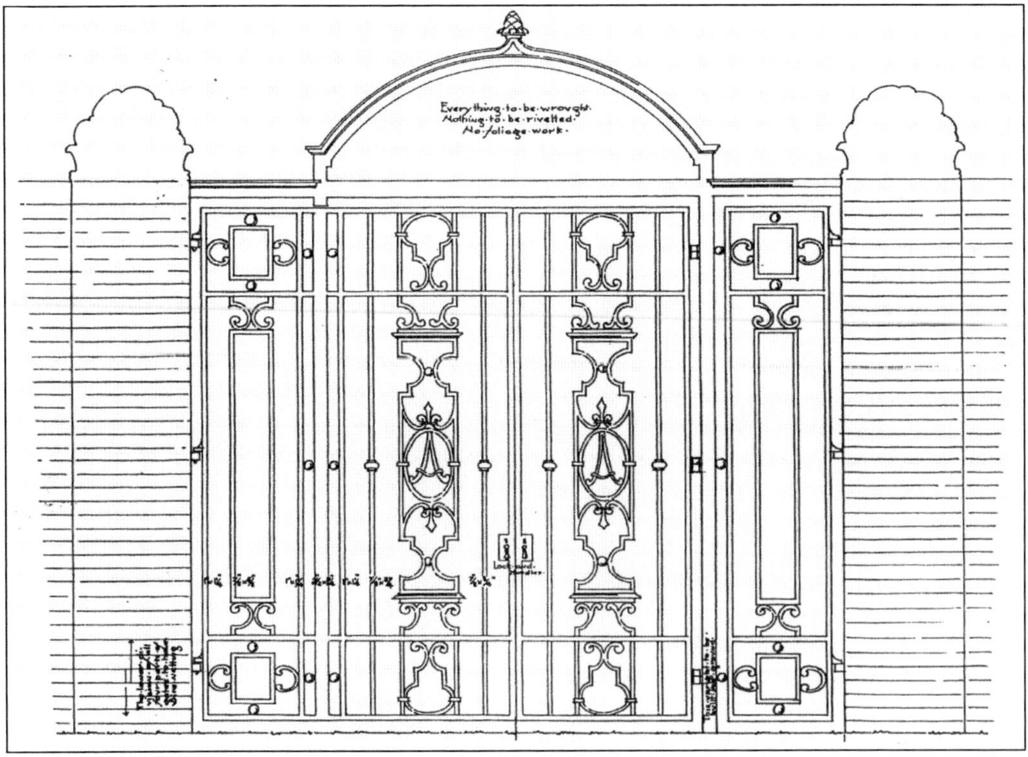

Of the gates to be placed between the rose garden and brick wall garden, John Borie wrote on his 1905 sketch, "Everything to be wrought. Nothing to be riveted. No foliage work." Over the years, these gates were shifted to various locations on the estate. They now separate the seasonal gardens from the Avenue of Chinese Musicians. (APRC.)

A dog stands between a set of Borie's black-painted iron gates at the entrance to the brick wall garden. An "A" is visible in the center of the gates. Fruit baskets sit on top of the columns. The same "A" appears in the mansion's iron balconies overlooking the terraces and entrances. (APRC.)

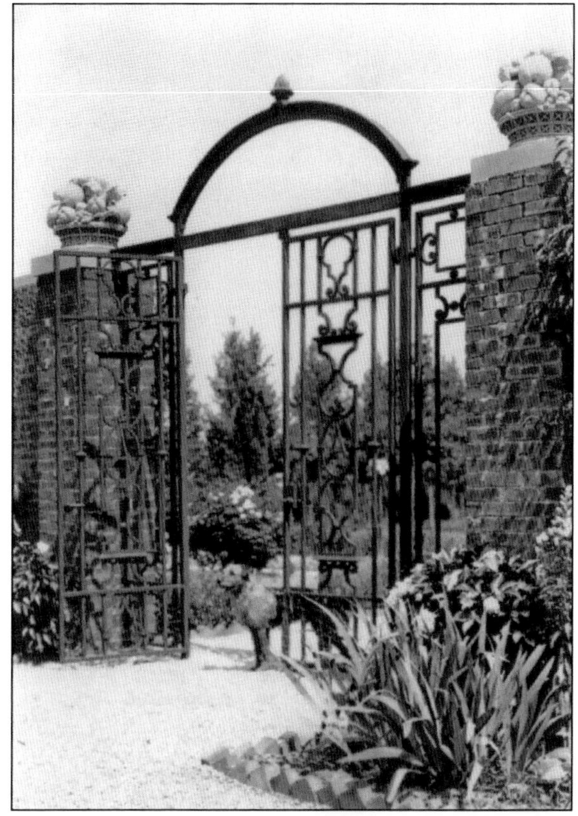

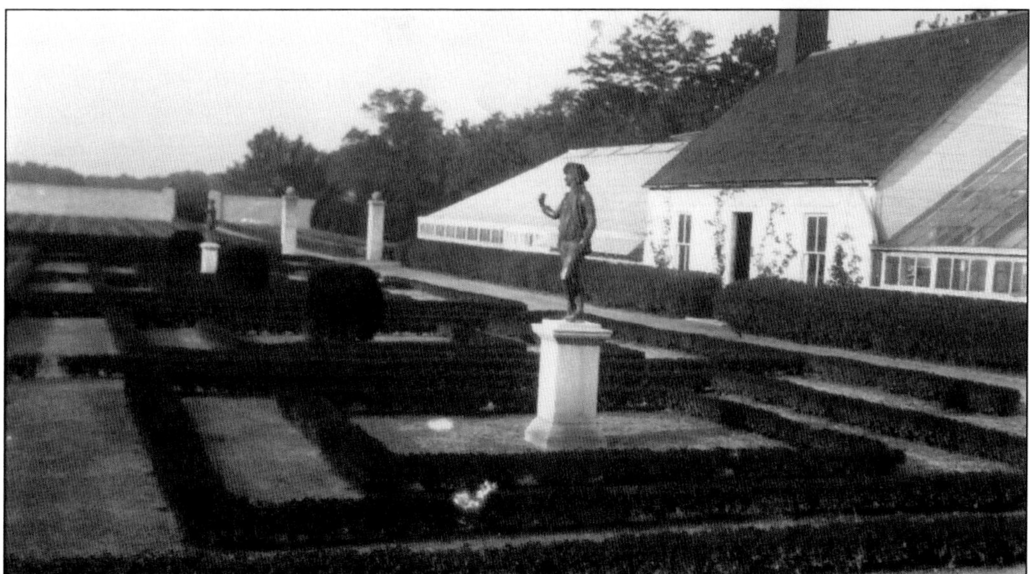

This 1920 photograph shows the square parterre, French for "along the ground," with greenhouses and, to the right, the current visitor center. Planted in 1918 to replace topiaries, over 2,000 privet shrubs made up the garden's square hedges. Orb finials top the gateposts seen left of the west greenhouse. The shepherd and shepherdess later stood in front of the gatehouse and the House in the Woods. (APRC.)

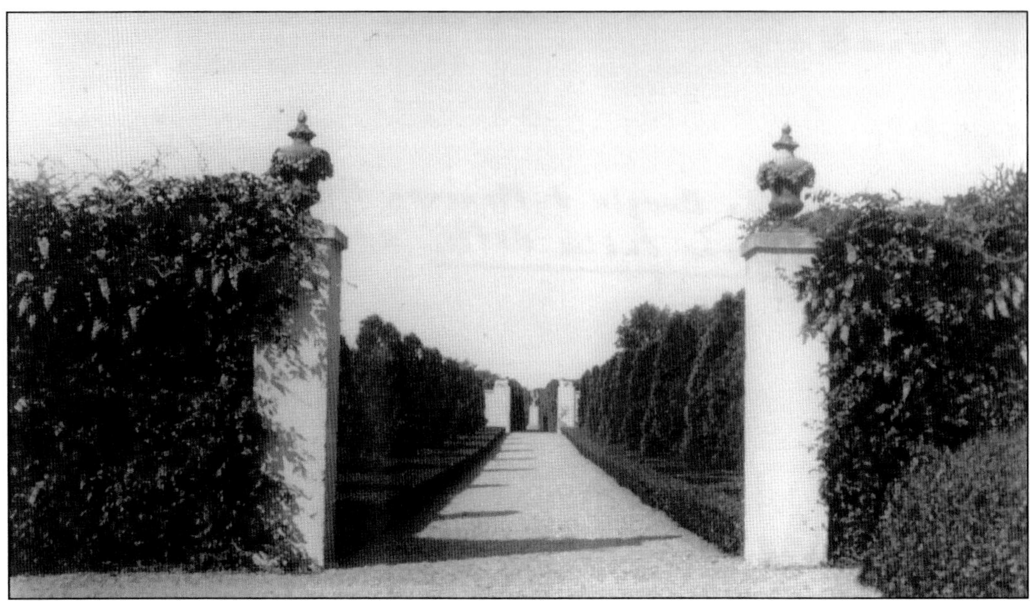

By 1930, the triangle parterre had been planted with equally-spaced arborvitae along a gravel path between the square parterre garden and the seasonal gardens. The low shrubs are amur privet, replaced by maintenance-friendly boxwood hedge in 2019. Foreground columns, topped with lead urns, were built in 1918. Limestone Assyrian lions sit on the distant columns. The *Adam* sculpture appears at center. (APRC.)

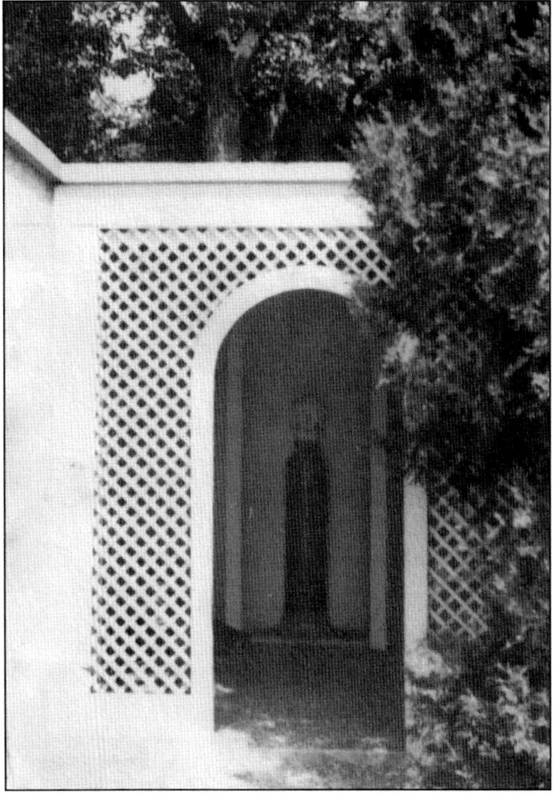

The entrance to a tower in the northwest corner of the triangle parterre leads to the tops of the north wall bordering the seasonal gardens. Built in 1920, the tower staircase was eventually closed to the public for safety reasons. In this photograph, a marble bust perches on a cylindrical granite pedestal. (APRC.)

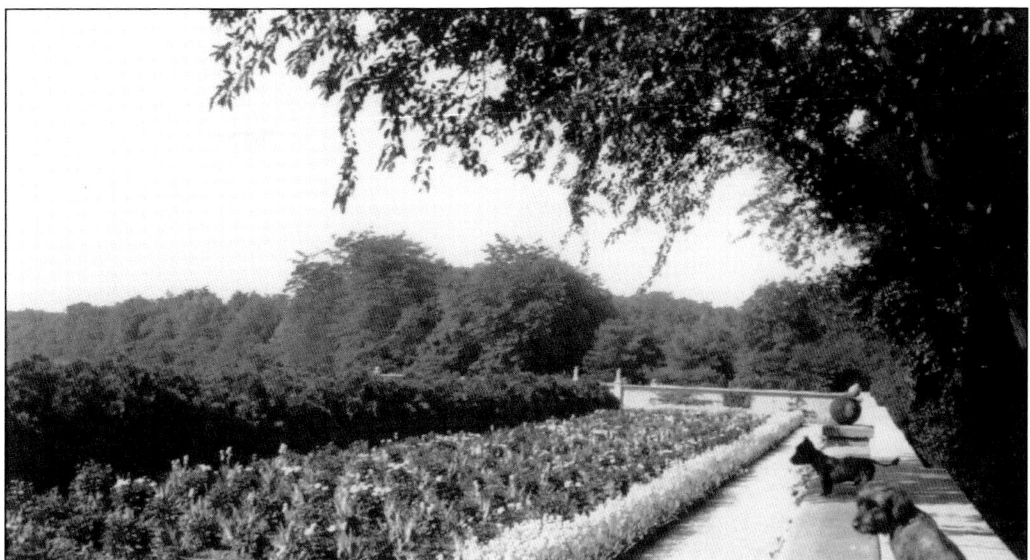

In this 1925 photograph, irises bloom in front of peonies, still a popular attraction every May. Orb finials are evenly spaced across the concrete walkway gracing the vine-covered northern wall. Two of Robert Allerton's dogs stand on the walkway. Allerton and friends would wander along, eating grapes from the vines. On the other side of the background wall is the Chinese parterre. (APRC.)

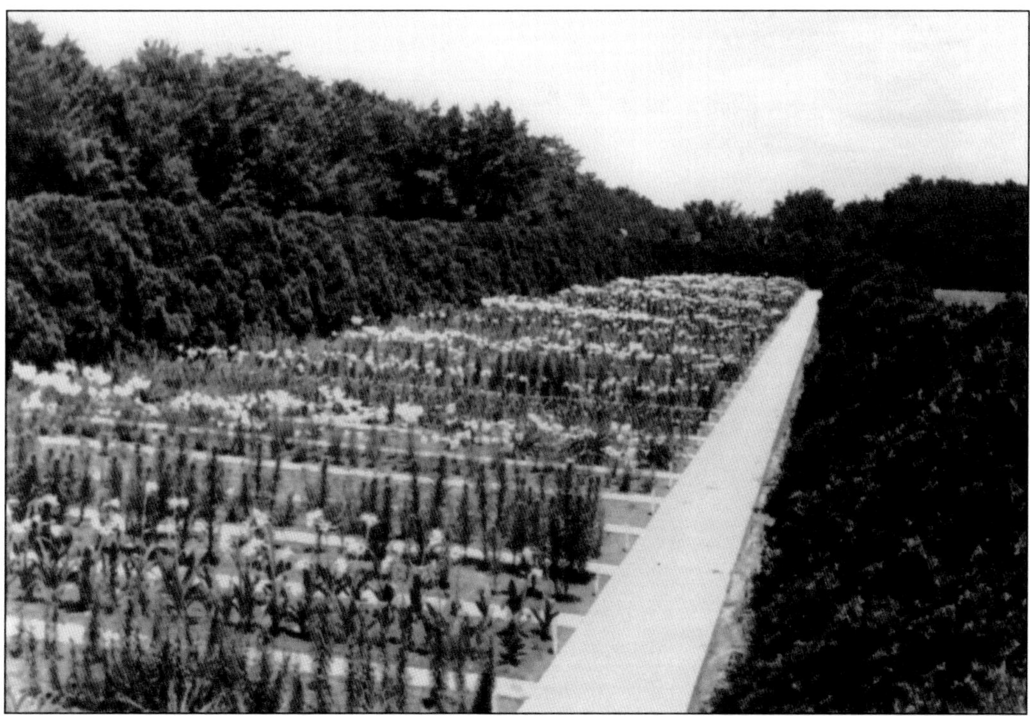

Guests could wander through the perennial garden on the other side of the arborvitae from the spring garden. In this 1935 photograph, lilies are blooming. The cypresses to the right have since been removed as part of a complete garden redesign in 2018. At that time, new winding sidewalks were installed in addition to plantings of new bulbs and herbaceous perennials. (APRC.)

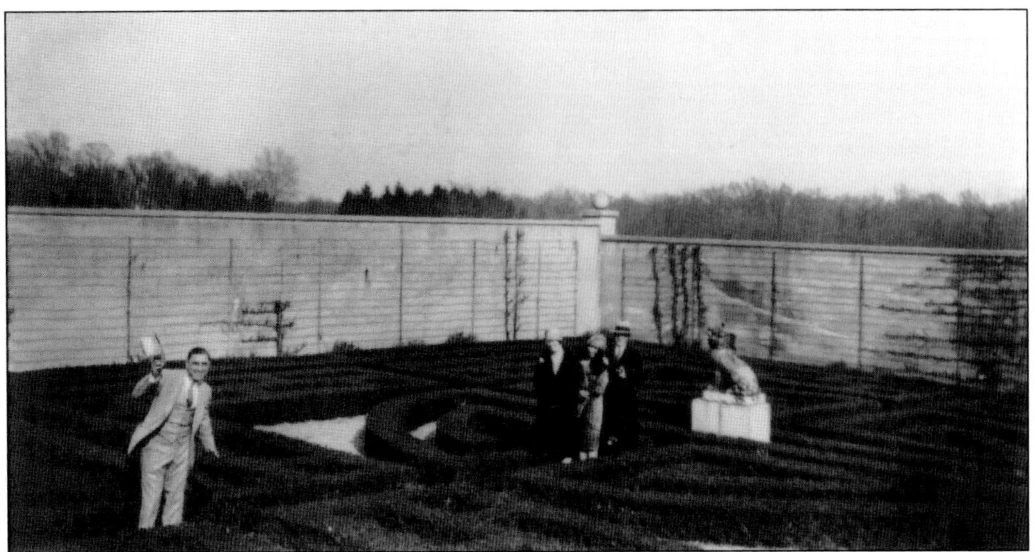

Elmer Priebe waves his hat at the camera in 1920. Behind him stands three unidentified people. The Chinese parterre is surrounded by concrete walls displaying espaliered fruit trees. The hedges follow a geometric design, reportedly based on a pattern from Allerton's favorite silk pajamas. A fu dog statue guards the center of the maze. (APRC.)

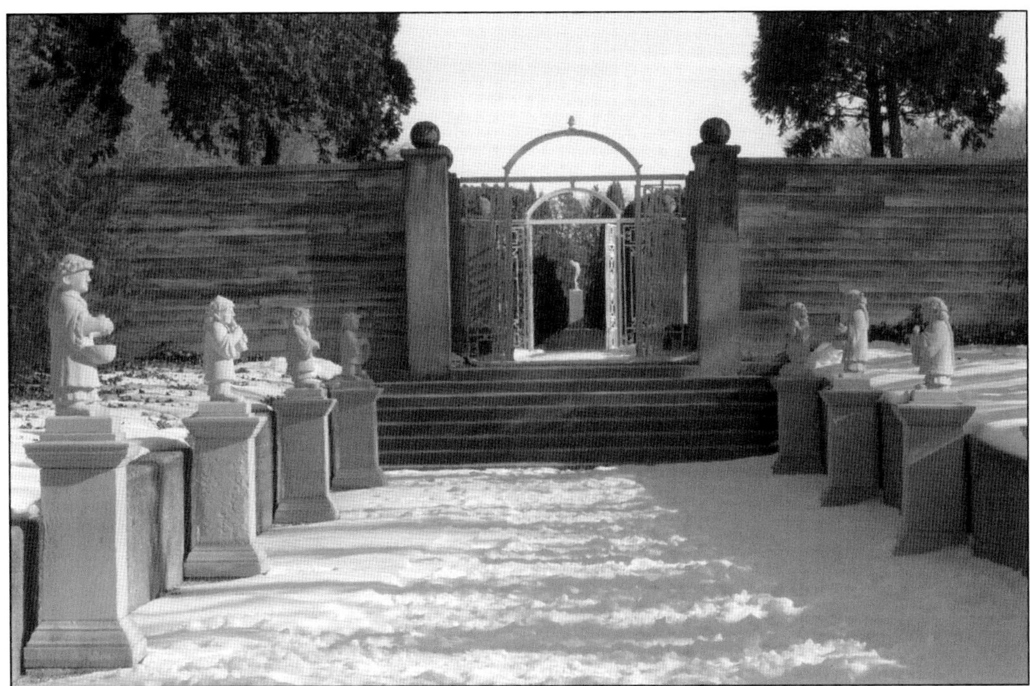

The Avenue of the Chinese Musicians stands in snow, with *Adam* in the background. Allerton purchased 10 musician sculptures in England sometime before 1923, later commissioning local tombstone carver Lew Wagy to produce two more. The statues were located near the rose terrace walls until 1932, when Allerton moved them across the river to a path lined with red cedars—the "Lost Garden." (MH.)

The Chinese musicians shifted around the estate from time to time. Sadly, as decades passed, vandalism, erosion, and squirrels needing to sharpen their teeth did their damage. These current statues are copies of the originals. Six original sculptures are kept safe on the second floor of the library. (MH.)

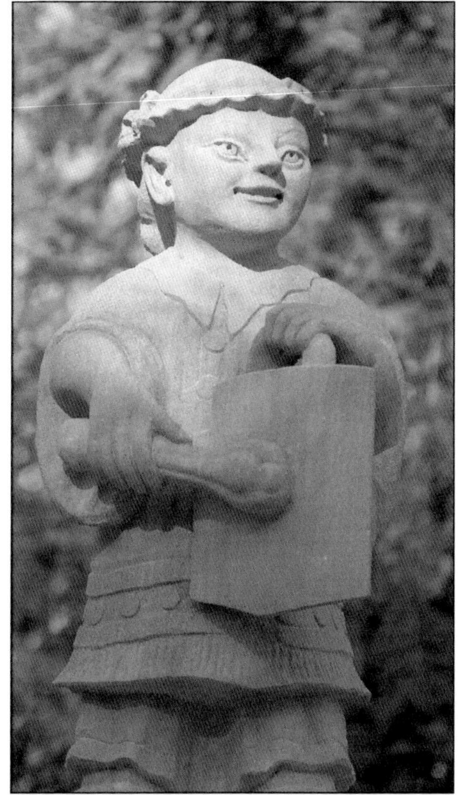

James Shield, Robert Allerton's head gardener, worked at the Farms until 1935, creating a trial garden behind the area near the icehouse across Old Timber Road. Seen here are flower beds, grapevines in the center, the welding shop, the car shop, the woodshop, and a swinging gate by the welding shop bench. (APRC.)

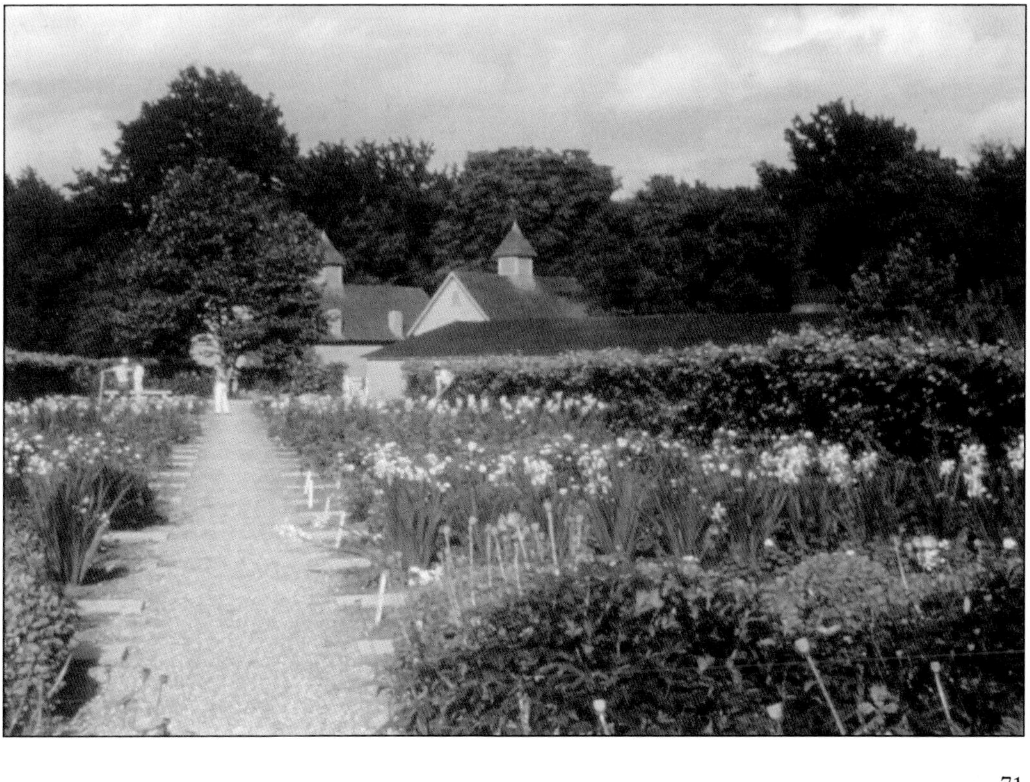

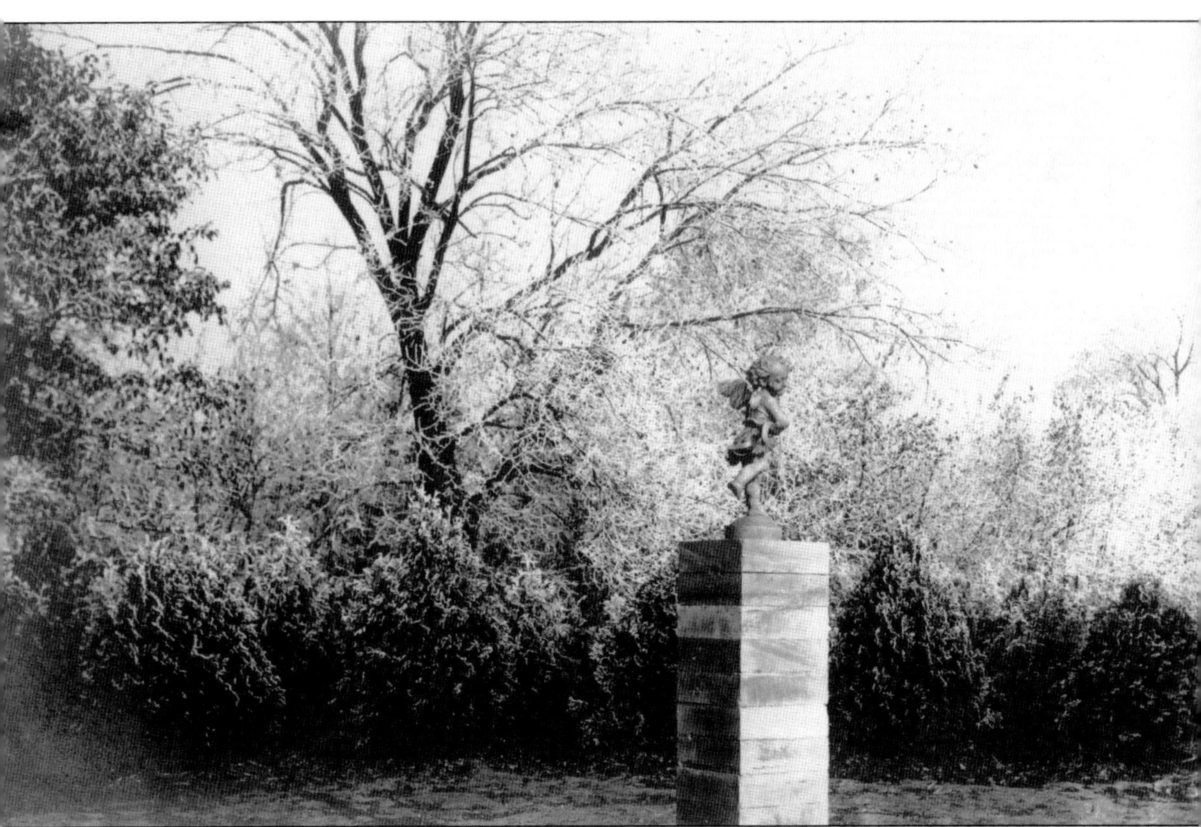

The trial garden was also home to several sculptures. This cherub with dolphin resembles a bronze sculpture, *Putto with Dolphin*, from before 1476 by Andrea del Verrocchio, found in Florence's Palazzo Vecchio museum. Del Verrocchio's piece was originally commissioned for a fountain in the Medici villa in Careggi, near Florence. (APRC.)

# *Five*

# An Artistic Touch
## 1914–1925

Allerton continually enhanced his property and outbuildings. In December 1915, he also partially funded a farm-to-market road into Monticello. The side of the road leading to Monticello—to market—was paved with brick to hold the weight of loaded wagons. The other side of the road—returning to the farm—did not require paving because the wagons would be empty.

During Robert Allerton's winter trip to Tahiti in late February 1914, he learned of his father's death in Pasadena. Long ailing, Samuel Allerton had succumbed to complications from diabetes. It took Robert several weeks to return home. The funeral was finally held on March 14 in Chicago, with burial at the Graceland Cemetery.

One of the last of the country's great meatpacking pioneers, Samuel Allerton had served as a director of the First National Bank of Chicago until his death, still holding his original 3,000 shares. His estate was valued at approximately $4 million, approximately $103 million in 2020. Robert took over his father's directorship positions with banks and other businesses.

After selling the Prairie Avenue house to the Hump Hair Pin Factory, which was replaced with townhomes in 1999, Robert Allerton placed the proceeds into a trust fund honoring a doctor who took care of his father. Still operating today, the fund benefits Chicago's Northwestern Memorial Hospital. Needing a Chicago home, Robert's stepmother purchased an apartment at 1315 Astor Street.

Throughout the 1920s, Allerton served as a trustee and vice president of the Art Institute of Chicago, purchasing art, organizing exhibitions, and loaning and donating his acquisitions. His gifts to the Art Institute began in 1922 with, among others, a graphite drawing of a jockey by Edgar Degas and Auguste Rodin's bronze *Head of Pierre de Wissant*, a study for Rodin's *Burghers of Calais*. For a 1922 exhibition, he loaned the museum two Rodin drawings, a 14th-century gold lacquer Korean Buddha, and an Édouard Manet drawing. Other loans and gifts included textiles; antique silver and furniture; works by Paul Gauguin, Camille Pissaro, Amedeo Modigliani, Henri Matisse, Vincent Van Gogh, and Georges Seurat; and many more.

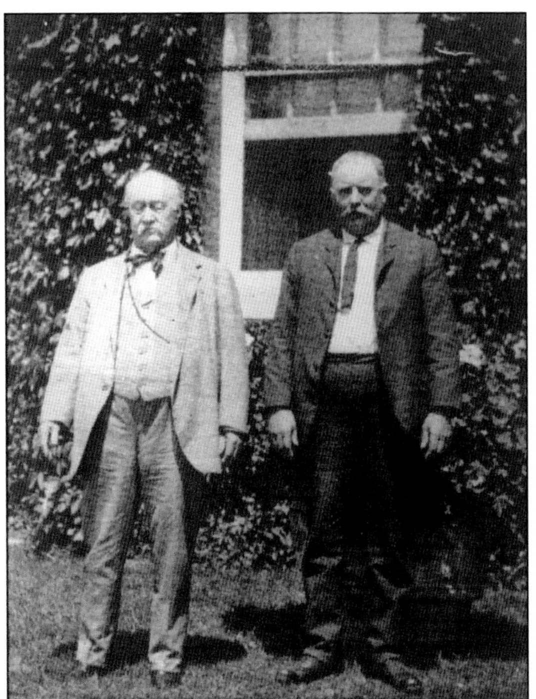

Samuel Allerton and his longtime farm manager, John Phalen, stand together in 1913. Before Phalen died in 1919, he joined Robert Allerton and other local residents, including Allerton family friend William F. Lodge, in establishing the Piatt County Fairgrounds at the north end of State Street in Monticello. Today, the site is known as Forest Preserve Park. (APRC.)

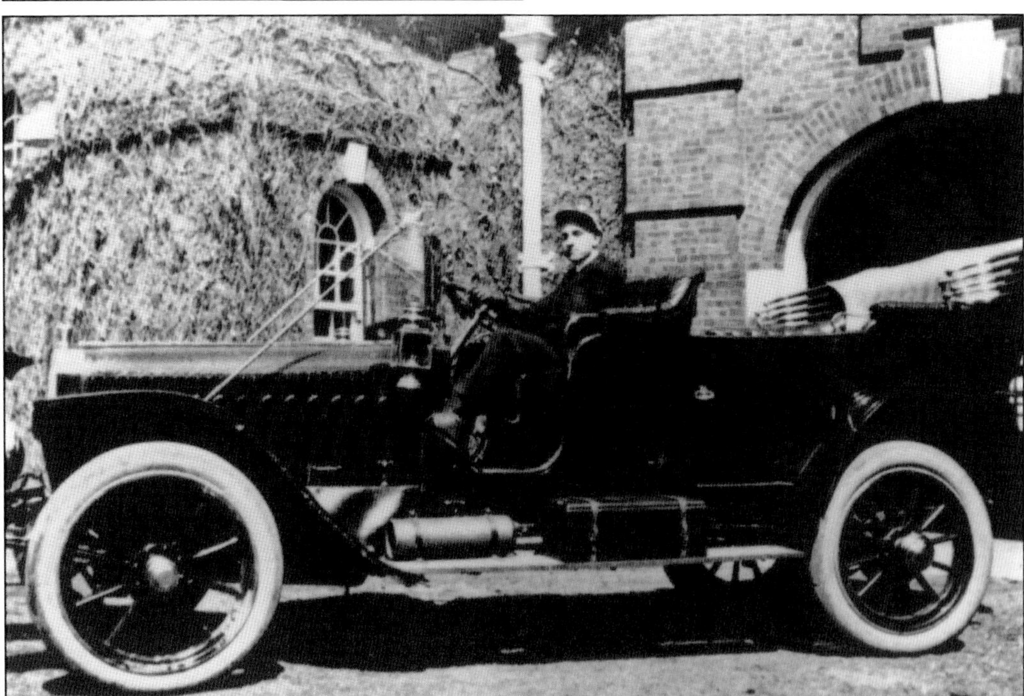

In 1914, Elmer Priebe, Robert Allerton's chauffeur, sits in a seven-passenger 1907 Stevens-Duryea Big Six touring car, a secondhand crank-start vehicle that Samuel Allerton gave to his son. Back then, chauffeurs had to fix their own vehicles. This led to Priebe staying at the Prairie Avenue house during the winter of 1904 while taking maintenance classes. Robert replaced the Stevens-Duryea in 1907 with a Packard offering a starter. (APRC.)

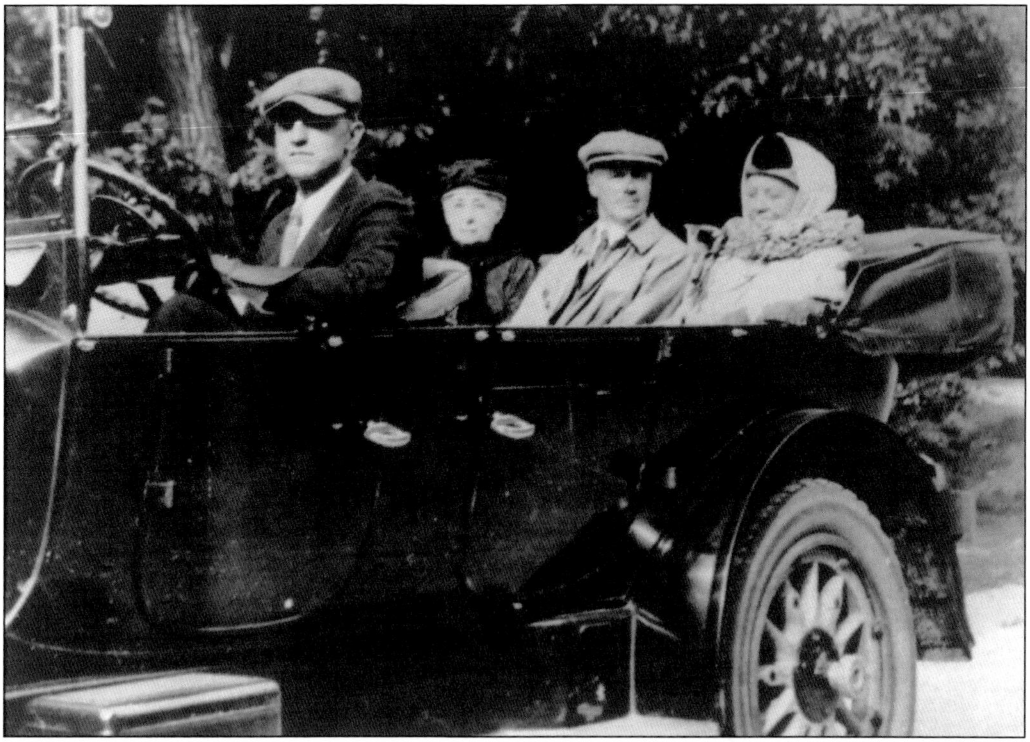

Chauffeur Elmer Priebe sits behind the wheel of Robert Allerton's new Packard in 1923. In the backseat, from left to right, are Robert's paternal aunt Lois Allerton, Robert, and Anna Rathbone. His aunt Lois was 97 years old in this photograph. She died in 1926 at the age of 100. (APRC.)

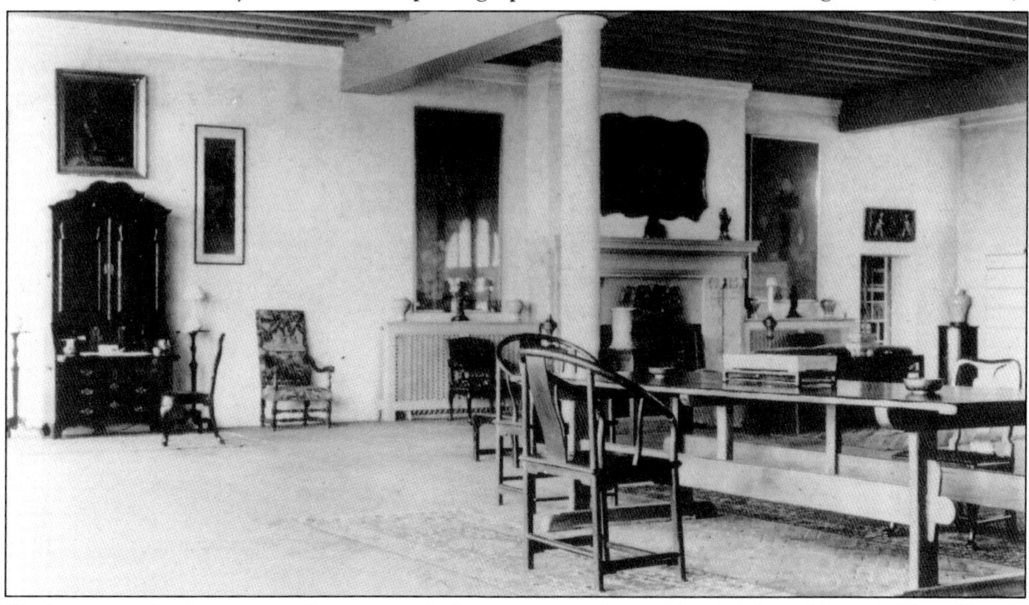

With more vehicle usage, Allerton needed to renovate the stables. He hired Joseph Llewellyn to make the plans and supervise the work. The main floor was modified into a studio/library with bedrooms and bathroom, keeping the brick floor. The lower level would serve as the garage. Part of the work involved the removal of a manure pile from behind the stables. (APRC.)

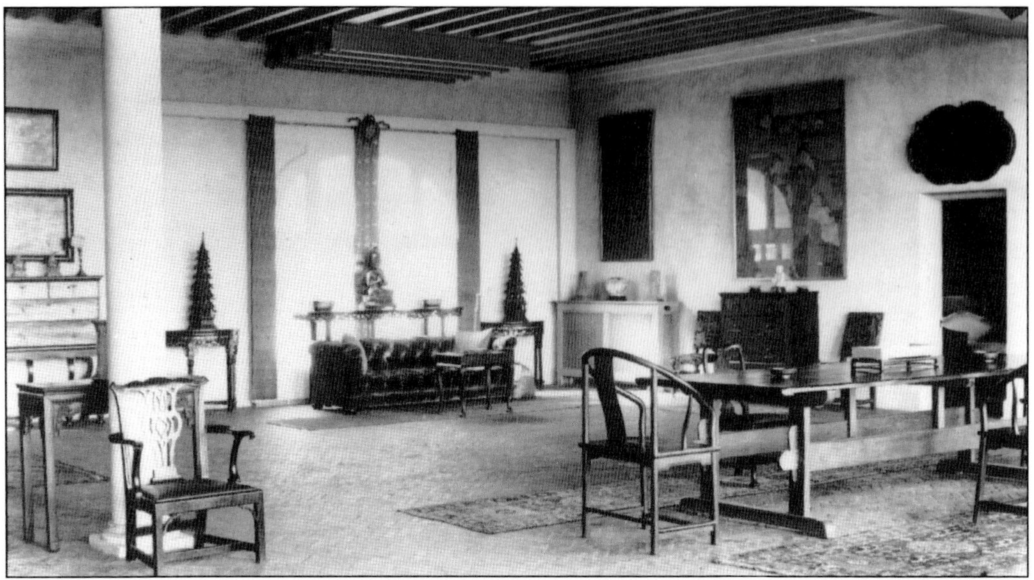

This 1915 photograph offers another view of the 2,600-square-foot renovated stables. Allerton filled the room with furnishings from Asia and Europe, such as the Jacobean chest. The curtains behind the sofa are sheer enough to barely see the shape of the arched doorway where the horse and buggies once entered. (APRC.)

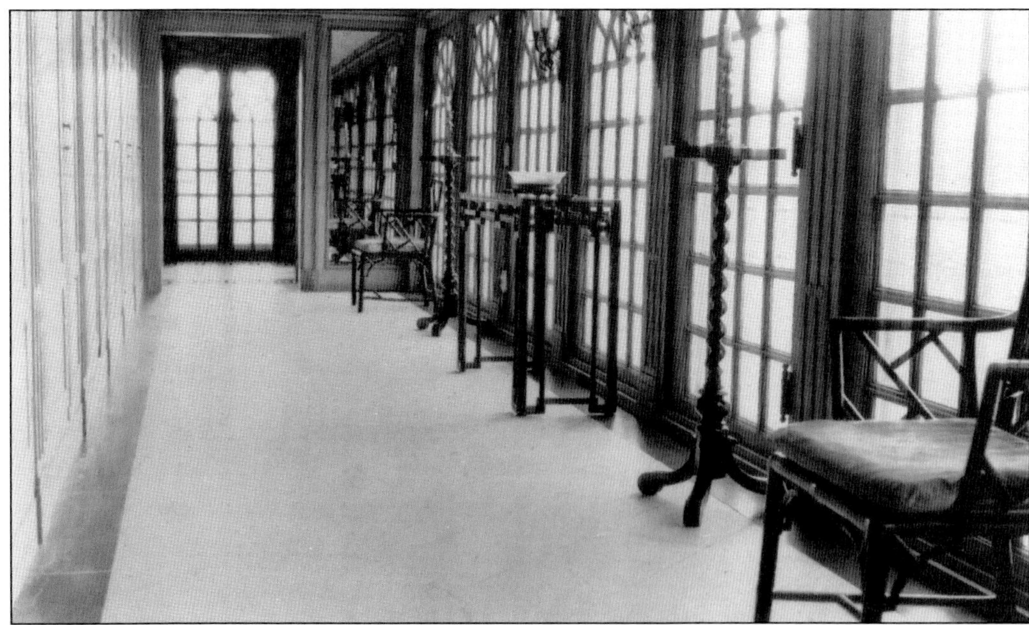

The stable's conservatory became a repository of closets for housing the costumes Allerton collected during his world travels. His costumes came from Greece, Spain, Mexico, the Middle East, and Asia, among other countries. After being placed in various locations in the house, the closets eventually wound up here. (APRC.)

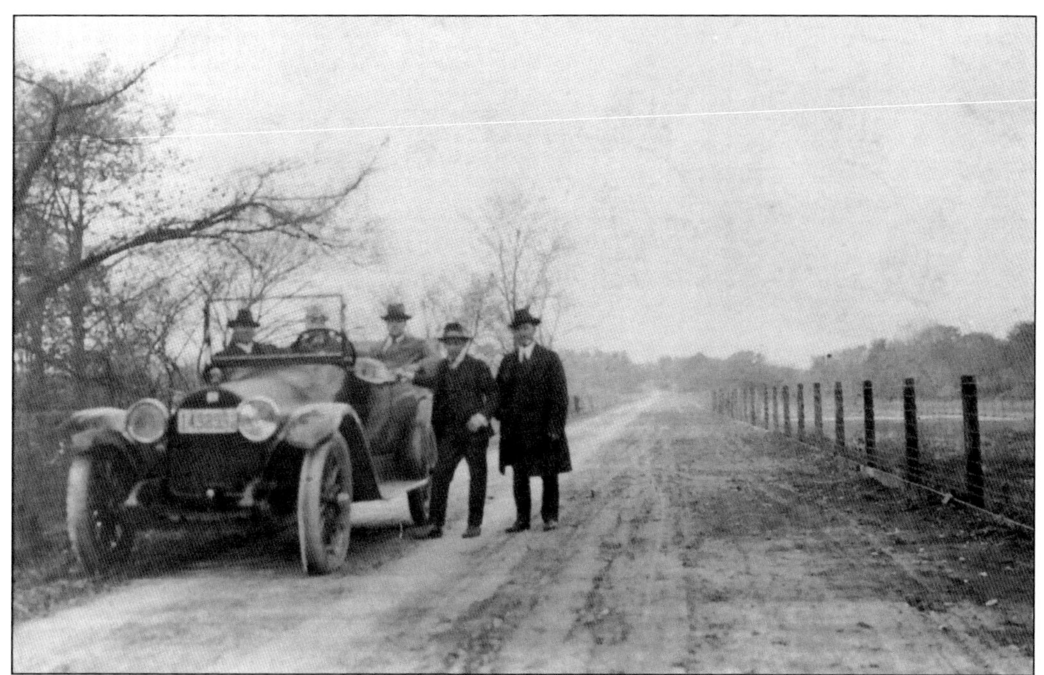

In 1915, Robert Allerton is pictured with the design team he commissioned to construct a new bridge across the Sangamon River. In the Maxwell's front seat are architect Joseph Corson Llewellyn (left) and the chauffeur. Robert Allerton is in the backseat. Standing are Ed Nitschke (left) and engineer Arthur T. Porterfield, members of Llewellyn's design team. (APRC.)

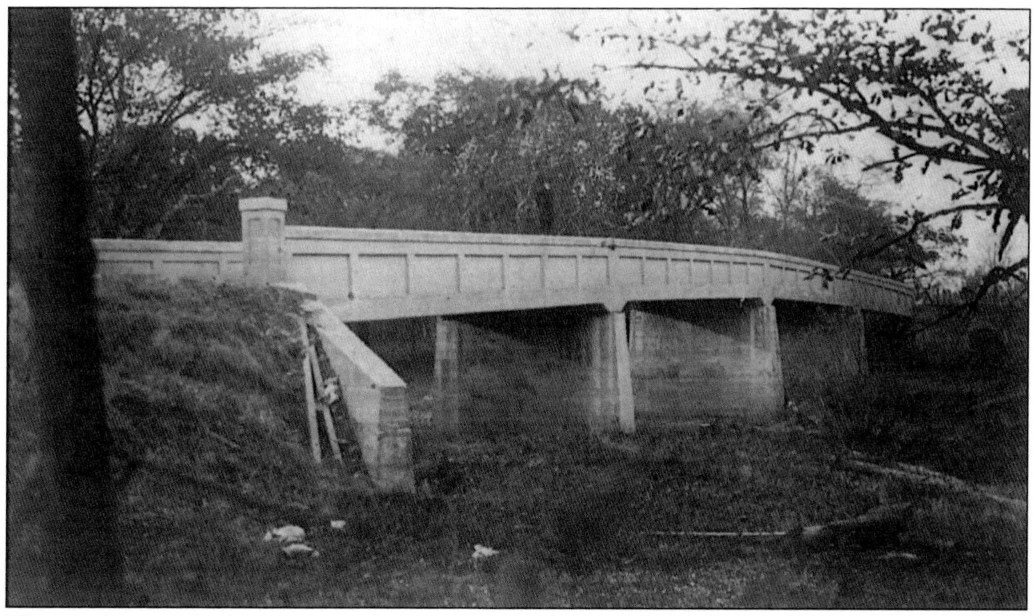

The one-lane arched concrete bridge over the Sangamon, seen here in 1918, replaced the river ford. The bridge lasted until 2001, when its deterioration made it unsafe. For a few years, visitors entered the area via a longer, alternate north route. A new metal bridge was finally constructed in 2012 at a cost of $1.6 million. Sources included state capital funds. (APRC.)

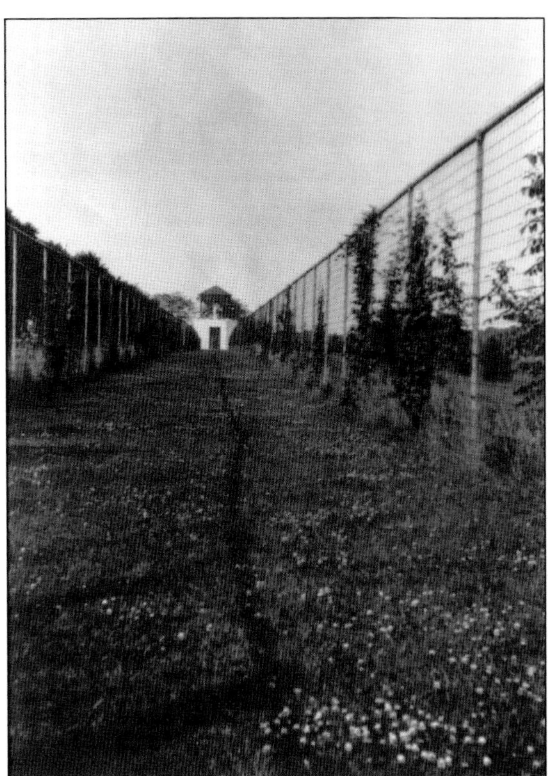

In 1915, Allerton designed the vine walk leading from the gatehouse to a new concrete gazebo. Bordered by wire trellises covered in vines, the vine walk would be shaded by cedar trees planted on each side. This 1925 photograph shows the gazebo with a second story of cast-iron fencing that Allerton found in Chicago in 1924. (APRC.)

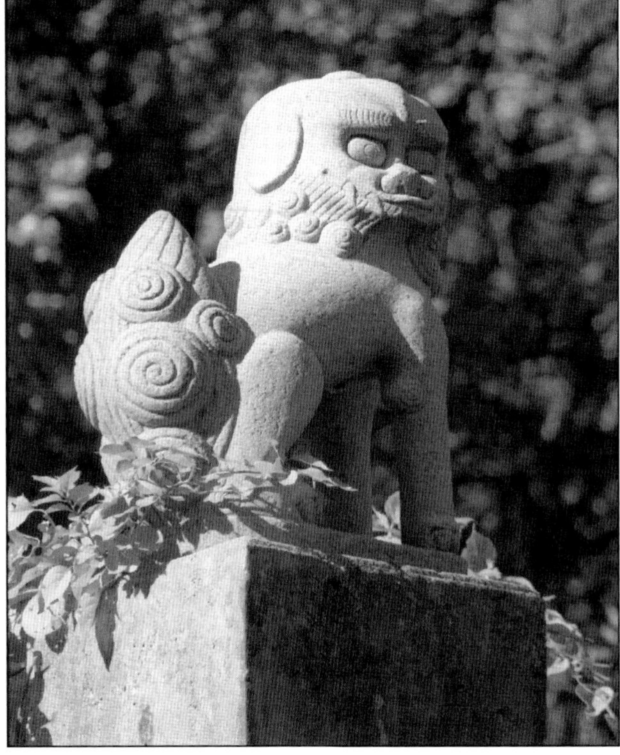

Allerton placed two granite Korean fu dogs on columns at the eastern end of the vine walk, facing the gazebo. With origins in China, the mythological creatures were said to offer protective benefits and were often used as "guardian lions." Other fu dogs were used as architectural ornaments, as seen throughout Allerton's estate. (MH.)

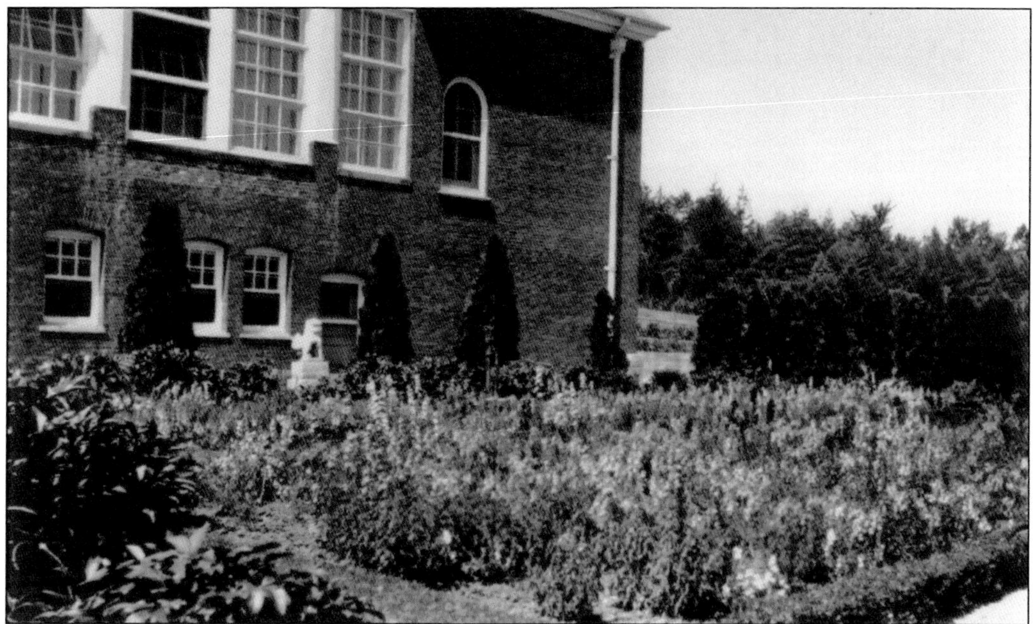

In this 1920 photograph, a granite Korean fu dog stands watching over flowers in the kitchen garden at the northeast stable façade. Collected for years, most of the fu dogs scattered around the estate are either blue or granite. Currently, a green fu dog stands in the kitchen garden overlooking the vegetables and herbs. (APRC.)

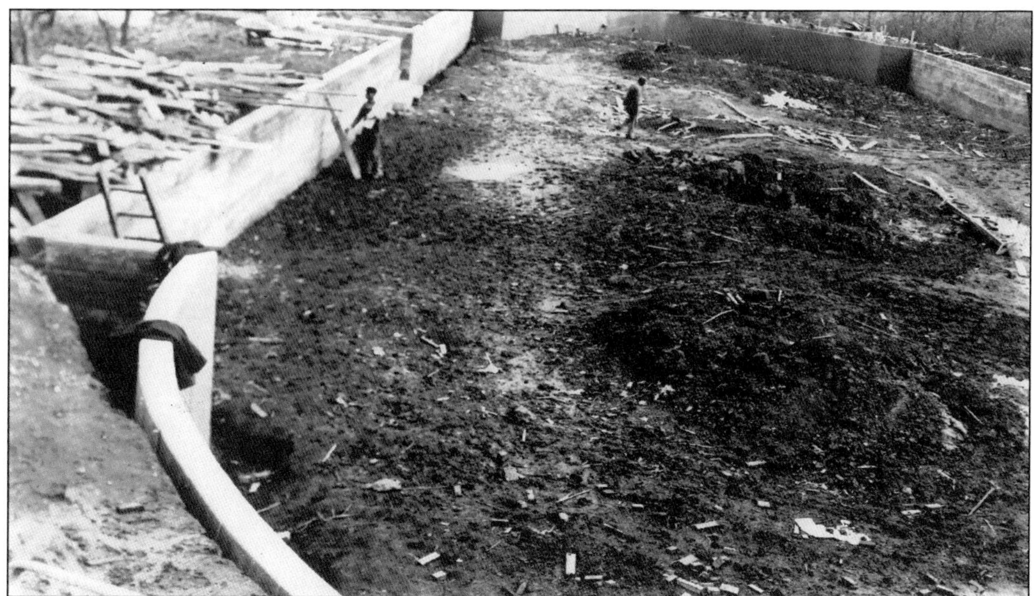

As Allerton's garden projects expanded, he eventually reached his landfill beyond the Avenue of Chinese musicians. An architect friend, David Adler, helped Allerton begin a new garden there in 1915. Allerton hired Monticello contractor William F. Lodge to lead the sunken garden project, lay draining tile, and level the area before pouring concrete walls, the first in Piatt County. Here, two unidentified workers labor on the project. (APRC.)

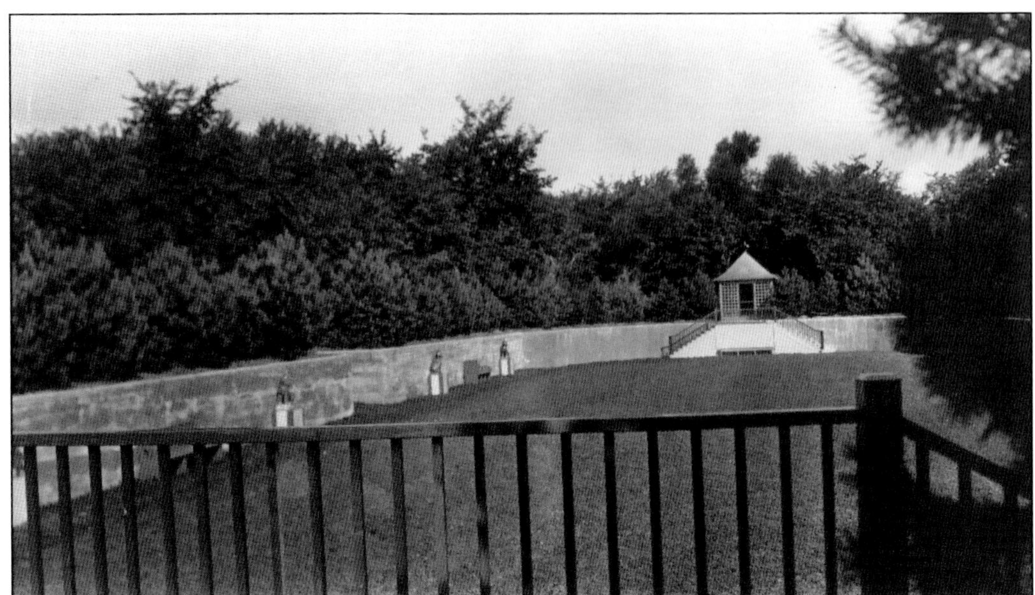

By 1917, the sunken garden had been completed, with lattice gazebos above the walls and double stairways with railings at the north and south ends leading down to the grass. Two low wooden benches sit between the stairs, and four fu dogs stand on pedestals against the concrete wall. Over the next few years, Allerton pursued more extensive modifications in the garden. (APRC.)

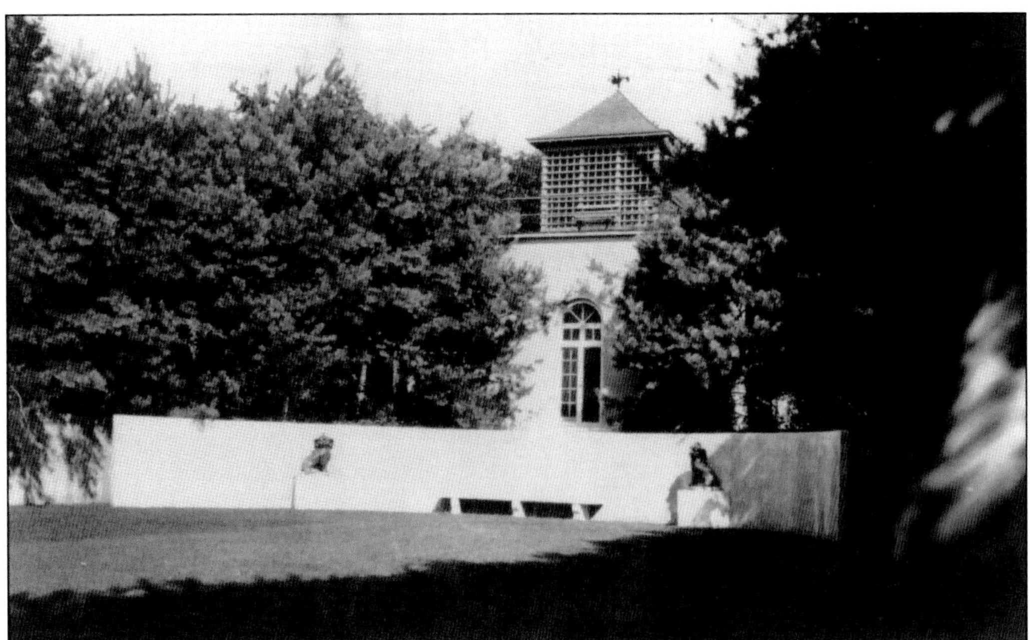

The sunken garden underwent more modifications in the mid-1920s. As of 1925, the lattice gazebo from the 1917 photograph was removed and placed on top of a newly-constructed square tea house with French doors. A weathervane perches above the gazebo. Two fu dogs sit on medium-height pedestals flanking a stone bench. (APRC.)

After the 1916 death of his maternal aunt Reinette McCrea, Allerton commissioned stone carver Charles Laing to copy Germain Pilon's *The Three Graces* for his aunt's Lake Geneva gravesite. Later, Allerton commissioned Laing to create another copy, this one to be located at the Farms. Since 1970, it sits in the peony garden. Peonies were said to be Allerton's favorite flowers. (MH.)

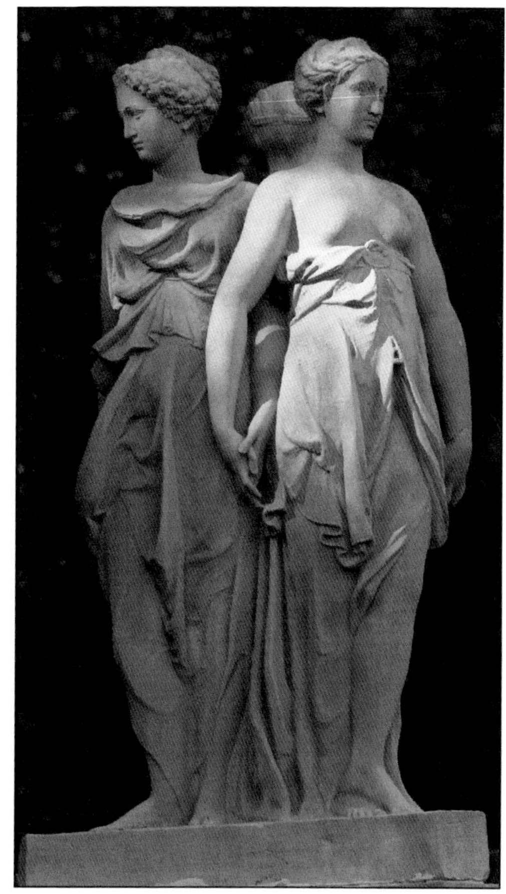

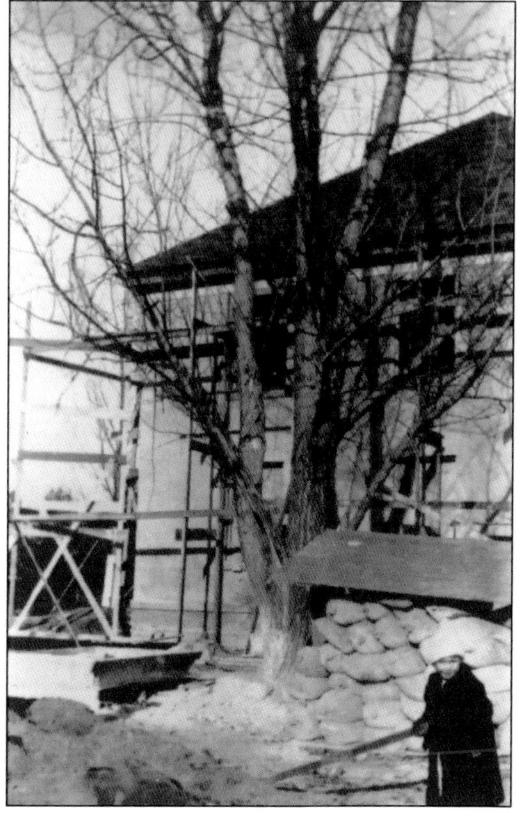

In 1917, Allerton commissioned Joseph Corson Llewellyn to design a home farther down Old Timber Road for the head gardener and his family. It would be called the House in the Woods. The unique construction included hollow tiles covered with stucco. In this 1917 photograph, three-year-old Pauline Ashby, daughter of the estate's cook and dairy barn operator, stands at lower right. (APRC.)

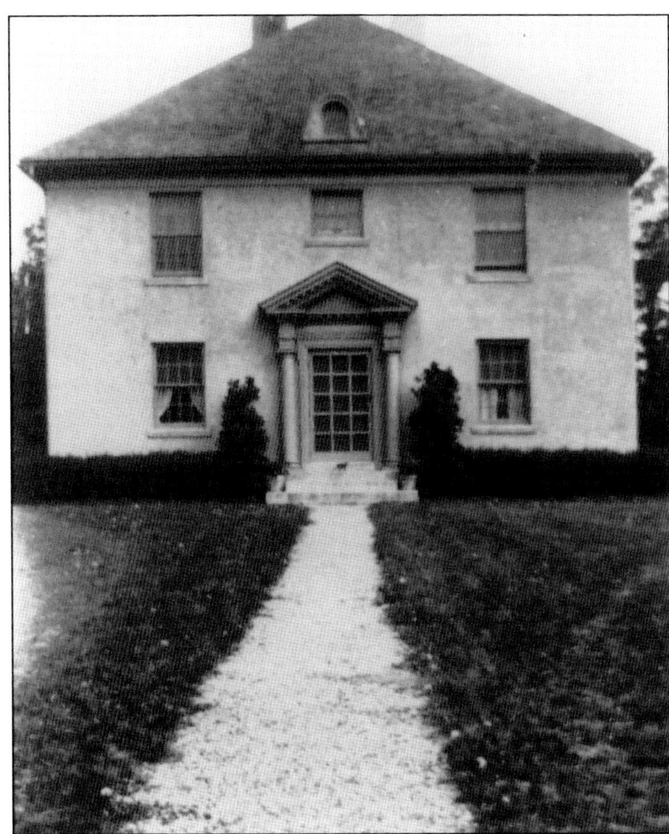

In 1925, a kitten sits on the steps of the House in the Woods. The front door was salvaged from the mansion when the marble hallway joined it to the stables. Ten years after Allerton built the House in the Woods, he relocated the shepherd and shepherdess sculptures from their positions in the square parterre to here, later placing them atop columns facing the gatehouse. (APRC.)

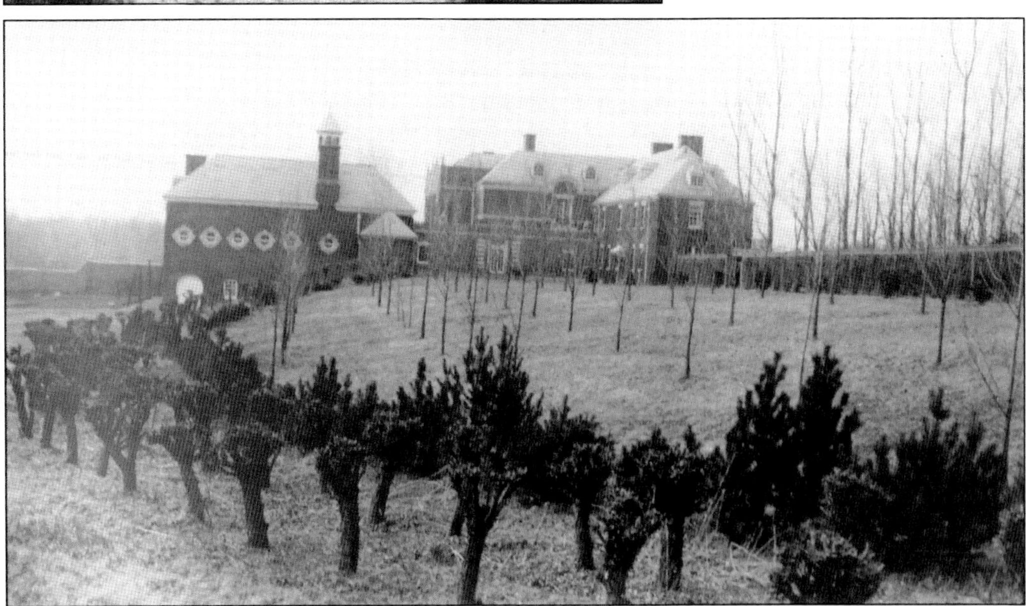

This 1918 photograph shows the mansion's entry court, the east wall, the northwest stable and mansion façades, and the northeast façade of the servants' wing. By this time, the stable had been joined to the mansion, and the parapet was removed. To the right of the newly planted trees and shrubs, a trellis fence runs along the carriage drive. (APRC.)

Glyn Warren Philpot revisited Allerton in 1921. During his stay, he created a small plaster model of a primitive man, pushing through the earth. Afterward, Allerton commissioned Charles Laing to sculpt Philpot's model into two symmetrical limestone *Primitive Man* statues facing each other on the Avenue of the Formal Gardens. In 1923, Philpot exhibited the plaster models at London's Grosvenor Galleries. (MH.)

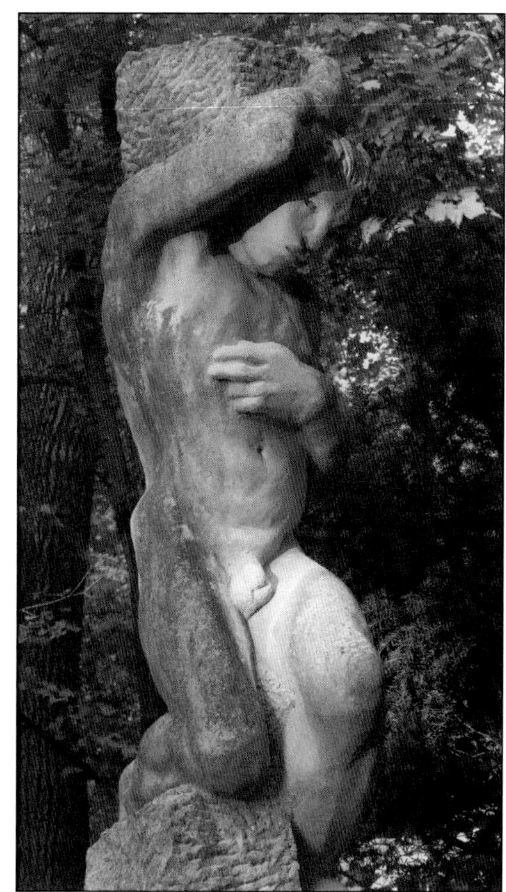

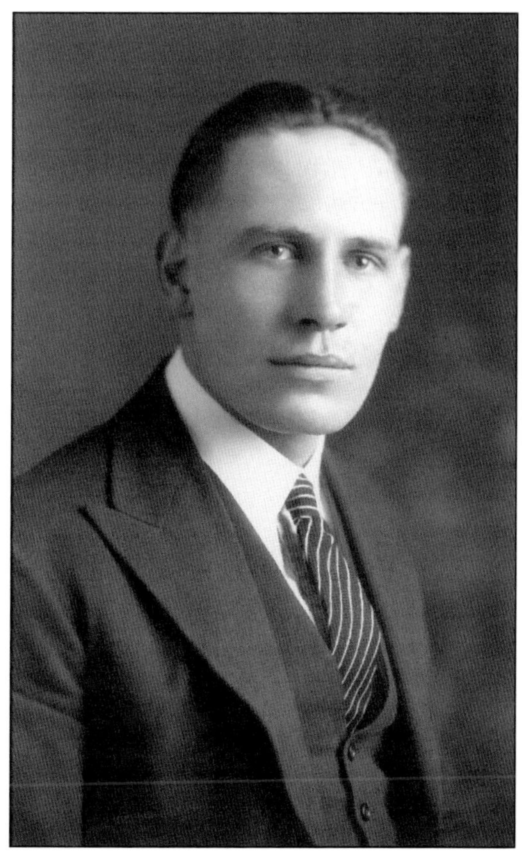

Allerton's butler, Edward Page, was the model for Philpot's *Primitive Man* sculpture. Page posed nude in the cold studio for hours every day, balancing a load of heavy books on his shoulder. In exchange for his efforts, he earned $5. As his son-in-law later recalled, Page felt he should have been paid more. (JG.)

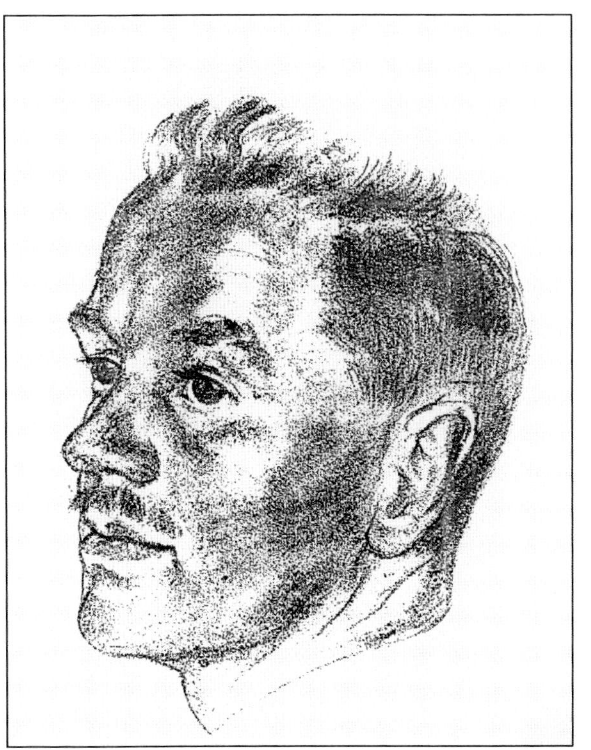

When Glyn Philpot returned in 1921, he brought his close companion of six years, artist and poet Vivian Forbes. While there, Forbes made a charcoal sketch of Allerton. An engaging young man, Forbes was emotionally unstable, and his poetry usually dwelled on his relationship with Philpot. In December 1937, the day after Philpot's funeral from a sudden stroke, a grief-stricken Forbes committed suicide with sleeping pills. (APRC.)

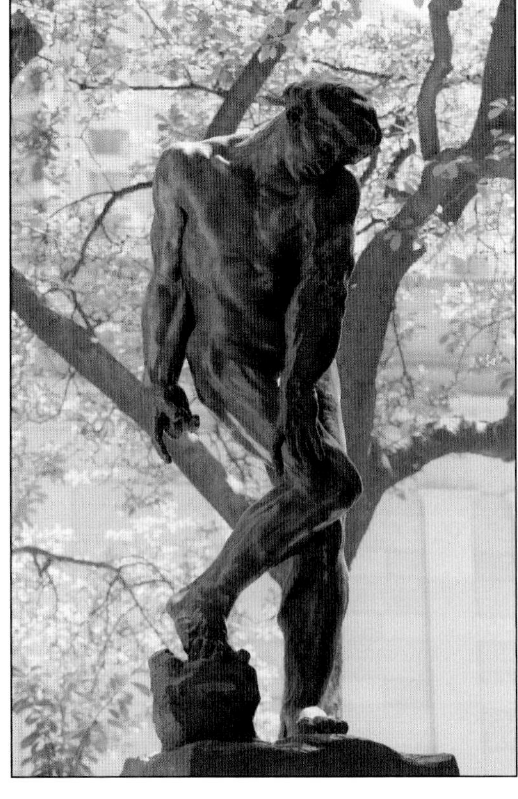

In 1924, Robert Allerton purchased a bronze statue for the Art Institute from the studio of Auguste Rodin. Inspired by Adam stretching on the Sistine Chapel ceiling, the agony shown by *Adam* exemplifies the sufferings caused by original sin. In this casting at Philadelphia's Museum of Art, *Adam's* pointing right arm is similar to the one on the Sistine ceiling, receiving life from God. (MH.)

Allerton commissioned Charles Laing, the carver of *Primitive Man* and *The Three Graces*, to make a reproduction of the original *Adam* for his estate, seen in this 1925 photograph. Damaged in transport, it was finally toppled by a visitor in 1975. Allerton commissioned Laing to make another reproduction. Rather than leave the stone uncut, in an attempt to strengthen the piece, Laing connected both hands to the body. (APRC.)

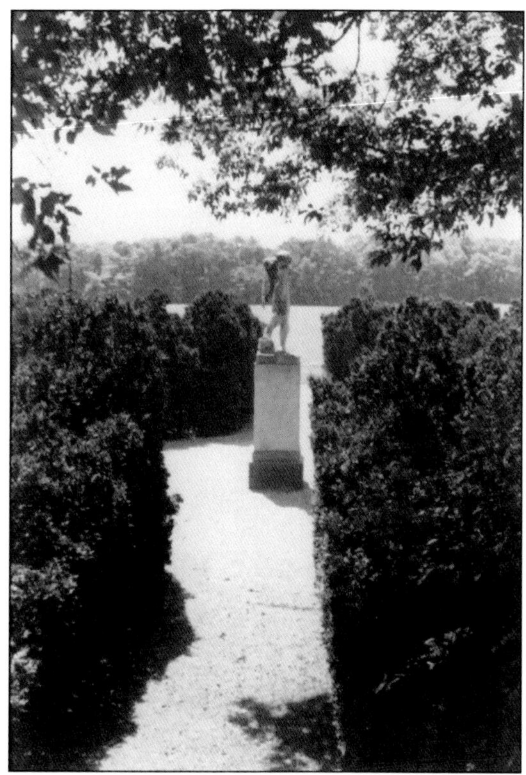

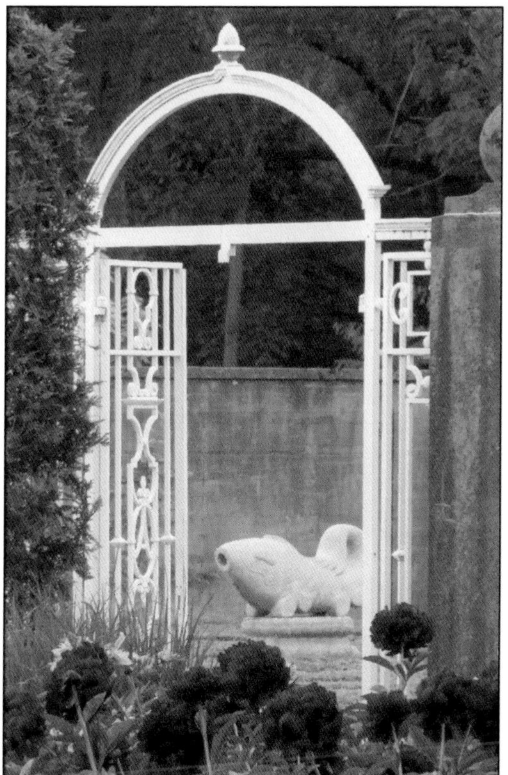

During his travels in China, Allerton purchased two marble goldfish fountains, supposedly from a prince's garden, through a dealer in Peking (Beijing). In 1925, Allerton shuffled statuary in the Chinese parterre, replacing fu dogs with the two goldfish sculptures, never utilizing them as fountains. He moved Borie's gates to the Chinese parterre in 1930. (MH.)

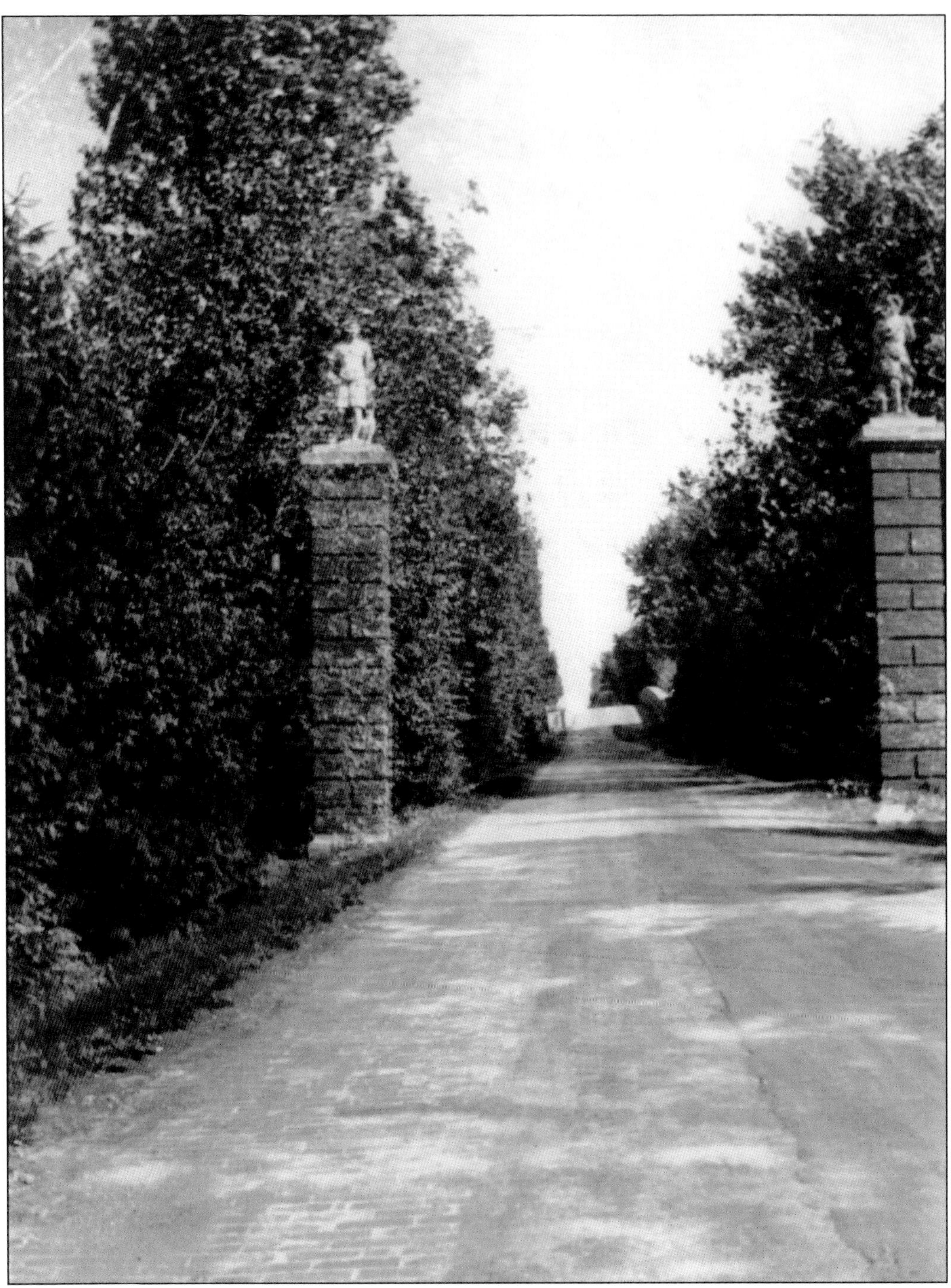

Allerton referred to the five-foot-tall concrete statues of Diana and her male companion, an ephebe, as "Charlie" and "Frances" because they were given to him by his friends Charles and Frances Pike. The statues first stood in the square parterre before being moved in 1925, finally standing on columns at the south entrance to the estate. The difference in paving in the farm-to-market road is visible. (APRC.)

# *Six*

# Love, Death, and Changes 1920–1941

As the decades progressed, Robert Allerton participated more with Chicago's Art Institute. Meanwhile, his gardens bloomed with more sculptures. Modifications also followed in his mansion, including two music room renovations. The first involved repainting the room and installing jungle-like murals on the upper half of the walls. Frederic Clay Bartlett created the murals, which were similar to Henri Rousseau's work. A second and later renovation turned the room into a library, involving removal of the murals and adding shelving and a walkway along the upper part of the room.

Allerton's personal life took a turn when, through a Monticello relative in 1922, he met John Wyatt Gregg, a young architectural student at the University of Illinois. As Gregg quickly grew in importance to him, Allerton began referring to him as his "adopted son" and helped him in his career. Through Allerton's friendship with Chicago architect David Adler, Gregg began working in Adler's office in 1926. After Adler closed his office in 1932, Allerton suggested Gregg come to live at the Farms to assist Elmer Priebe in managing the property.

In 1924, Allerton's beloved stepmother, Agnes, suffered a slow and painful death due to sclerosis of the liver. As with his father, he inherited well from her estate. Four years later, he opened and funded a new wing in the Art Institute's decorative arts department, dedicated to Agnes Allerton.

In June 1929, Robert learned that his nephew, Allerton Johnstone, had leaped from the fifth-floor window of a Los Angeles hotel. With a history of mental illness, the 28-year-old amateur wrestler had grown despondent over a relationship with a woman. A few years later, on December 31, 1937, Kate Allerton Johnstone passed away in Pasadena after suffering from brain cancer. She was buried at Graceland Cemetery in Chicago, joining her son, father, and stepmother in the family plot. She left another son, Vanderburgh Johnstone, and twin grandsons. In her will, she left a $600 monthly allowance to her ex-husband, Hugo Johnstone.

At the time of her death, Robert Allerton and Gregg were on a life-changing trip that took them to Kauai in mid-February 1938.

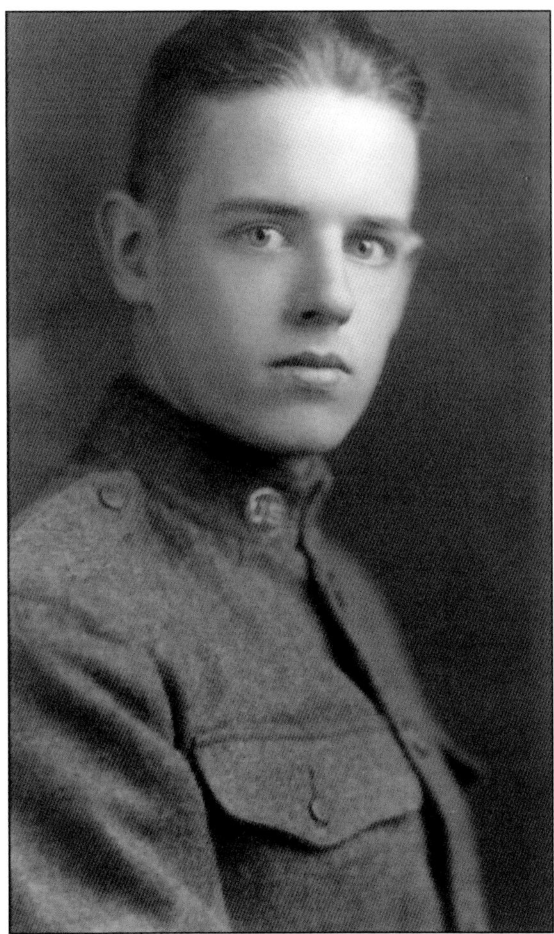

Born in 1899, John Wyatt Gregg served in World War I before attending the University of Wisconsin, studying chemical engineering. Upon his father's death in 1921, Gregg quit college to join an architectural practice and support himself. In 1922, he enrolled at the University of Illinois's architecture school, living at the Zeta Psi fraternity, working part-time jobs as the fraternity's bookkeeper and commissary steward and as a teaching assistant. (APRC.)

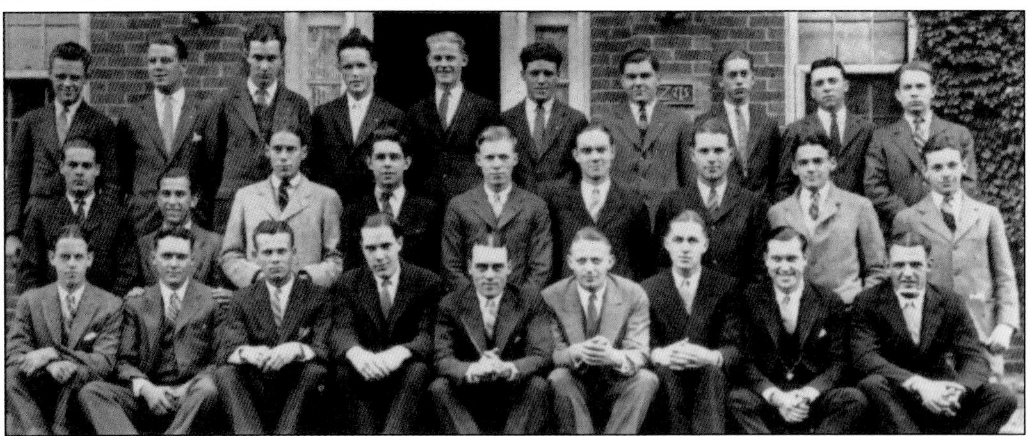

John Gregg's fraternity roommates were Robert Allerton's second cousin Asler C. Dighton and William T. Lodge, both from Monticello. Another fraternity brother was "Red" Grange. Gregg sits in the first row at far left, Dighton is in the second row third from left, and Lodge is in the third row at far left. In November 1922, during the campus Dad's Day celebration, Lodge suggested that Allerton substitute as Gregg's father for the fraternity lunch, setting off a lifelong relationship. (APRC.)

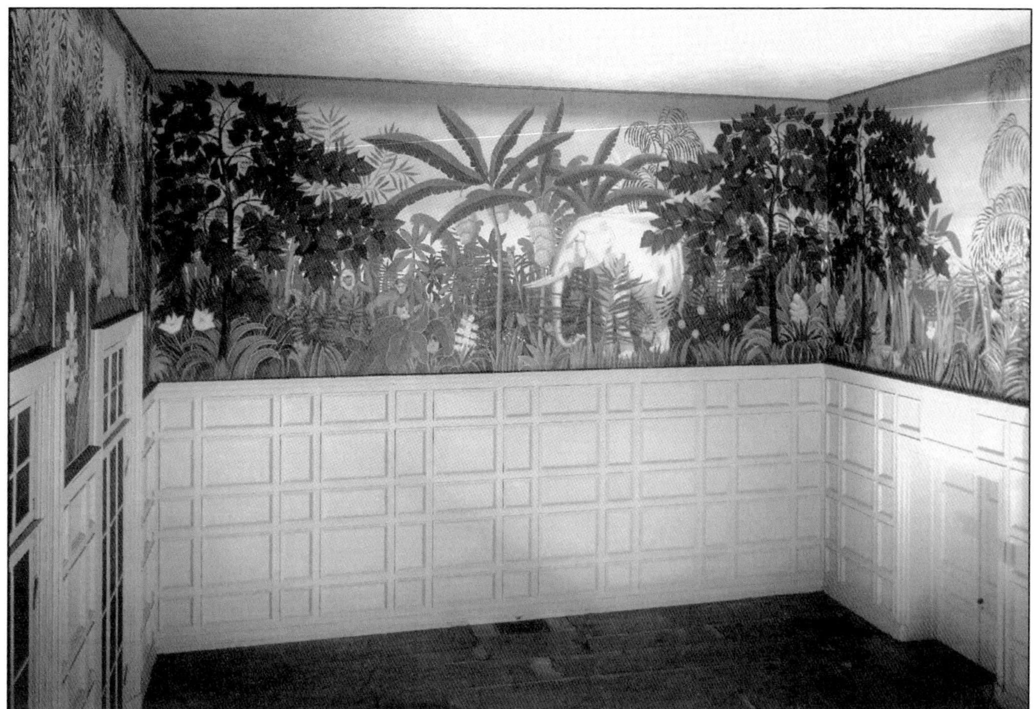

Two years after the death of Frederic Bartlett's first wife, Dora, in 1917, he married her friend Helen Birch. When Birch died in 1925 from cancer, Bartlett was subject to depression. To take his mind off his loneliness, Allerton suggested that Bartlett could help redecorate the music room with a jungle fresco that included tropical plants, elephants, and mandarin-yellow paneling. (BH.)

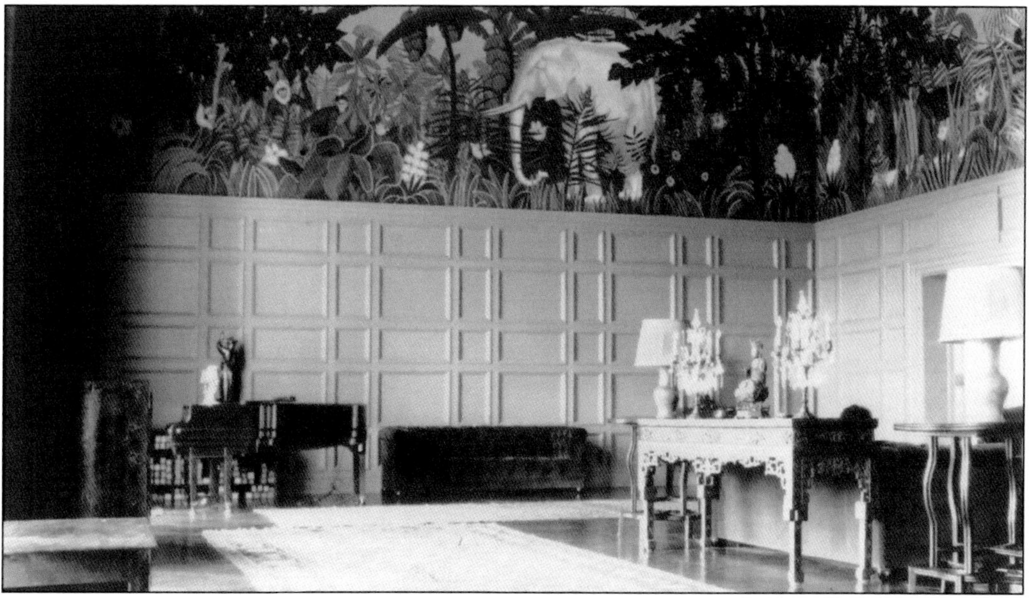

In this 1927 photograph, Allerton has moved furniture back into the room, including his Steinway Model B piano. In time, he learned that his guests did not care for the overpowering jungle appearance, nor the plush peach-colored furniture, and would avoid the room. Over the years, the mural began to deteriorate. It was time for another change. (APRC.)

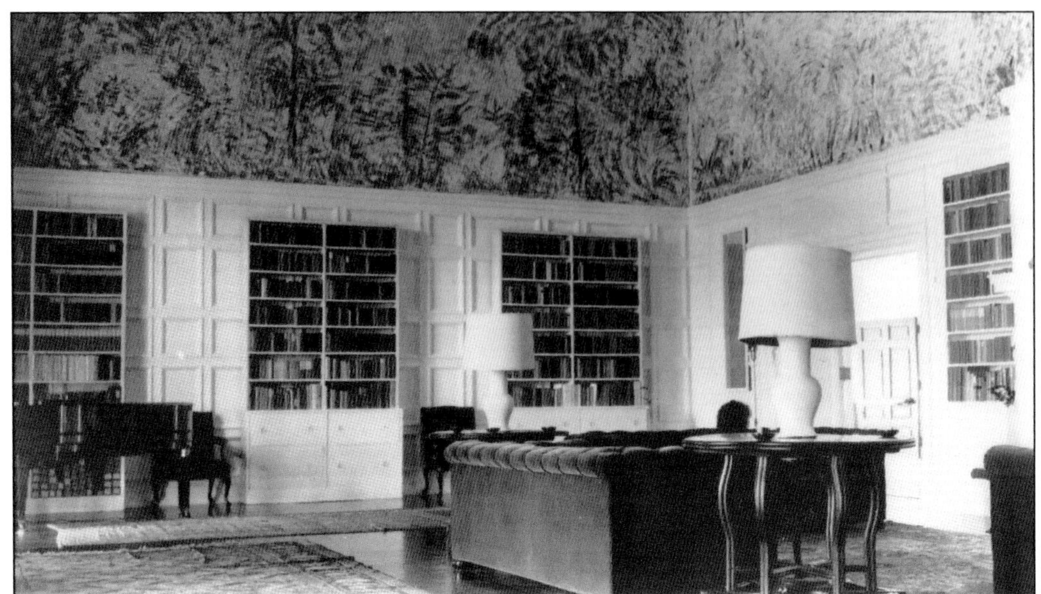

In 1940, Allerton lightened up the music room, remodeling it into a library. Frederic Bartlett's murals were removed, rolled up, and stored, and the plaster was painted white. This photograph shows the room with the murals gone. The bookshelves lining the room are free-standing, taken from the marble hall. The piano was earmarked for John Gregg's sister. The sofas were reupholstered and currently can be found in the gallery. (APRC.)

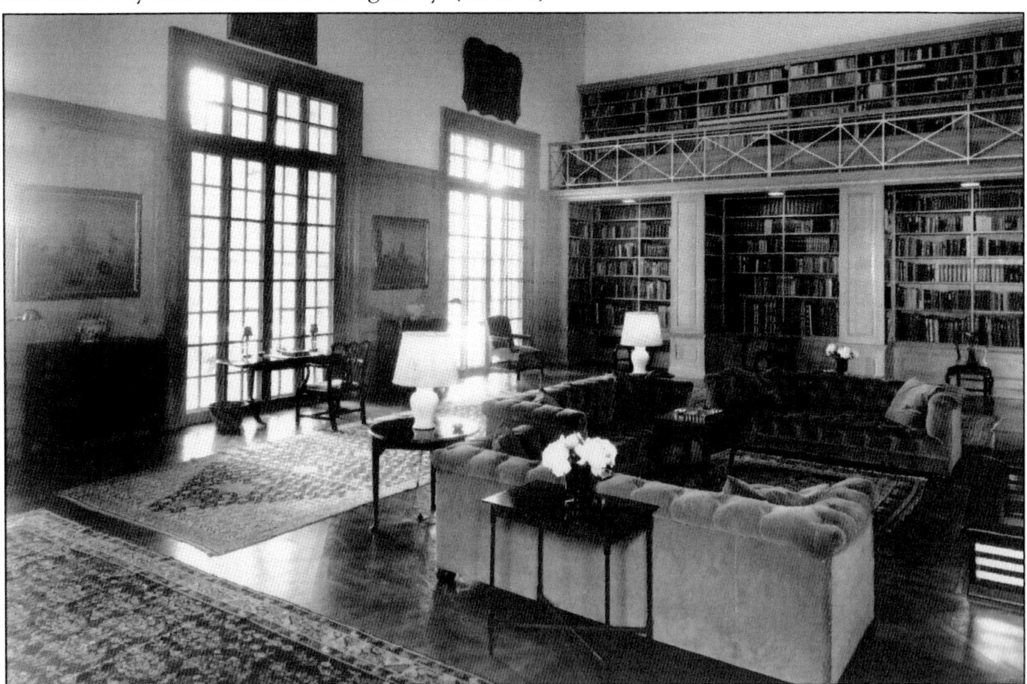

The music room's overhaul was complete by September 1940. The panels and library shelves around three sides are varnished yellow pine. The free-standing shelves, ceiling panels, and marble fireplace designed by John Borie were donated to the University of Illinois, and a new and simpler fireplace was installed. Only the flooring is original. (APRC.)

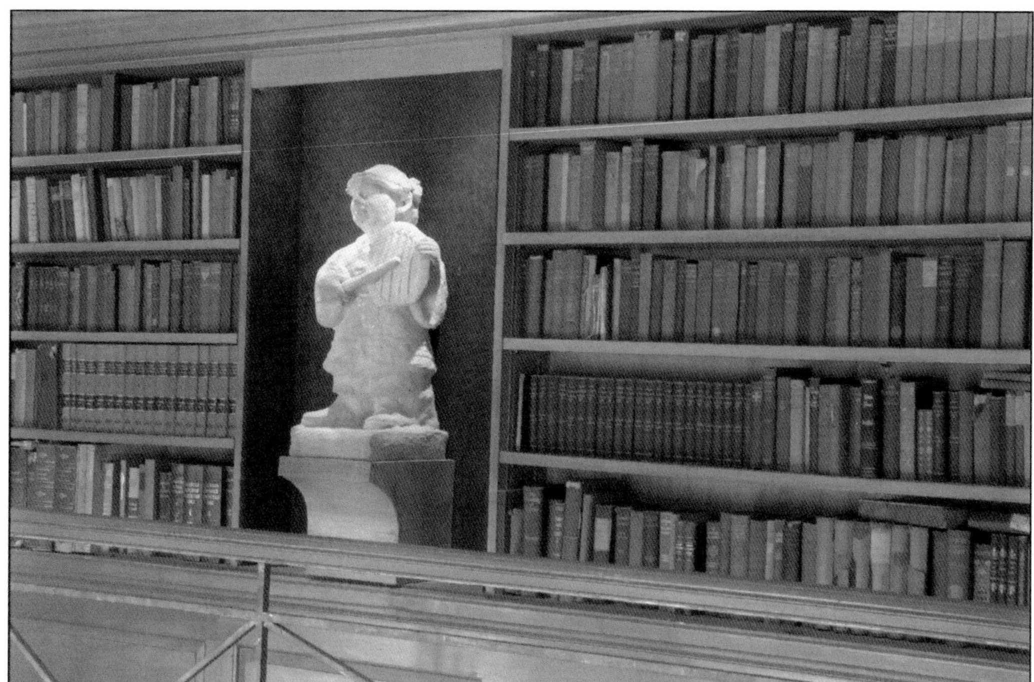

Additional shelves above the main floor of the refurbished music room are accessible only through a locked mirrored door on the stairway landing. Currently, several original fu dog statues stand in niches surrounded by books Allerton collected during his overseas travels. He would mark each book with the city where it was purchased. (MH.)

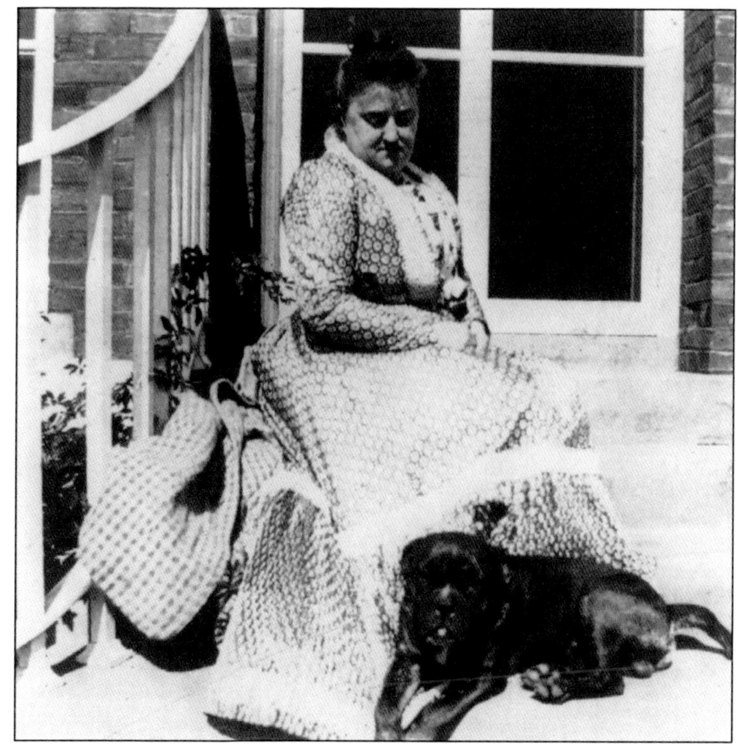

Agnes Allerton is seen here in 1920 at the Farms. She died in 1924, leaving most of her $2 million estate to Robert, including the Lake Geneva and Pasadena houses and her Chicago apartment at 1315 Astor Street. He brought some of her belongings to Monticello, but others, including a silver tea set, he threw away or tossed into Lake Geneva. He sold the Pasadena house and razed the Folly. (APRC.)

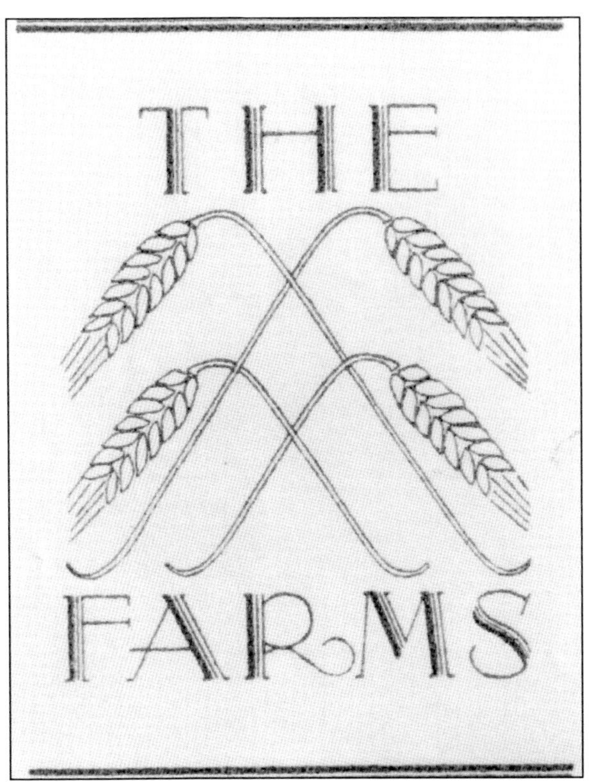


This logo for Allerton's stationery letterhead may have been designed by John Wyatt Gregg. The two crossed shafts of wheat, originally in cobalt blue, highlight the Farms' agricultural focus, as noted by a comment from Samuel Allerton when his son remarked on a sunset's beauty: "Look at the corn and wheat. That's where the money is." (APRC.)

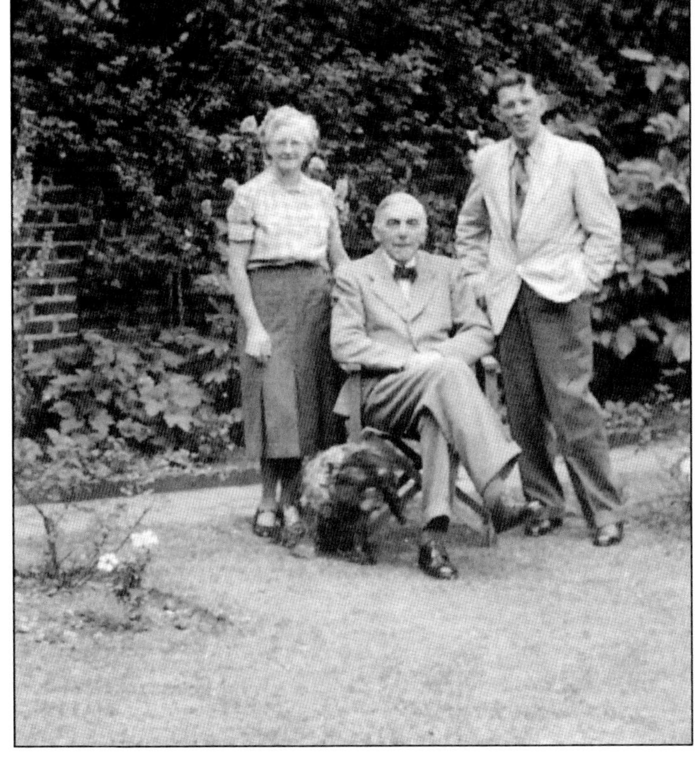

In 1928, Allerton's close friend in England, Roger Quilter, compiled a new piece of music entitled "I Arise from Dreams of Thee," based on a poem by Percy Bysshe Shelley. The composition, arranged for tenor voice with orchestra, was dedicated to Allerton. In this photograph, Quilter sits between employees Ada and Harry Heaton. (VL.)

A pair of limestone *Charioteer of Delphi* sculptures stand on the gazebo steps in 1930, with Peri Snyder near the base of the right sculpture. Both are based on a bronze statue found in 1896 in Delphi, Greece, now at the Delphi Museum. Allerton's sculptures were modeled from a terra cotta copy owned by the Art Institute. A sculpture of *Diana of Gabii* stands on the gazebo's second story. (APRC.)

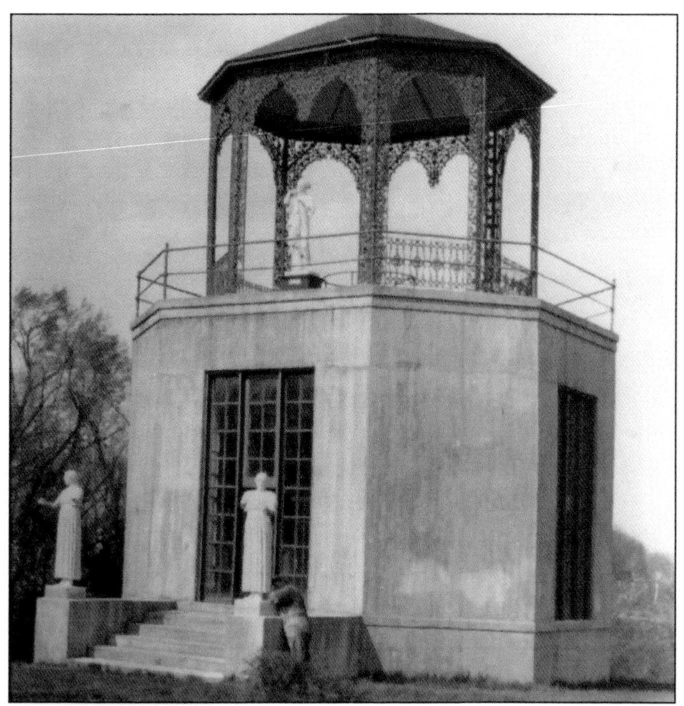

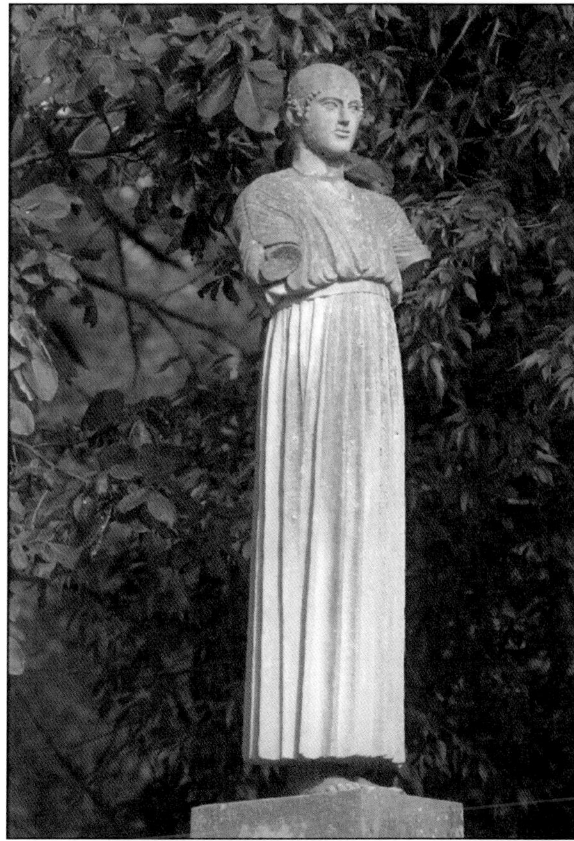

The original *Charioteer in Delphi* only had one arm, a look that Allerton chose to emulate, visible in the previous photograph showing the missing arm of the statue to the right. However, Allerton did not like the one-armed look, and preferring symmetry wherever possible, he had both arms removed. (MH.)

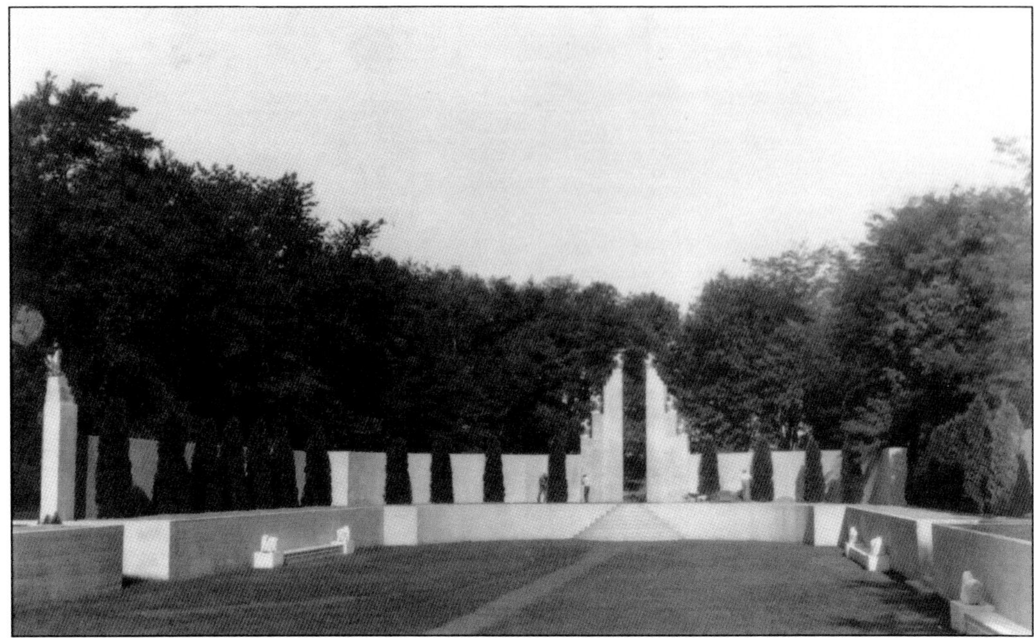

By the 1930s, Allerton and Gregg had added more outside art to the existing gardens and paths. In 1931, Allerton shipped 16 guardian fish sculptures from Japan. This 1935 photograph shows the sunken garden, redesigned with upper walls and circular stairs, and guardian fish placed on 24-foot-tall columns. Eight goldfish sit on the benches. Three gardeners and a dog work atop the wall. (APRC.)

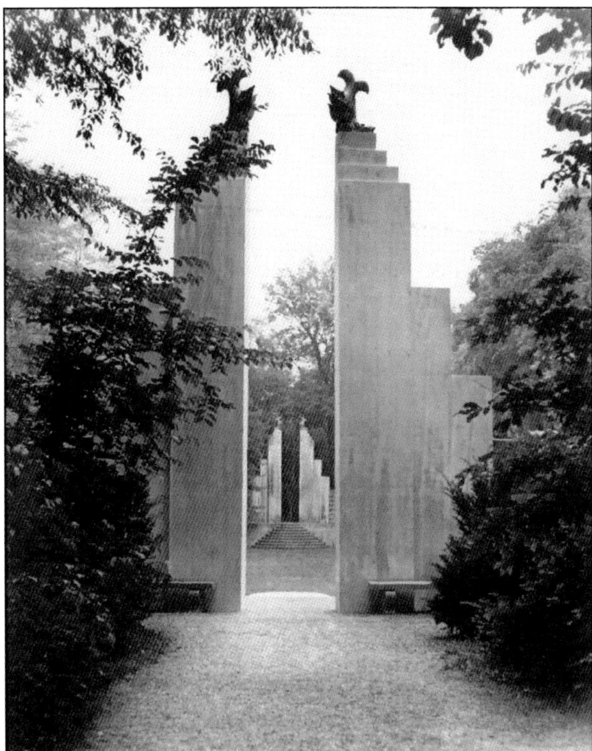

After noticing the "tiger-headed" guardian fish on the rooftop of Japan's Nagoya Castle, Allerton commissioned Yamanaka and Company to create several bronze fish covered by three layers of gold leaf for his estate. The mythological fish from Japanese folklore combine the head of tiger with a carp body. Called *shachi*, they were charms to ward off fire from Japanese palaces and castles. (APRC.)

During a Paris trip in the late 1920s, Allerton visited the studio of Émile Antoine Bourdelle, Auguste Rodin's student and friend. Among Bourdelle's work was his 1914 sculpture the *Death of the Last Centaur.* Before Bourdelle's death in 1929, Allerton commissioned a bronze casting, one of five copies. Seen in a recent photograph, a plaster centaur model still stands in Bourdelle's museum studio in Paris. (MH.)

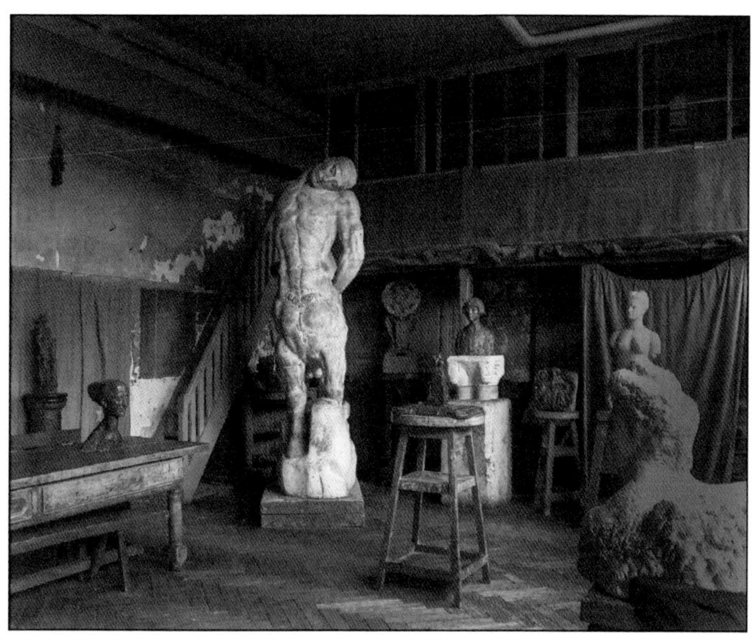

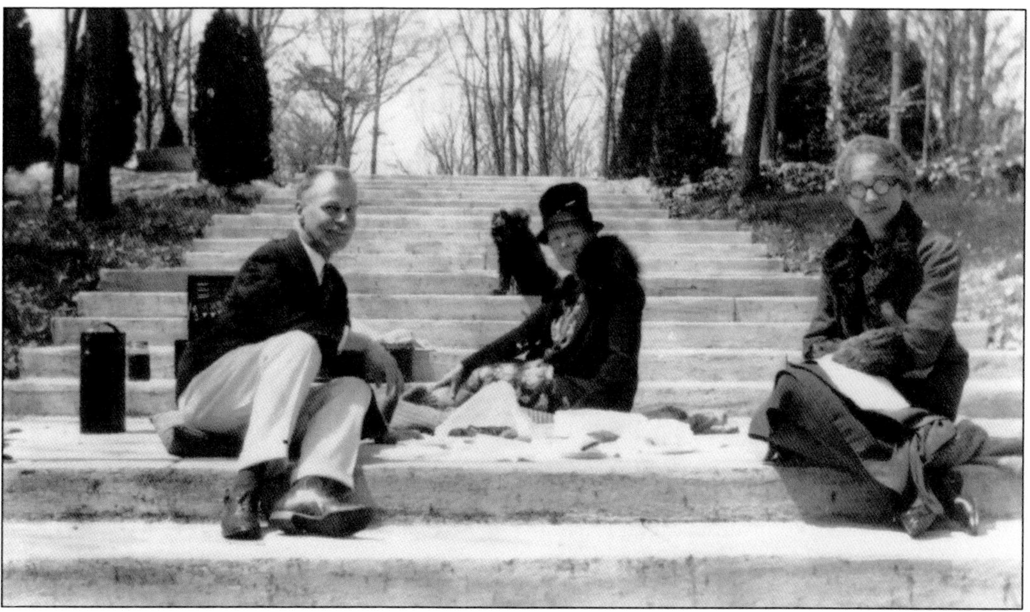

Allerton, one of his dogs, and two unidentified women enjoy a picnic in 1927 at the intersection of a path from the sunken garden. Sixty steps lead down to the river, with every fifth step forming a landing. Allerton chose this spot as the location for the *Death of the Last Centaur.* (APRC.)

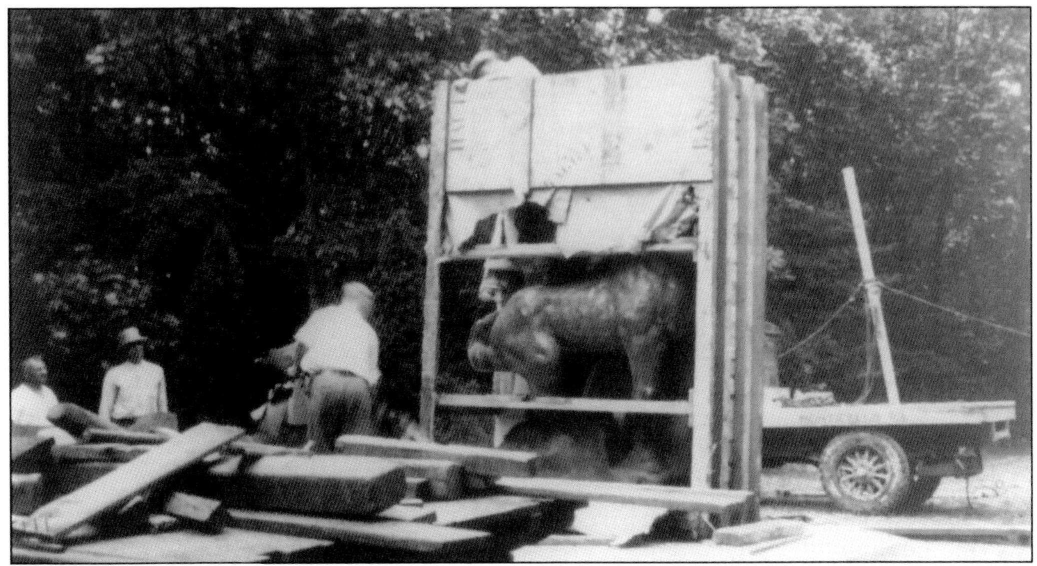

In 1932, the *Death of the Last Centaur* arrived in Monticello, ready to be placed on a two-tiered octagonal base created by John Gregg. Two men watch as two others take apart the wooden crate, unveiling the bronze sculpture. The man second from left, with what seems to be a mustache and wearing a hat and tie, may be Allerton. (APRC.)

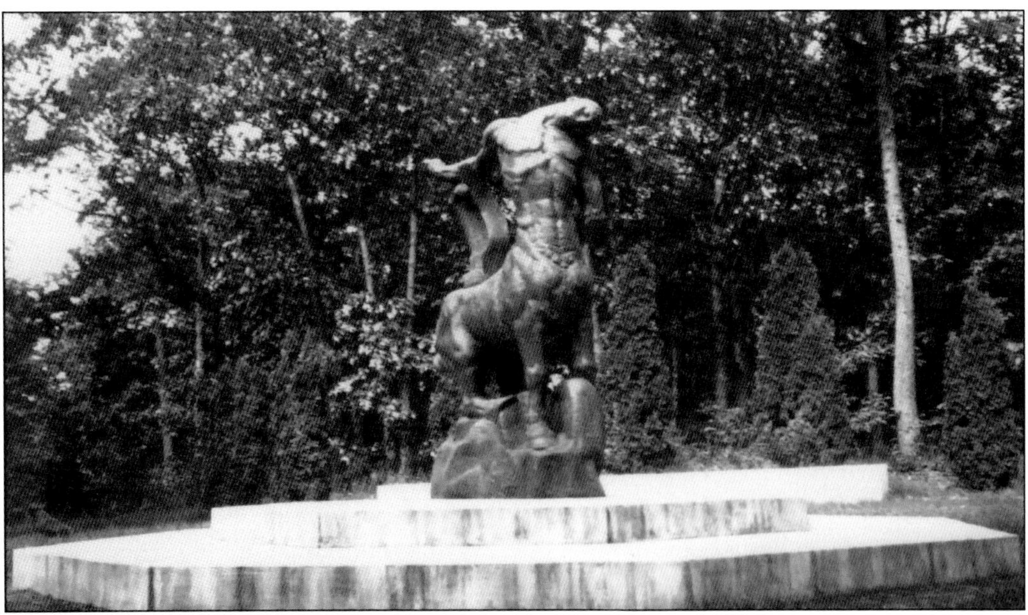

The creature in the *Death of the Last Centaur* holds a lyre, representing the melancholy artist dying because people no longer listen to him. According to Greek mythology, Chiron was the last centaur. Although immortal, he exchanged his life for that of Prometheus. Other castings can be seen in Athens, Paris, and Buenos Aires. (APRC.)

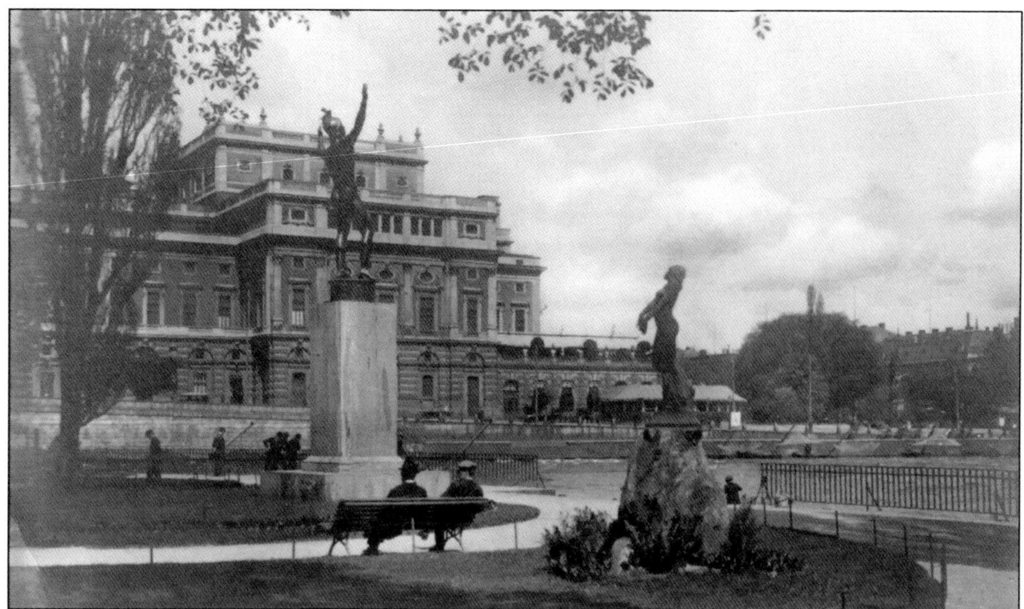

While visiting Stockholm in 1929, Allerton noticed the *Sun Singer* in Strömparterren Park near the harbor. In a visit to the artist, Carl Milles, Allerton saw Milles's much smaller statue in his garden, but it was missing its head and arms. Allerton commissioned the same small version but insisted it must have the head and arms. Because of a translation error, the artist thought Allerton wanted the same as at the harbor. (AO.)

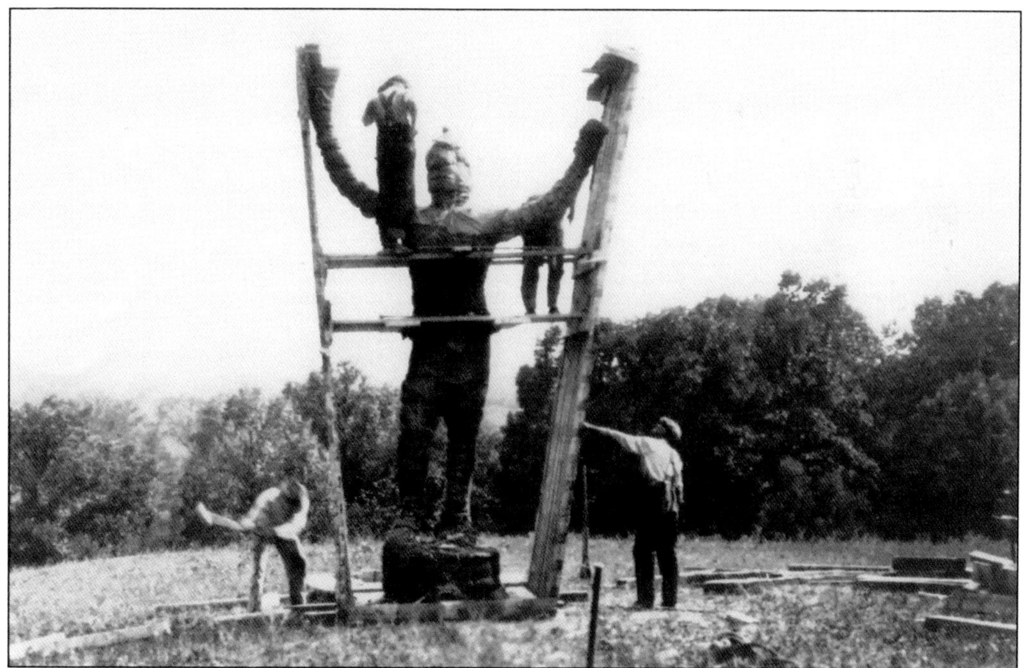

In 1931, the *Sun Singer* arrived, mummy-wrapped and much taller at 15 feet than the one commissioned. Allerton had originally planned to place the statue on the library terrace, but when it arrived, he realized a giant version would obscure his bedroom window. It needed a more monumental location. He bought property down the road for its placement. (APRC.)

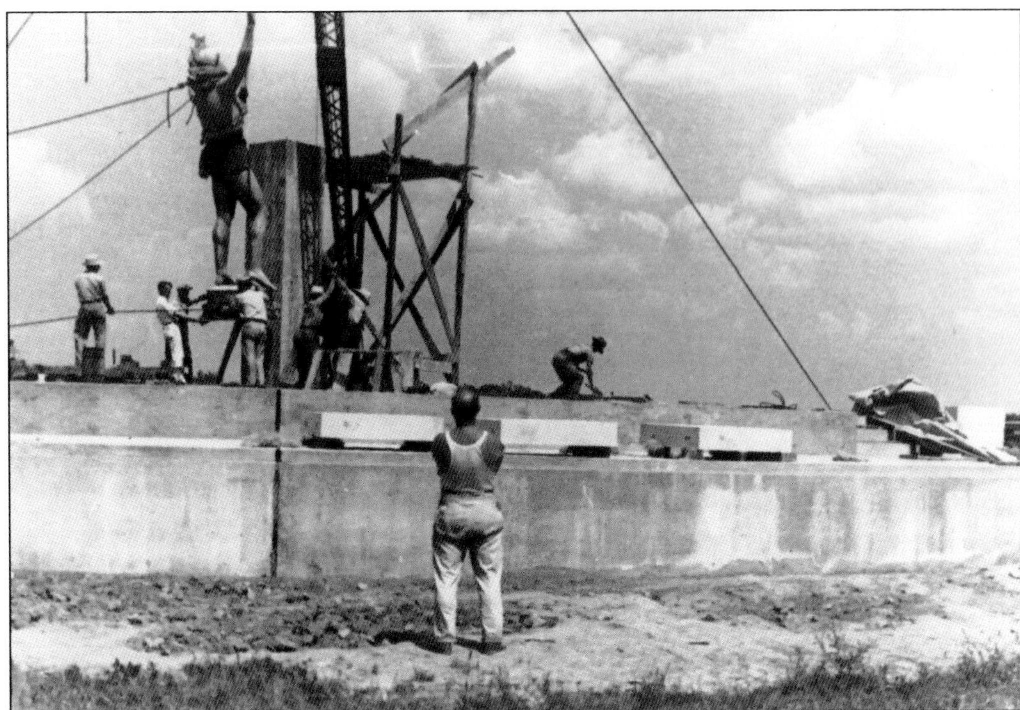

Allerton requested that Gregg design a three-tiered base for his *Sun Singer.* In this 1932 photograph, eight men hoist it to its pedestal. During the installation, before Allerton arrived, workers placed a condom on the *Sun Singer.* A home movie made of the event was later called "the Big Erection." (APRC.)

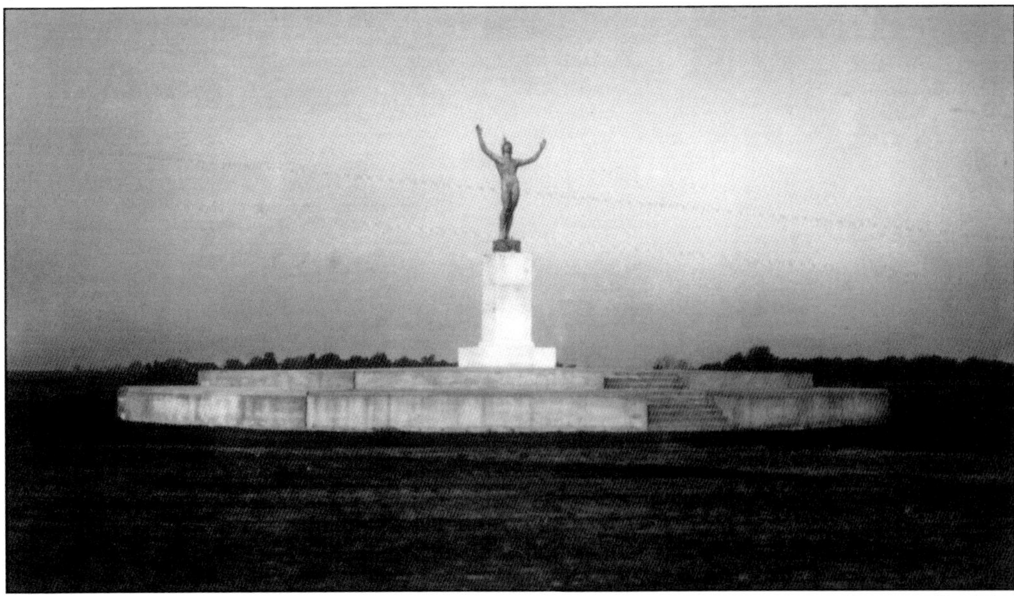

By 1932, the *Sun Singer's* installation was complete. When Allerton wrote to Milles to tell of the setting, Milles replied that a water location would have been more appropriate. In a later visit to the Farms, Milles changed his mind, telling Allerton that the setting was better than at the Stockholm harbor. The statue was restored in 2007. (APRC.)

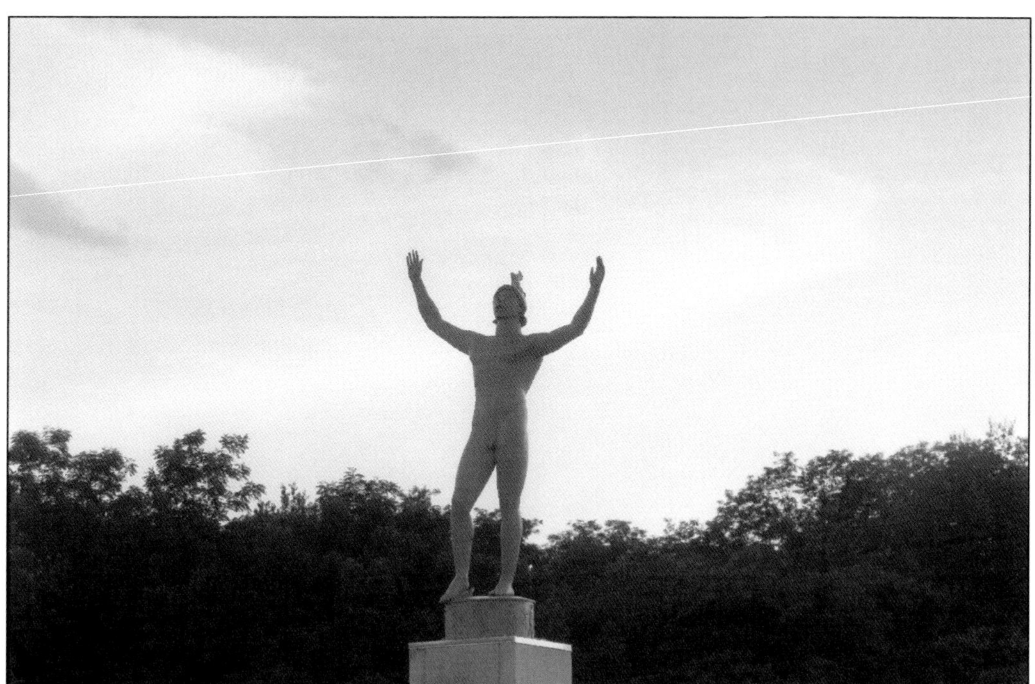

Carl Milles designed the statue after the Swedish Academy requested a monument commemorating the writer Esaias Tegnér. Illustrating Tegnér's poem *Address to the Sun*, Milles sculpted Apollo—the Greek god of light, poetry, and music—singing to the rising sun. Nine muses are sculpted around the statue's base. Under Apollo's right heel is a tortoise, possibly referencing the lyre made from a tortoise's shell. (MH.)

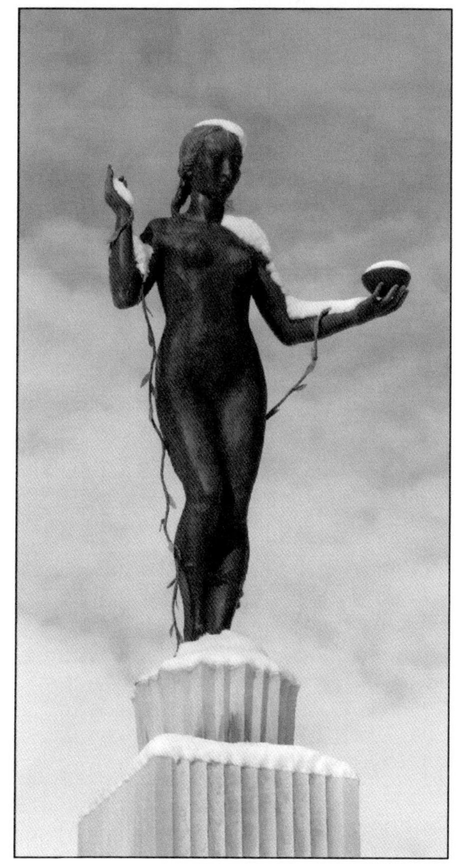

While visiting Hamburg, Germany, in 1930 with Gregg, Allerton noticed a sea maiden statue atop a kiosk holding a Viking longboat in an advertisement for a shipping company. Allerton sought out the artist, Richard Kuöhl, and commissioned him to create a pair of statues for the Farms. In lieu of the longboat, the statues offer "bowls of plenty" to hold grain but still drip with seaweed. (MH.)

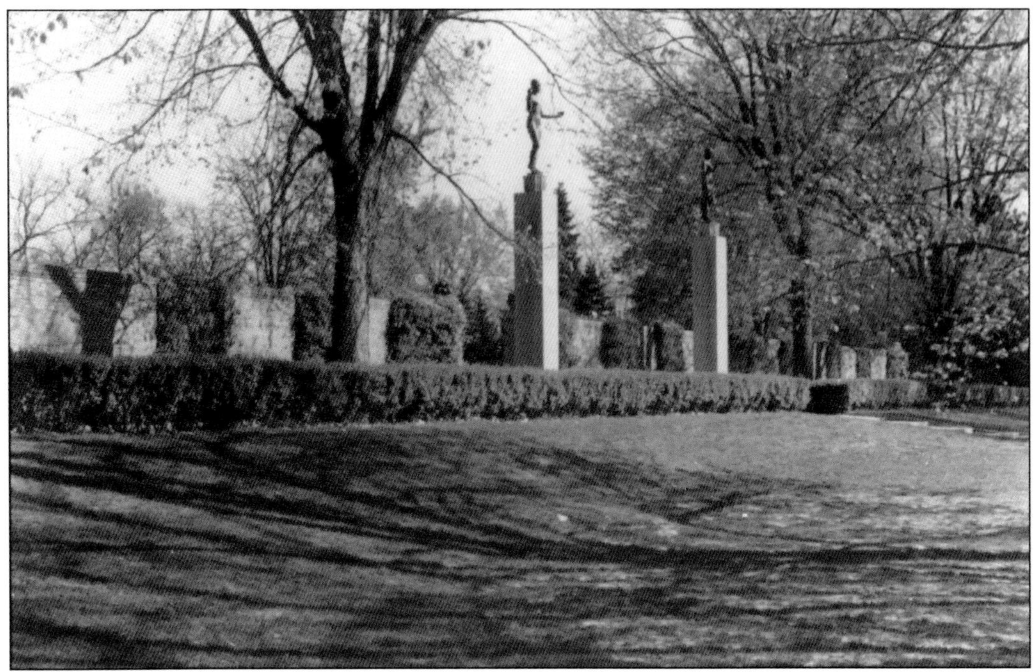

In this 1935 photograph, the sea maidens stand on pedestals designed by John Gregg near the brick wall garden. The artist specialized in architectural sculpture, working in terra cotta, stone, and ceramics. He is best known for Hamburg's Warrior Monument, commissioned by the Nazis in 1936 to honor fallen World War I German soldiers. (APRC.)

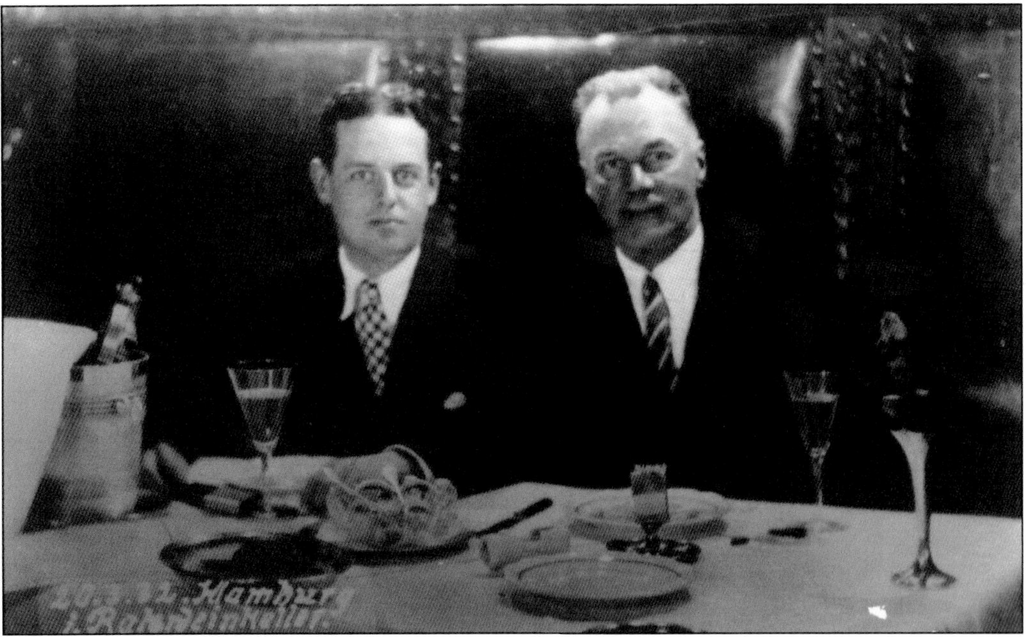


With architect David Adler's business closing in 1932 due to the Depression and Adler's despair after the death of his wife, John Gregg was unemployed. This, however, made him more available to accompany Allerton on his worldwide journeys. The photograph shows Gregg (left) and Allerton dining in Hamburg. It is dated March 20, 1932, Allerton's 59th birthday. (APRC.)

During a trip to Siam—now Thailand—Allerton commissioned two Siamese Buddhas made of teakwood logs. The logs required curing for two years before being carved and gilded. One sculpture's palms face outward while the other's cross its chest. After the sculptures were installed in 1931, the gazebo became the "House of the Golden Buddhas." (MH.)

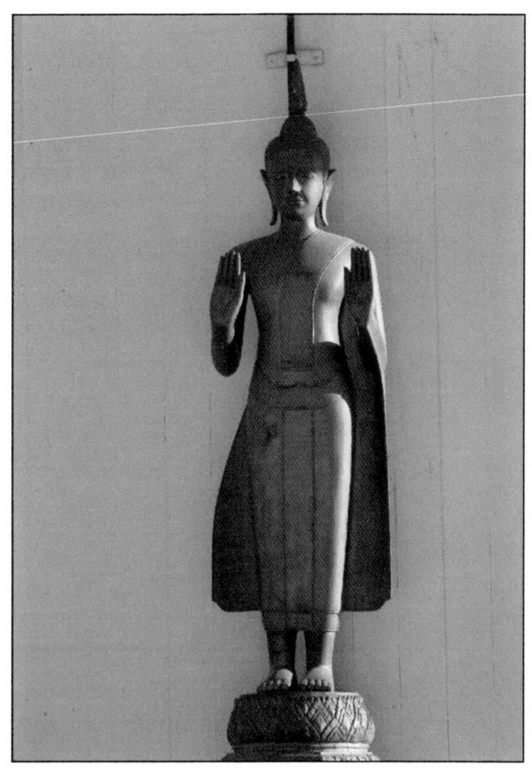

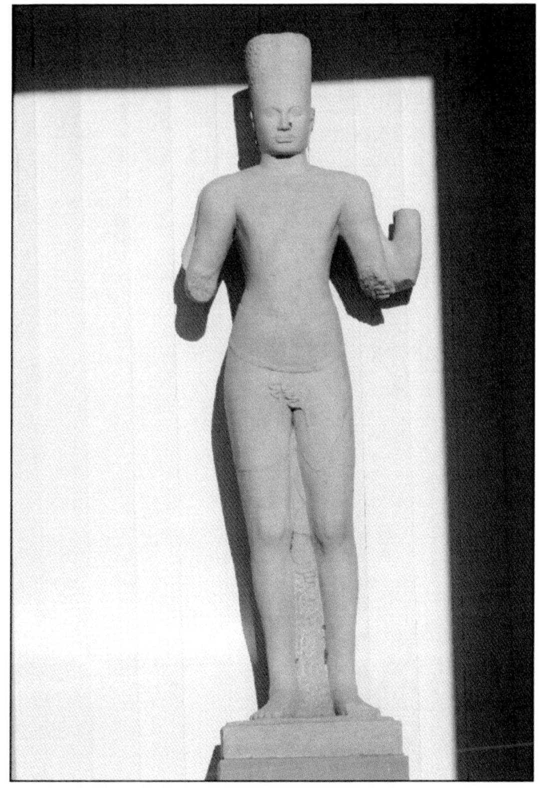

The hari-hara limestone sculpture standing in the House of the Golden Buddhas was copied from a plaster cast that Allerton purchased at Paris's Musée Guimet and later donated to the Art Institute. It represents the gods Hari and Hara and replicates a seventh-century stone statue in Phnom-Penh, Cambodia, which also had mutilated arms. (MH.)

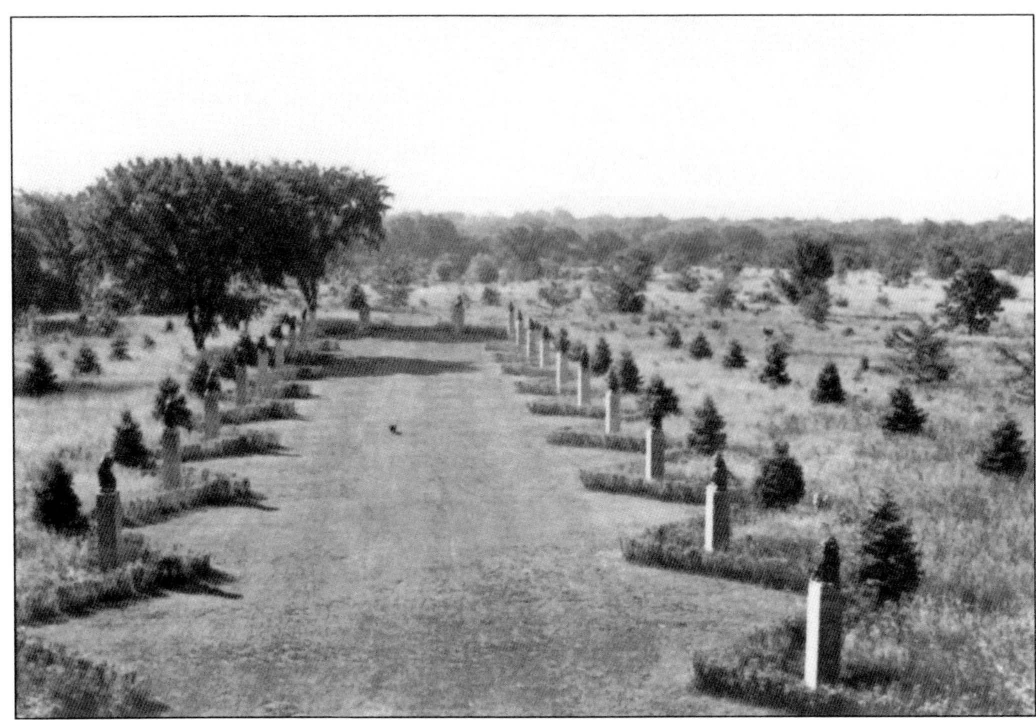

Allerton moved his collection of blue-glazed ceramic fu dogs to different gardens over the years. In the early 1930s, they sat east of the House of the Golden Buddhas in a setting that Gregg designed. Twenty fu dogs, perched on pedestals, face each other in this 1933 photograph. Privet hedges create a zig-zag, finishing with two more fu dogs at the end. (APRC.)

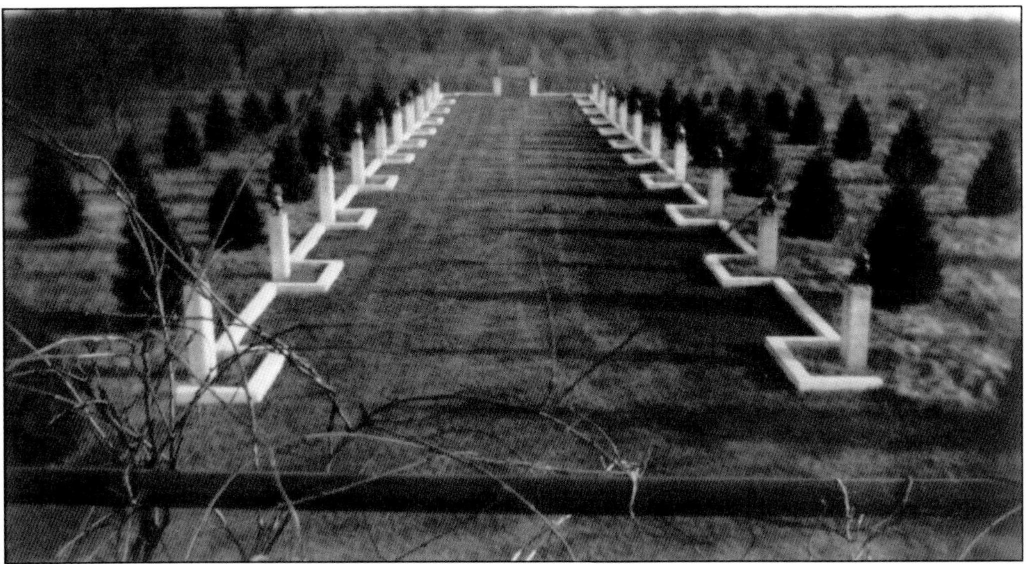

By 1935, Allerton's garden of fu dogs, as seen from the gazebo top, had been modified. Gone was the zig-zag pattern of privet hedges, replaced by squared concrete curbing. Over time, the statues were stolen or damaged by vandals, weather, and squirrels. The current fu dogs are reproductions by University of Illinois professor Donald Frith. (APRC.)

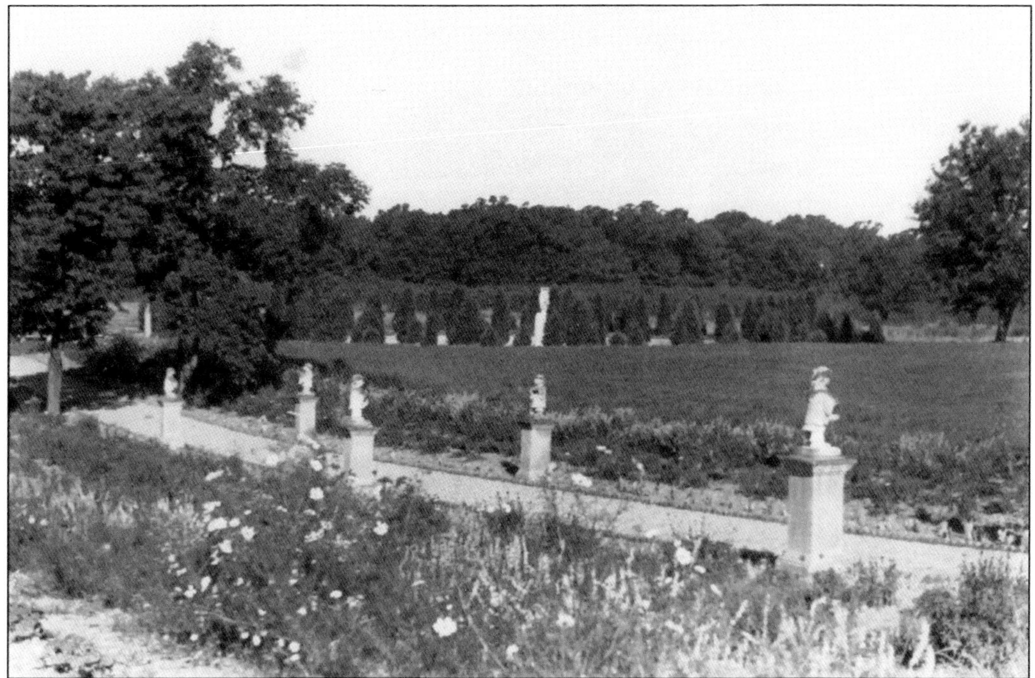

A picnic area lay across the river, accessible via a cable bridge or Allerton Road. There, in the early 1930s, Allerton created his Lost Garden, lined it with Chinese musicians, and placed *The Three Graces* at one end and the marble Diana at the other. This 1932 photograph shows Chinese musicians, *The Three Graces*, a dog on a cylindrical column, and brick sawtooth edging along a path. (APRC.)

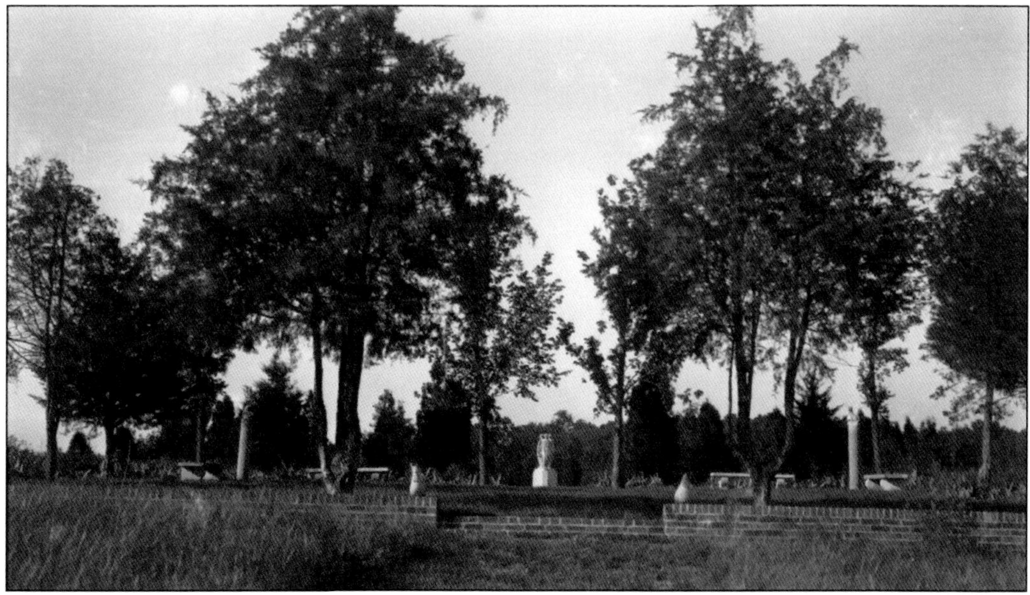

In the center of this 1935 photograph, *The Three Graces* stand on a concrete pedestal in an open area. Early on, the sculpture was surrounded by a circular wall, which was later removed. Dog sculptures on cylindrical columns are flanked by stone benches. Stone chickens sit on the brick wall. (APRC.)

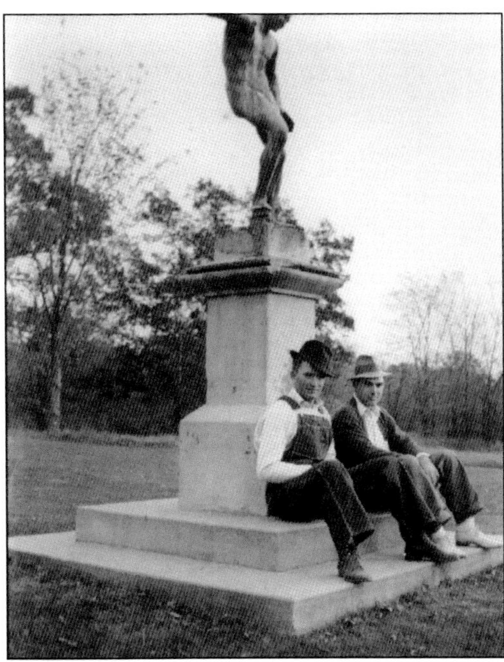

In 1930, two men sit by the Lost Garden's faun statue while the garden was being landscaped. As decades passed, the lead in the statue severely deteriorated. After unsuccessful attempts to repair it, the University of Illinois placed it in storage. The design is a fairly common figure in historic English gardens. (APRC.)

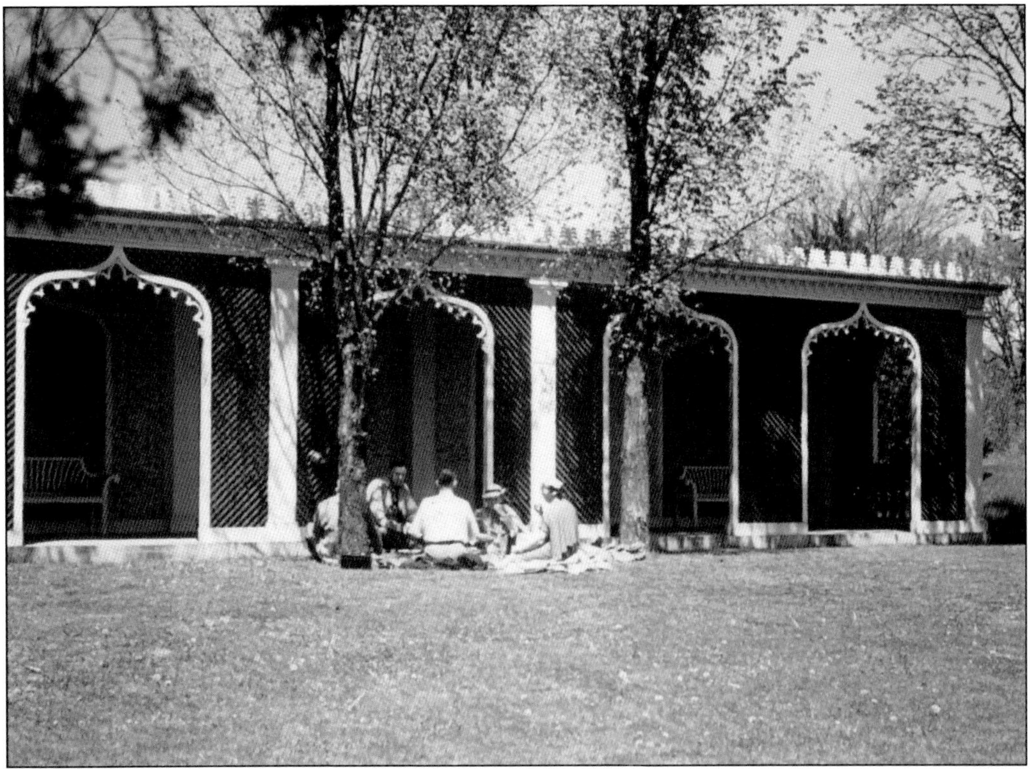

In 1936, Allerton's rectangular tea house, designed by Gregg, was complete. A group picnics in this 1937 photograph. Niches in four of the structure's openings displayed murals and benches constructed by Francis Brooks, responsible for all woodworking projects at the Farms. He also operated the projector at Monticello's Lyric Theater movie house. (APRC.)

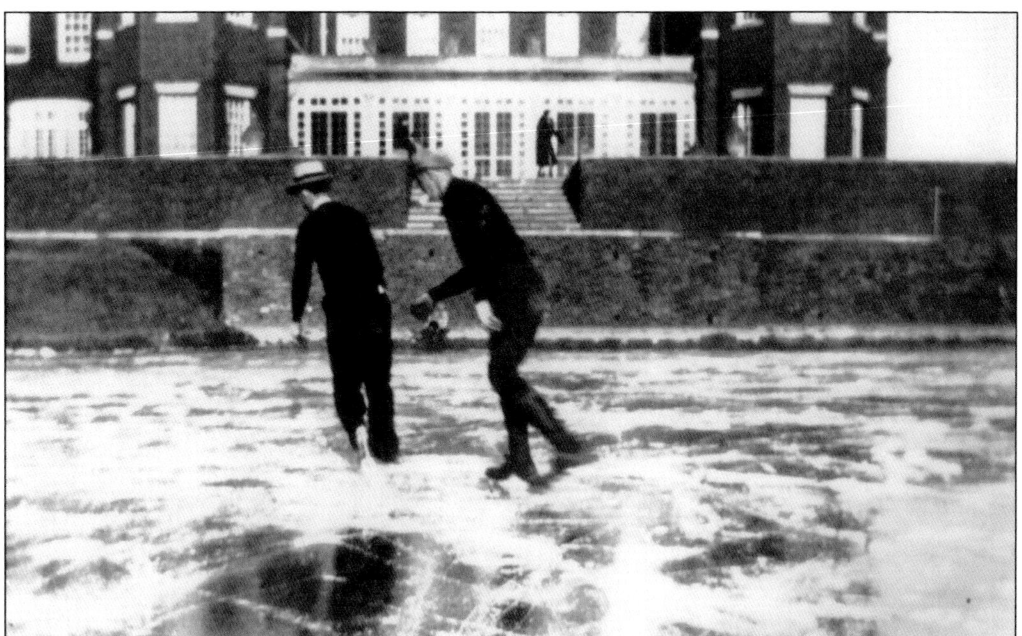

Employee Arthur Cackett (left) and an unidentified man enjoy skating in the winter of 1935 on the mansion's reflecting pond. In the background, a fur-coated woman walks at the right side of the swimming pool. Barely visible above the right skater's head is what appears to be another unidentified woman. (APRC.)

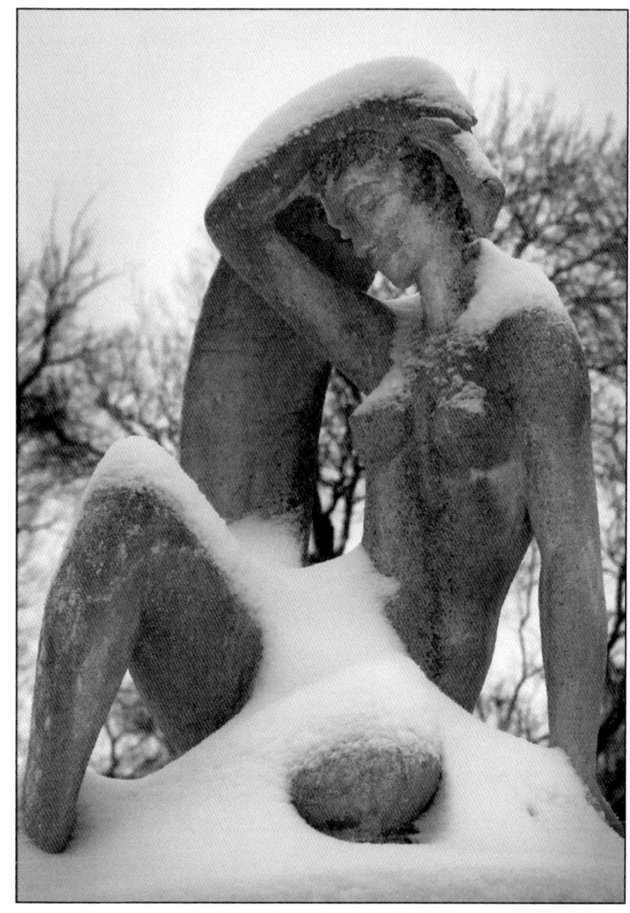

In 1941, while attending the Art Institute's annual Exhibition of American Painting and Sculpture, Allerton purchased Lili Auer's concrete figure *Girl with a Scarf*, the last piece he acquired for his Monticello estate. With the brick wall garden's dipping pool tilting due to the constantly wet ground, it was time for something else. He filled the pool in with gravel and broken concrete, placing the sculpture on top. (MH.)

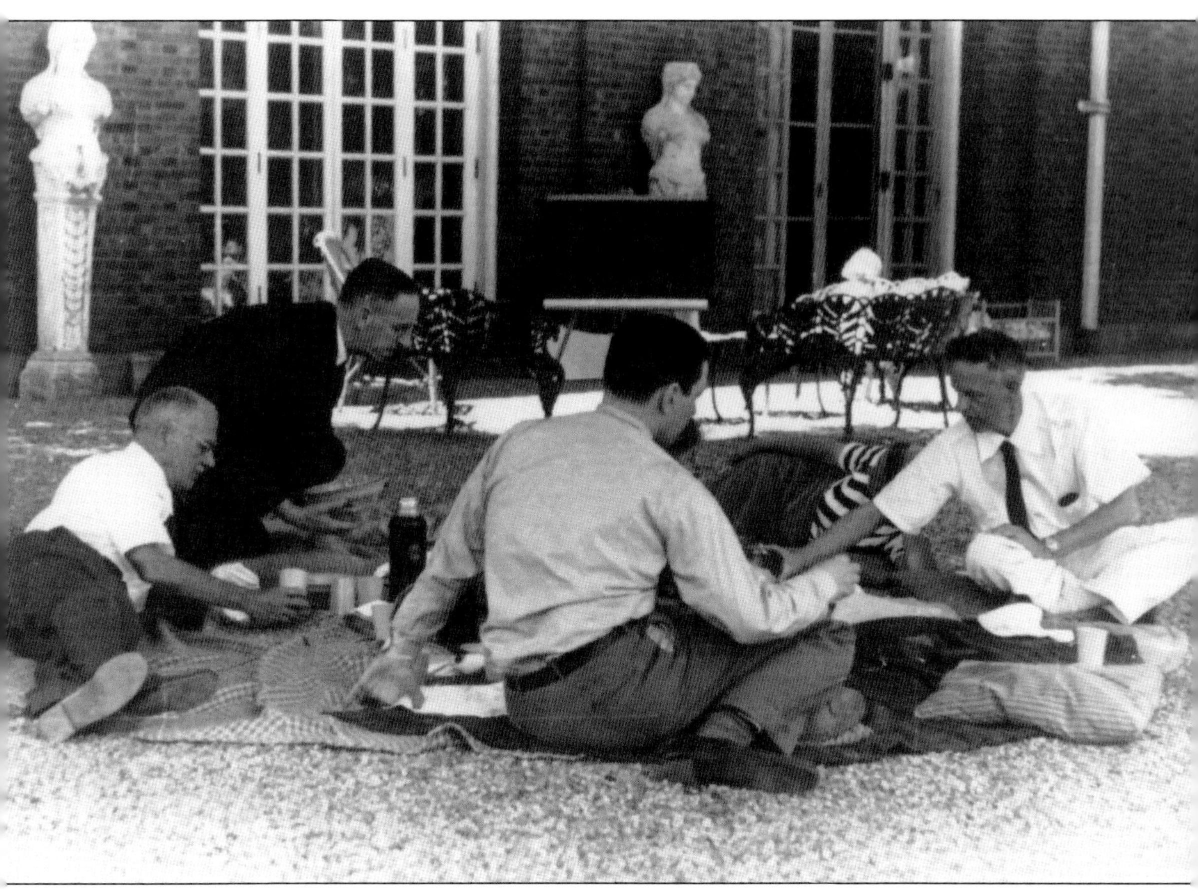

Allerton picnics with friends in the shade of the library terrace in 1941. Two caryatids stand guard. From left to right, the picnickers are Allerton, butler Arthur Cackett, artist Rainey Bennett, Ann Bennett (in the striped top), and John Gregg. At far right, a crib stands next to the doors while a bonneted child, assumed to be one of the Bennett children, sits on the iron settee. (APRC.)

# *Seven*

# Kauai and Monticello 1938–1986

In 1937, probably to avoid areas of conflict in Europe and Asia, Allerton and Gregg's winter trip took them to Australia and New Zealand. On their return in February 1938, they stopped over in Honolulu and visited an estate for sale on the island of Kauai. Suitably impressed and interested in a permanent winter home, Allerton purchased the property.

John Gregg designed a simple frame house, sitting flat on the ground, contrary to typical homes in Kauai that were raised on three-foot-high wooden supports. They used the river as the spine of their gardens.

On December 7, 1941, they received a telephone call from a neighbor that the United States was at war with Japan. They jumped into helping with the war effort. It was during their time there that Allerton decided that he would donate the Farms to the University of Illinois after the war ended. They would live permanently on Kauai.

In October 1946, Allerton donated 5,500 acres of the Farms to the University of Illinois, specifically for use as a public park and educational and research center. Before the university received the property, Allerton and Gregg shipped their favorite possessions to Lawai-Kai, offering many of their belongings to friends. They also donated art and antiques to the Art Institute, gave valuable books to a Chicago bookstore to sell, and arranged for Chicago furniture dealer John A. Colby & Sons to auction the remainder in November 1947.

In August 1964, through efforts and funding by Allerton and others, Congress established the Pacific Tropical Botanical Garden, later named the National Tropical Botanical Garden, as a nonprofit, non-governmental institution to perpetuate the survival of plants, ecosystems, and cultural knowledge of tropical regions. Allerton donated $75,000 toward initial expenses, later buying additional nearby land and donating another $1 million.

By the end of 1964, Allerton had died, and his ashes were spread over the bay. Twenty years later, Gregg died after heart surgery, and his ashes followed Allerton's over the bay. Together, they left an imprint on Kauai's role in enriching life through discovery, scientific research, conservation, and education.

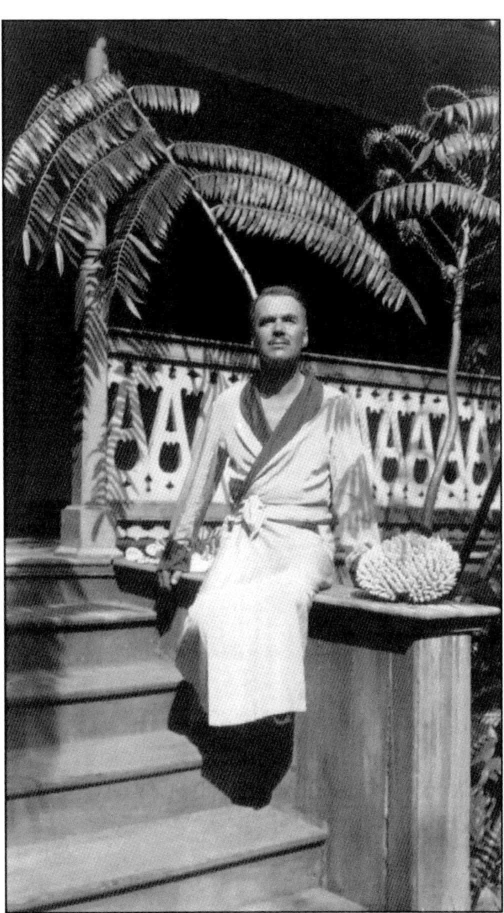

Robert Allerton poses in a robe in 1920 in Hawaii. He typically left Illinois every autumn for Europe or Asia, spending his time away from Illinois winters. In 1937, he and John Gregg traveled to Australia and New Zealand. In mid-February, they spent time in Hawaii, where their lives were about to change. (APRC.)

In early 1937, while staying in Honolulu, Allerton and Gregg visited a friend who mentioned an intriguing property with a crescent-shaped white-sand beach for sale on the island of Kauai. The area is seen in this photograph from the early 1900s. After visiting the property, Gregg said, "The charm and beauty of the place struck us dumb." By then, a permanent winter home was appealing. (AO.)

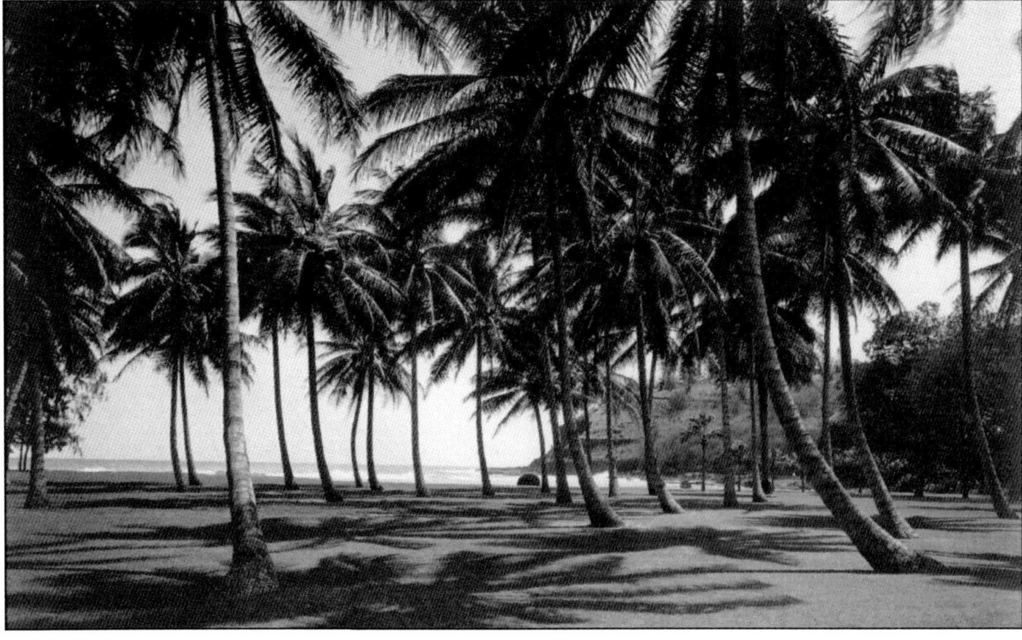

Queen Emma, King Kamehameha IV's widow, seen here in 1880, once owned the land Allerton and Gregg visited. Her cottage previously sat on a cliff overlooking Lawai Beach, which she planted with shade trees. The next owner, Alexander McBryde, built his bungalow near the beach. In 1938, Allerton purchased 83 acres for $50,000 from McBryde's estate. (AO.)

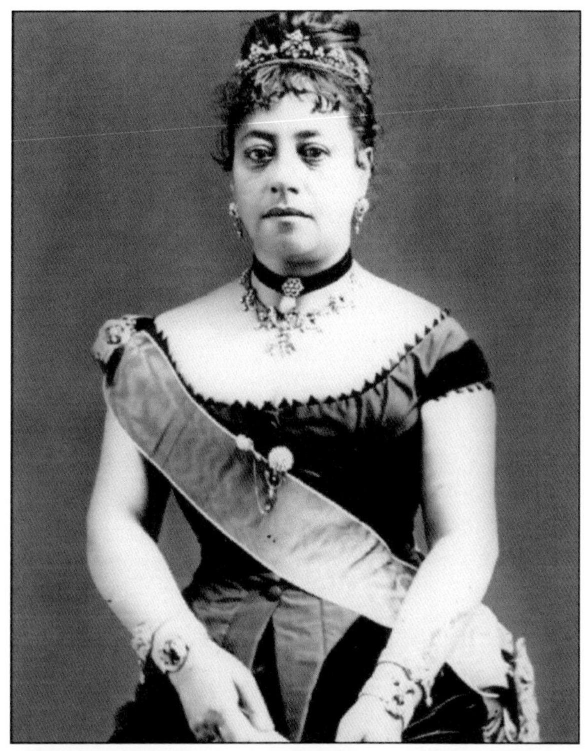

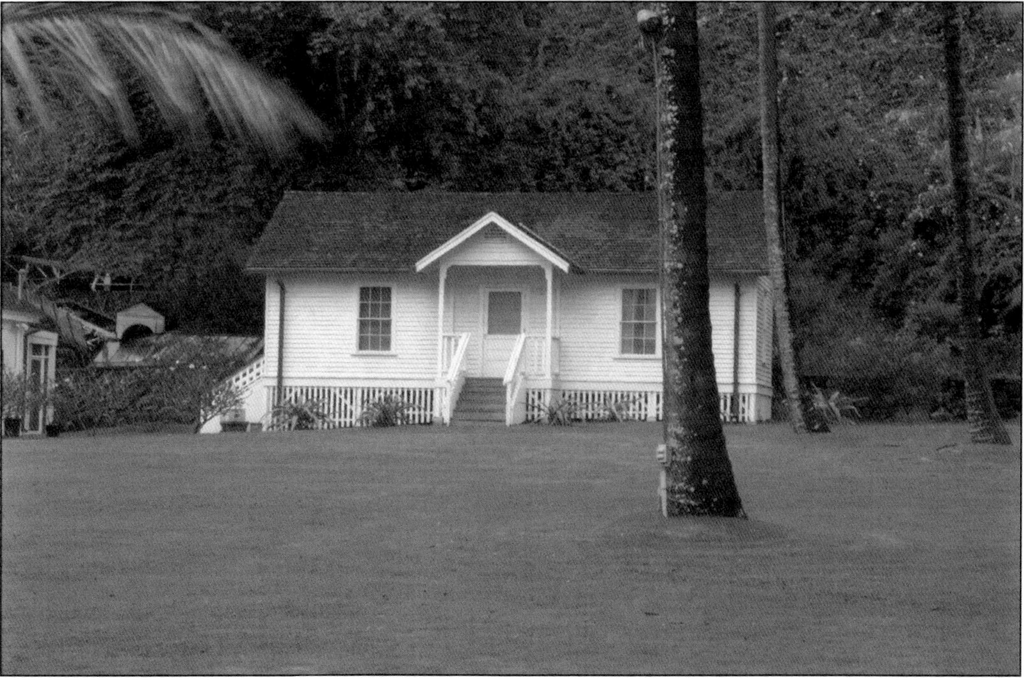

When Alexander McBryde bought the property, he lowered the queen's cottage to the valley floor, living there while building his bungalow. As Allerton constructed his home, he kept her cottage, covering over its green color with white to match his paint. Throughout his life on Kauai, Allerton treated her cottage as guest facilities, a residence for employees, or as storage space. (MH.)

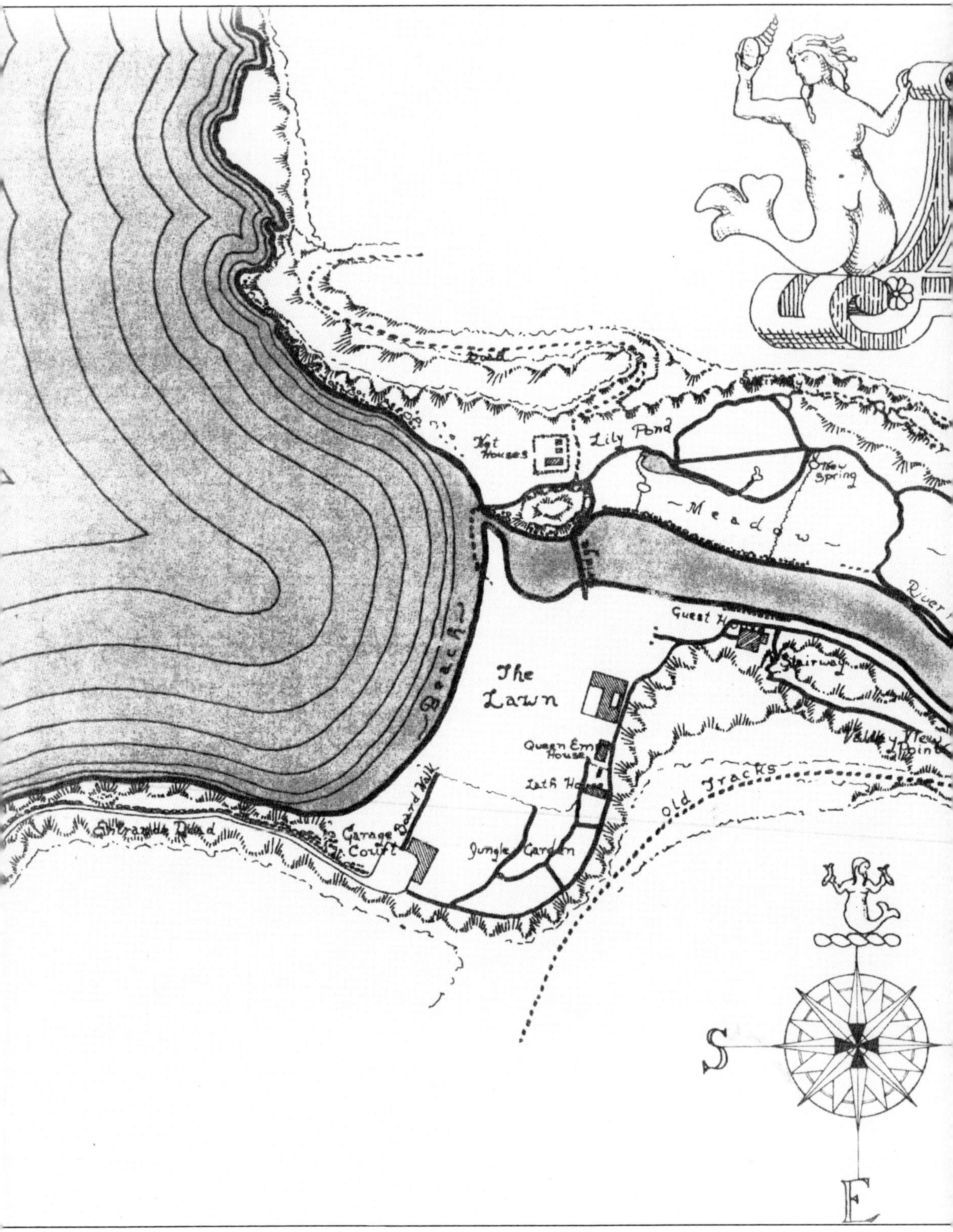
Road
Lily Pond
Hot Houses
New Spring
Meadow
River
Beach
The Lawn
Guest H
Stairway
Queen Em House
Lath House
Board Walk
Garage Court
Jungle Garden
Old Tracks
Valley View Point
S
E

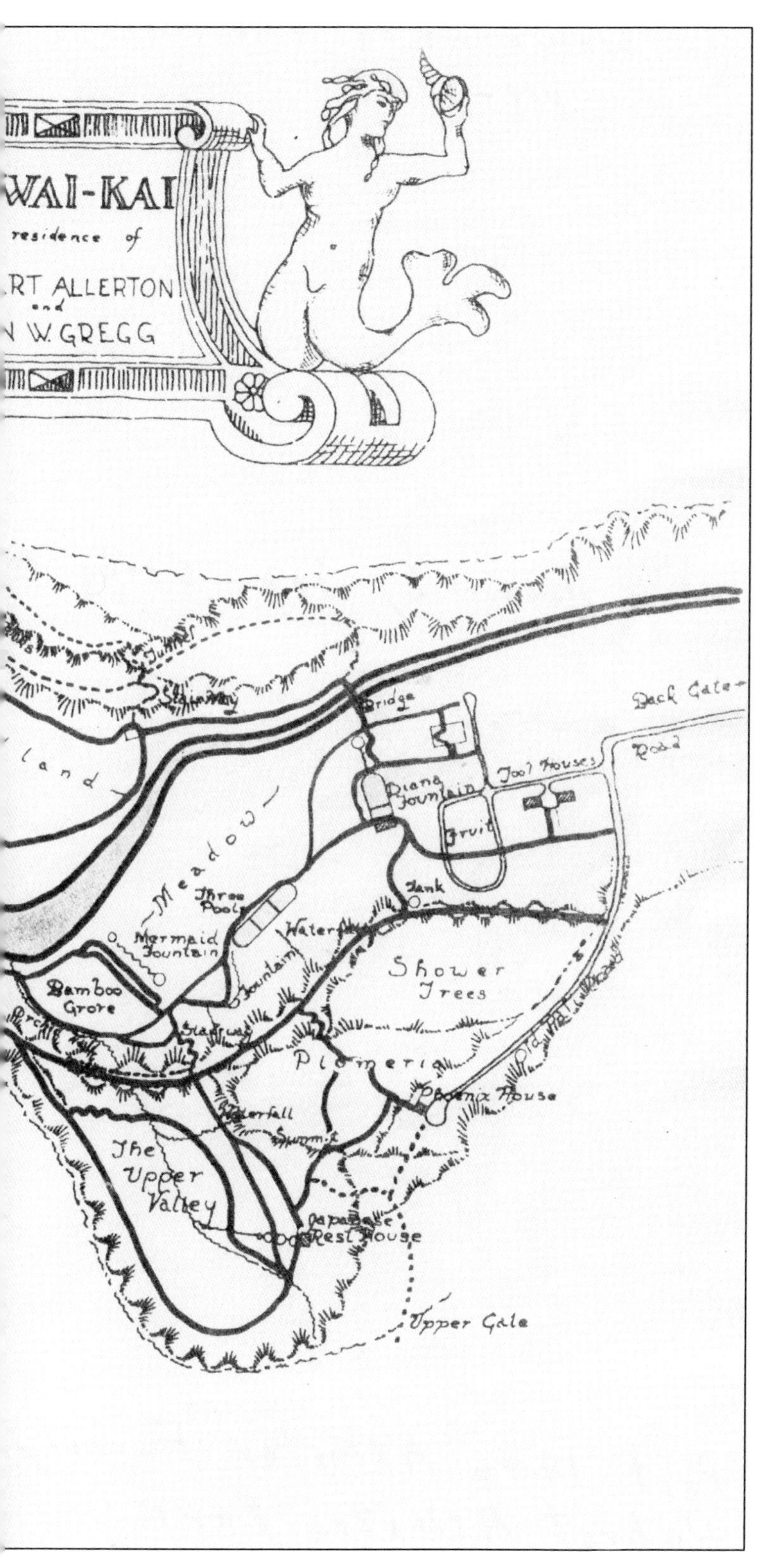


Gregg sketched a design for placement of the gardens and buildings for their new paradise, which they named "Lawai-Kai," meaning "valley of plenty." Note that the compass shows north to the right. They planned the house to face the beach, with Queen Emma's cottage sitting just east of it. The guest house lies out of sight along the road to the northwest. At the bottom of the left side of the sketch, the entrance road leads down to the garage court, boardwalk, and jungle garden. Most of the other gardens lie further beyond, between the river and the upper valley. The viewpoint lies just above the mermaid compass. (APRC.)

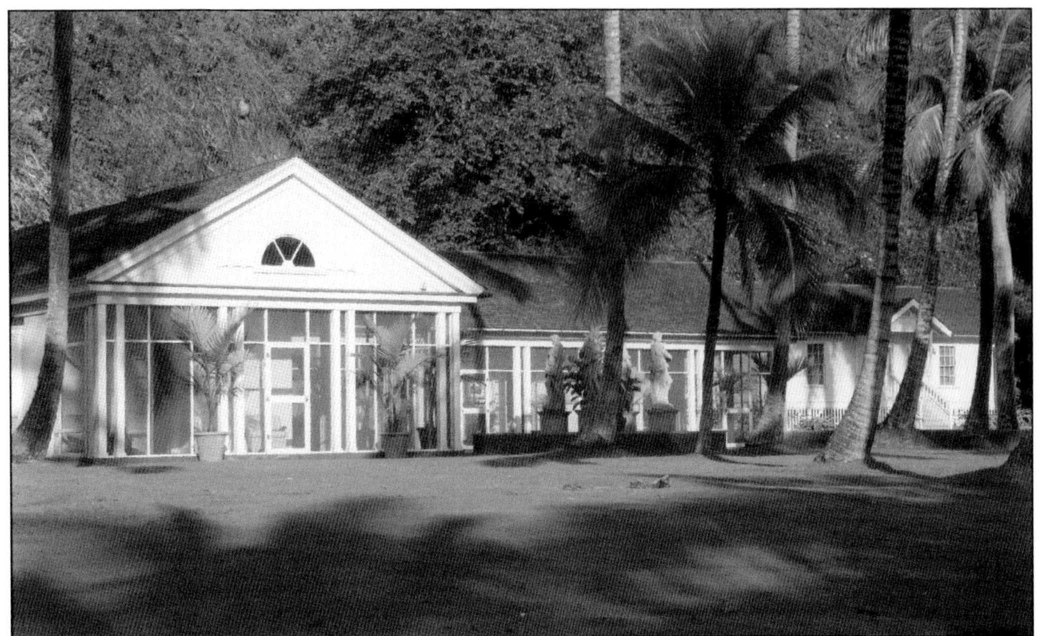

Gregg designed the house at beach level next to Queen Emma's cottage, which is seen to the right above. Due to an inadequate amount of building material on the island, they ordered hardware and plumbing from Crane Company in Chicago but utilized plywood and materials from McBryde's bungalow. They lived in half of the bungalow as they recycled the other half. The L-shaped design included a screened lanai to keep out the toads and mynah birds, two bedrooms—each with private bathrooms, a dining room, and kitchen. After completing their new home, they demolished and burned McBryde's cottage. This upset local residents who wanted to scavenge the remainder of the cottage. Gregg wrote to their bookkeeper about their new home: "I can't start telling you about the joys of this place. . . . It is beyond words." (Both, MH.)

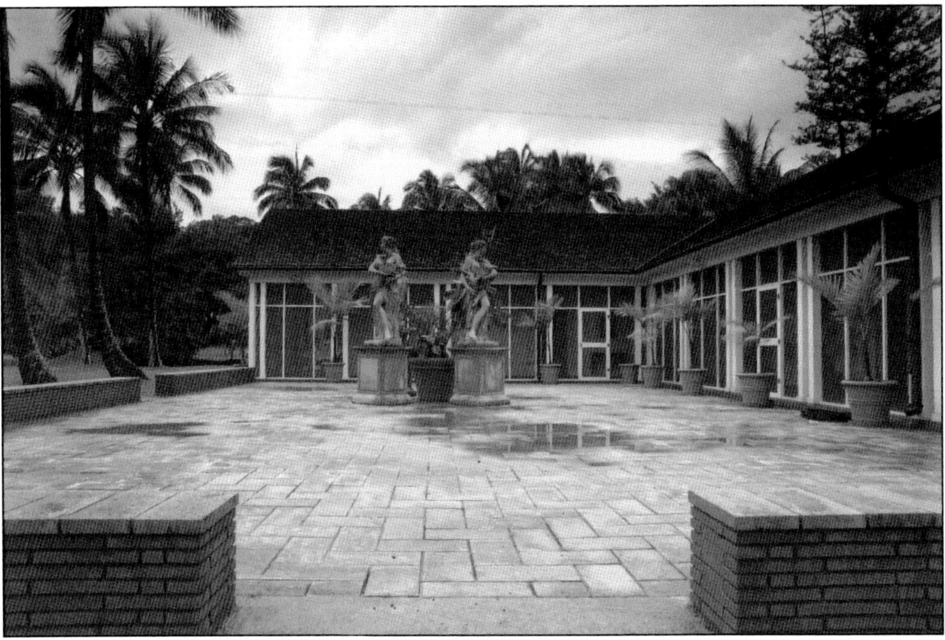

Allerton arranged for the shipment of several statues from the Farms to Lawai-Kai. Two of them, the cherub fountains seen in chapter four, took up residence in Kauai, facing each other across a small rectangular pool. The sculpture seen here carries a dolphin on his shoulder. (MH.)

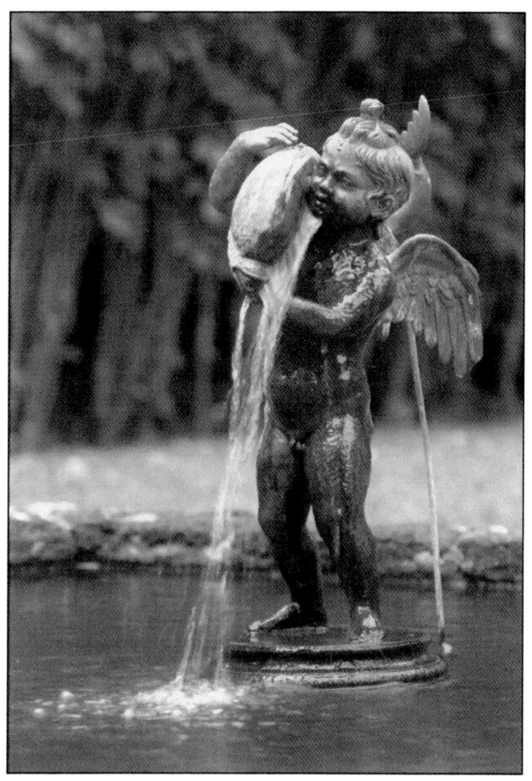

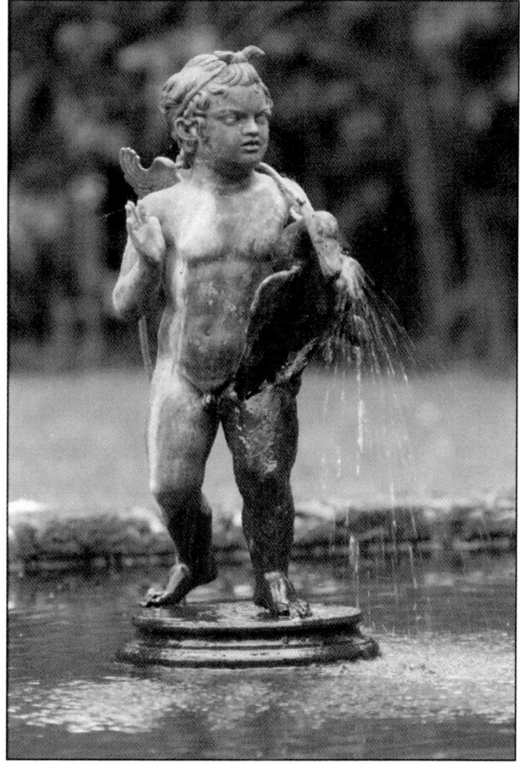

In its left arm, the second cherub fountain holds a squawking goose spouting water from its bill. Both statues were shipped from the Farms, where they had occupied prominent spots at the swimming pool and later at the Farms' trial garden. They were based on original sculptures from Herculaneum in Italy. (MH.)

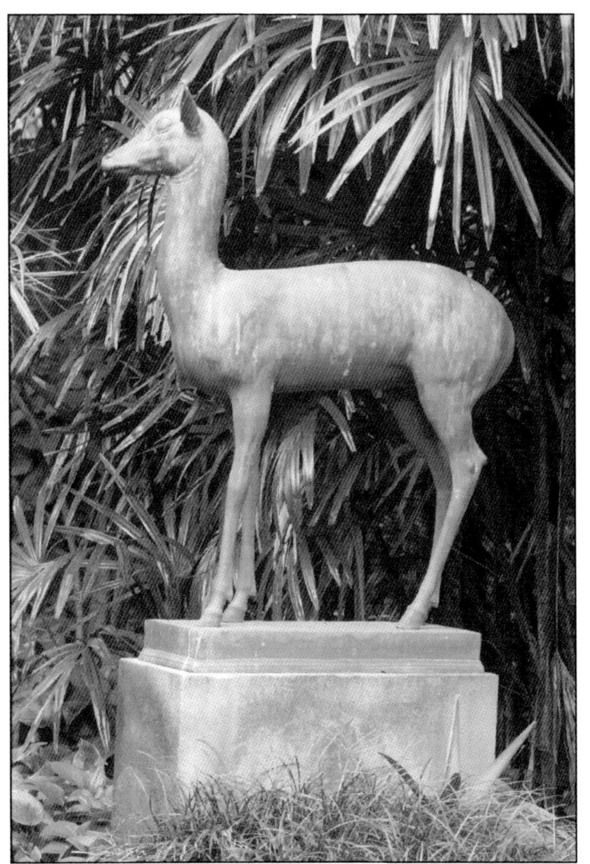

Beyond where the cherub fountains lay, Allerton situated the two "deer" that had once stood on the library terrace outside the Farms' office, seen in chapter four in a photograph with Elmer Priebe. The gazelles stand on small columns near an entrance to one of the Lawai-Kai gardens. Inscribed on a base is the name of the statues' foundry: "Chiurazzi, Naples, Italy." (MH.)

A bridge near the beach and another closer to the Diana fountain allows visitors to cross the Lawai River into woodland and meadow and up a cliff, encountering a lotus pond and a small cemetery. This sculpture of a reclining woman is supported by a pair of dogs under her right arm. (MH.)

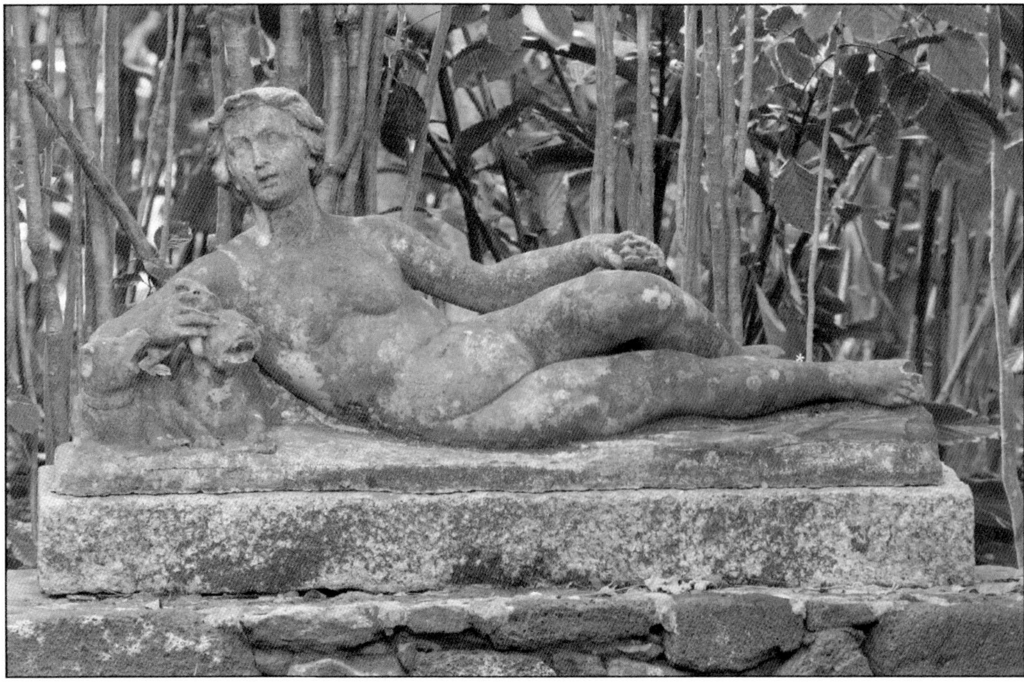

In 1942, the wrong statue was sent from the Farms, but Allerton found a lovely location for the one that arrived—his Diana that had last been placed at the Lost Garden. Behind it flows a fountain using lava rocks, with lava steps leading to the Lawai River. The original statue is in the Louvre and is attributed to Praxiteles. It represents Artemis, the goddess of hunting and the wild. (MH.)

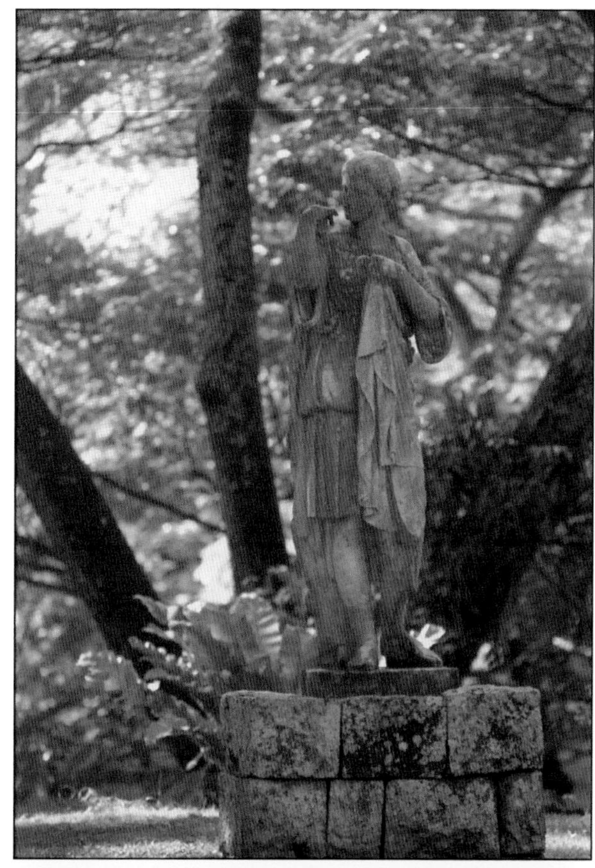

Across from a pool and Diana lies the Thanksgiving pavilion with niches housing marble statues, many shipped from the Farms. When Allerton first lived at Lawai-Kai, he decorated the pavilion using heads and busts copied from Italian originals found after the eruption at Mount Vesuvius. Today, some of those heads can be seen in some of the other Lawai-Kai gardens. (MH.)

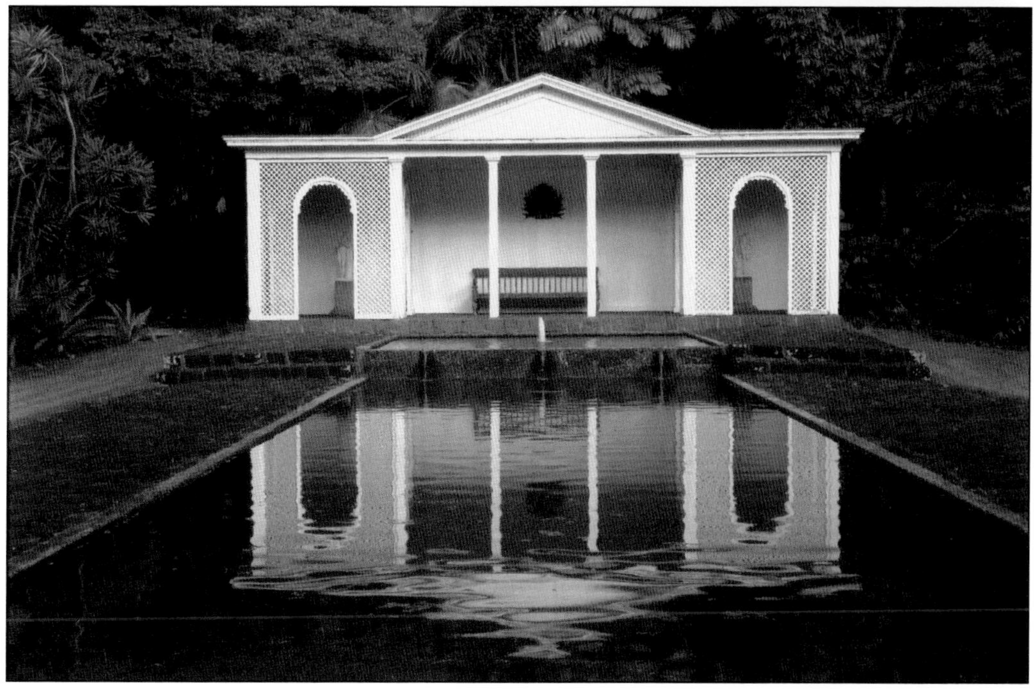

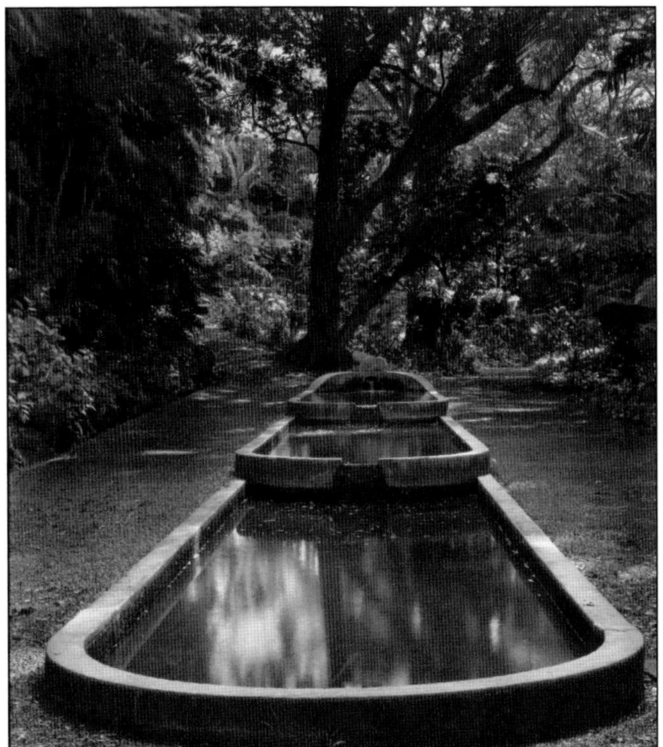

Moving toward the house beyond the Diana fountain, visitors encounter the area Allerton called "the Three Pools." A small amount of water spills out through an opening at the high end. As the water fills in one of the concrete pools, it dribbles out like a slow waterfall into the next pool and then the next. (MH.)

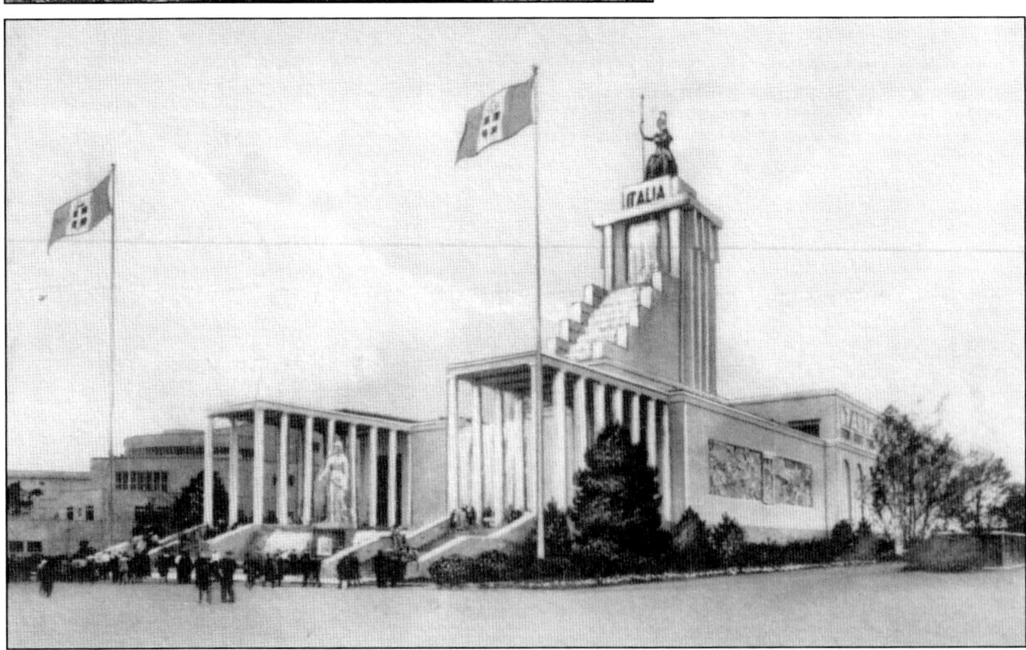


While attending the 1939 World's Fair in Flushing Meadows, New York, Allerton and Gregg noticed plaster mermaids in the foyer of a restaurant in the Italian Pavilion, shown in this postcard. The restaurant had been operated by the Italian Line cruise company, and the mermaids previously adorned one of its ships. Allerton sought out the Italian consul and commissioned bronze versions of the statutes for Lawai-Kai. (AO.)

When World War II broke out, Allerton assumed the deal for the bronze mermaids would not be honored due to Italy confiscating the metal for bullets. However, the deal went through. The mermaids were shipped first to Monticello, then arrived in Kauai in July 1940. The foundry information is inscribed at the base of the mermaid facing the one in this photograph: "L. Andreotti, Firenze, 1931." (MH.)

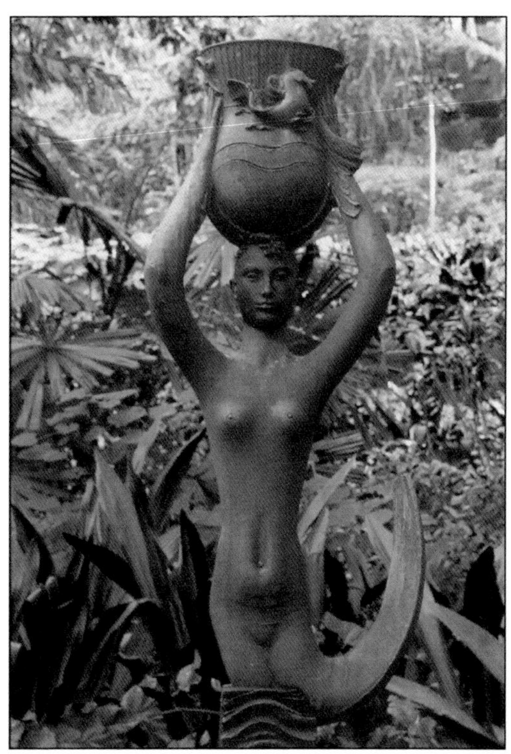

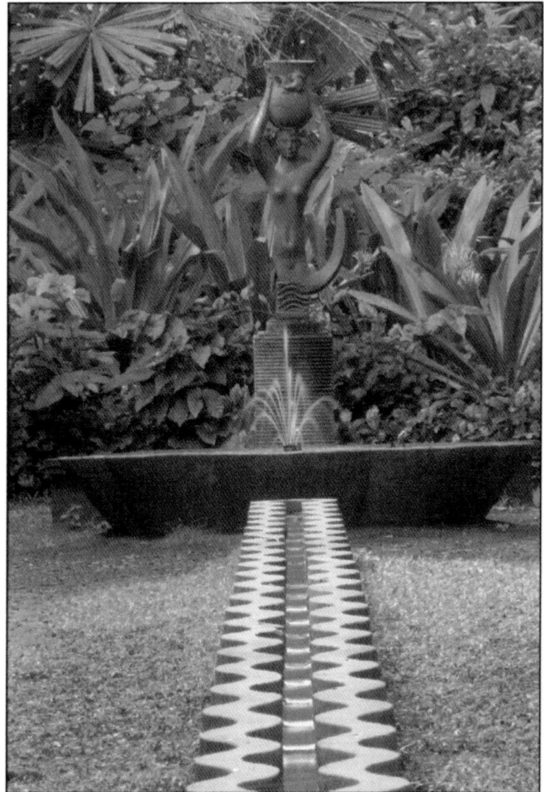

Gregg constructed a waterway between the two mermaid statues, with curvy concrete curbing. Small dams inside the waterway create waves as the water spills onward. Gregg copied the idea from a similar design at Villa Farnese in Caprarola, Italy. The end shell, constructed from a mold his contractor created, replicates one at Stockholm's capitol building. (MH.)

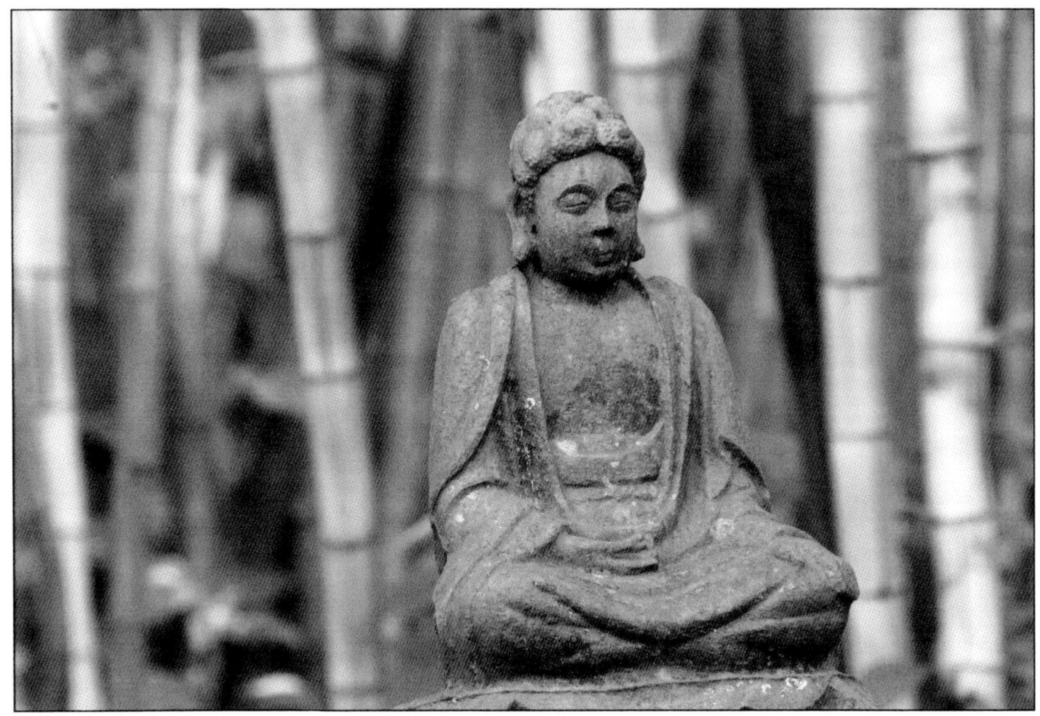

As visitors continue toward the house, past the sound of water flowing through the mermaid fountain, the next area encountered is the bamboo grove. The fastest-growing plant on earth, bamboo typically lives for approximately 75 years. This Buddha stands on a pedestal, towered over by the mature plants rising as tall as trees. (MH.)

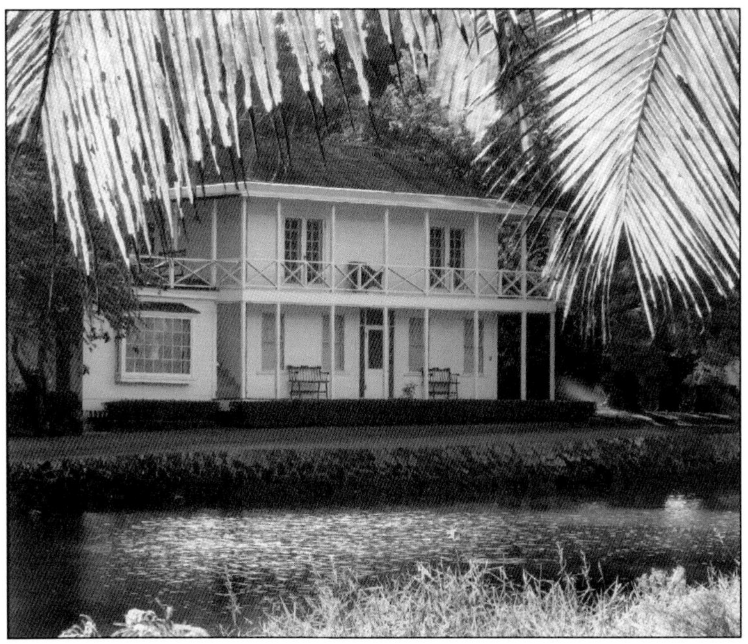

Following the river path beyond the bamboo grove and facing the river, the first building encountered is Lawai-Kai's guesthouse. It sits close to the cliff over which cascades Queen Emma's bougainvillea. Its location away from the beach has sheltered it from many hurricanes that battered the main house. It still houses guests staying on the premises. (MH.)

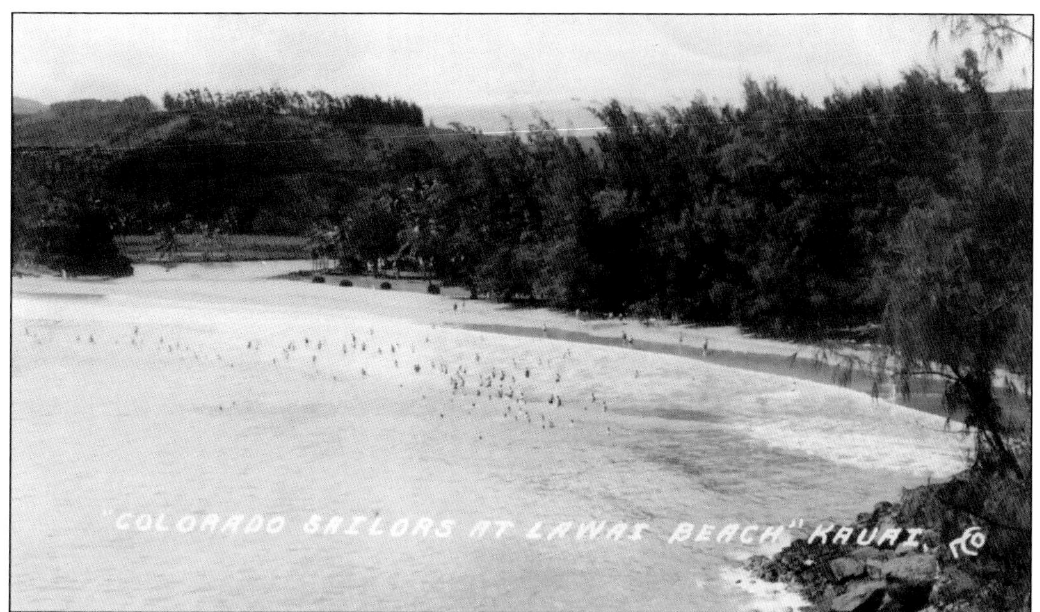


During World War II, the Army barb-wired the beach to hinder enemy attacks, but an opening was later cut to allow soldiers to enjoy the bay. USS *Colorado* sailors swim in this photograph. As part of his efforts to help the Office of Food Production, Allerton planted 15 acres of sweet potatoes. He also worked with Kauai's Red Cross, donating funds and a vehicle for an ambulance. (SC.)

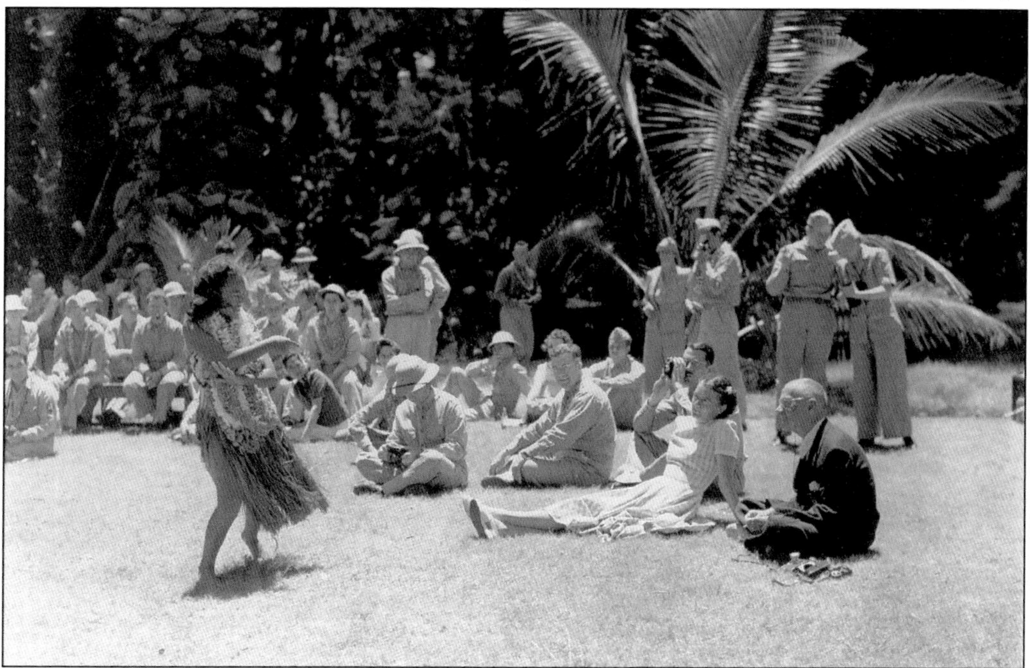

Gregg served as the sheriff's assistant and first lieutenant with the Kauai Volunteers. Meanwhile, Allerton hosted picnics and other events for convalescing soldiers. Entertainment for an August 1942 event included hula dancers and two orchestras, with attendance by over 100 soldiers and medical personnel. Wearing a dark suit, Allerton sits and watches a hula dancer. All parties ended before 7:00 p.m. to comply with blackout rules. (KHS.)

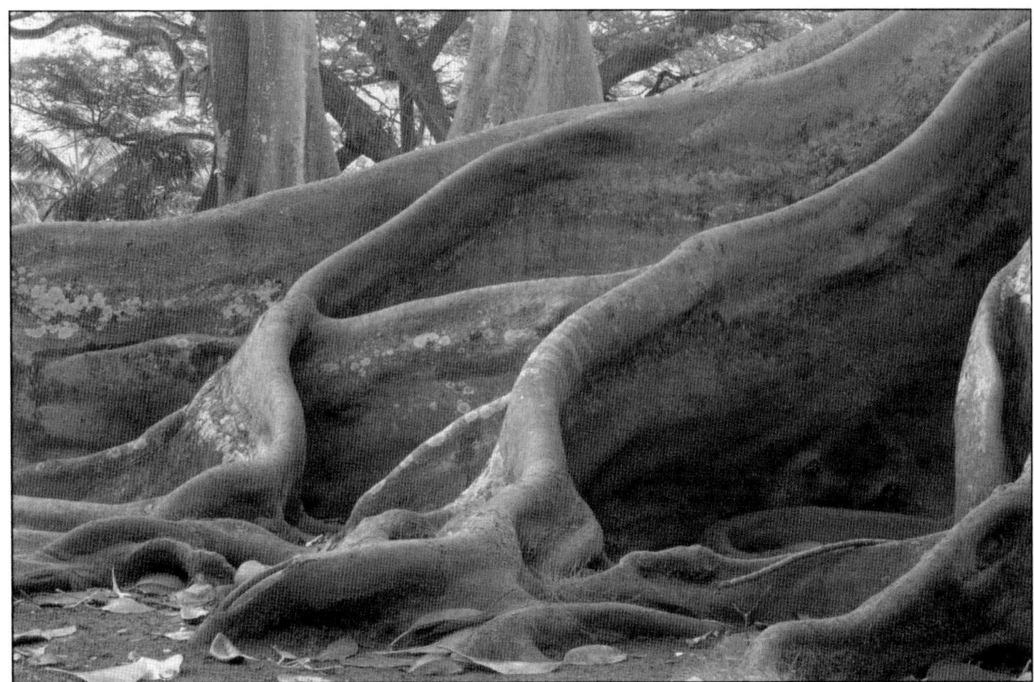

Hollywood enjoyed filming at Lawai-Kai. During the movie *Jurassic Park*, a raptor's egg was found among these raised roots of a Moreton Bay fig tree. Additional movies and series filmed on the property included, among others, *Donovan's Reef* with John Wayne, *South Pacific* with Mitzi Gaynor, and *The Thorn Birds*. (MH.)

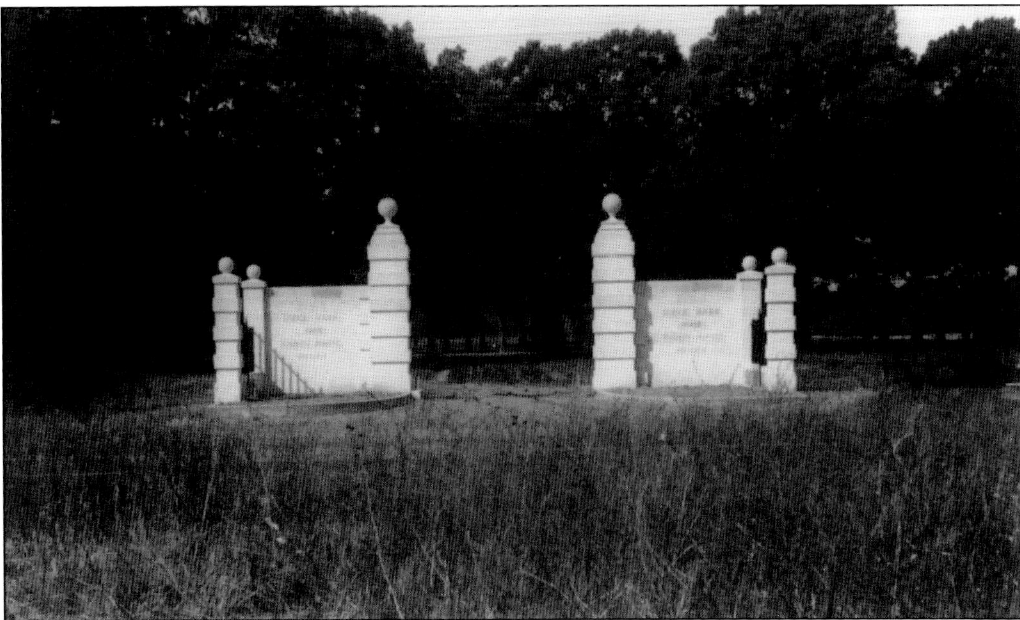

During the same time that Gregg was designing their Lawai-Kai paradise in 1938, he also designed a set of entrance columns on Monticello land once owned by Allerton's family friends: the Lodges. The gates still stand, opening into Lodge Park Forest Preserve past the north end of the town. (APRC.)

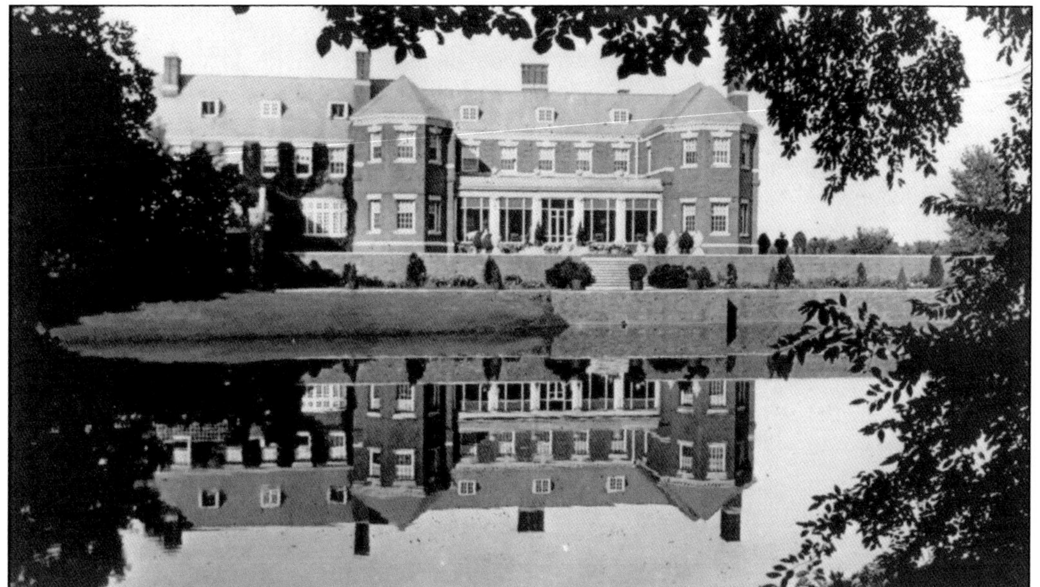

In October 1946, the University of Illinois became the new owner of 5,500 acres of Allerton's Piatt County property. The donation included eight farms and the 1946 corn crop, which was estimated at $51,000. In all, Allerton's gift was estimated at approximately $1.3 million. Allerton had originally decreed that none of the statuary was to ever be moved. (APRC.)

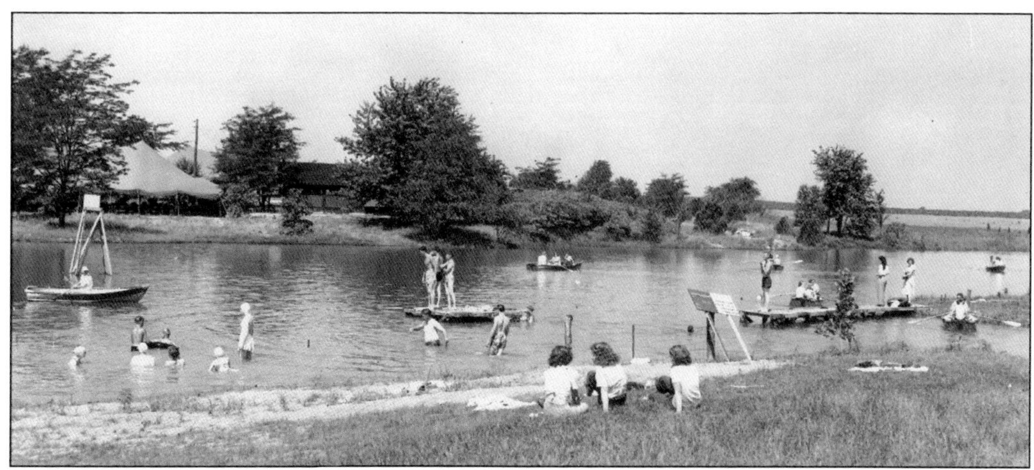

Across from the Monticello mansion, Allerton gave 250 acres to the 4-H as a memorial to Illinois 4-H servicemen and women who lost their lives in World War II. The camp opened on June 30, 1948. Since that time, the camp has served thousands of 4-H youth with work in nature studies, general recreation, aquatics, and handicrafts. (APL.)

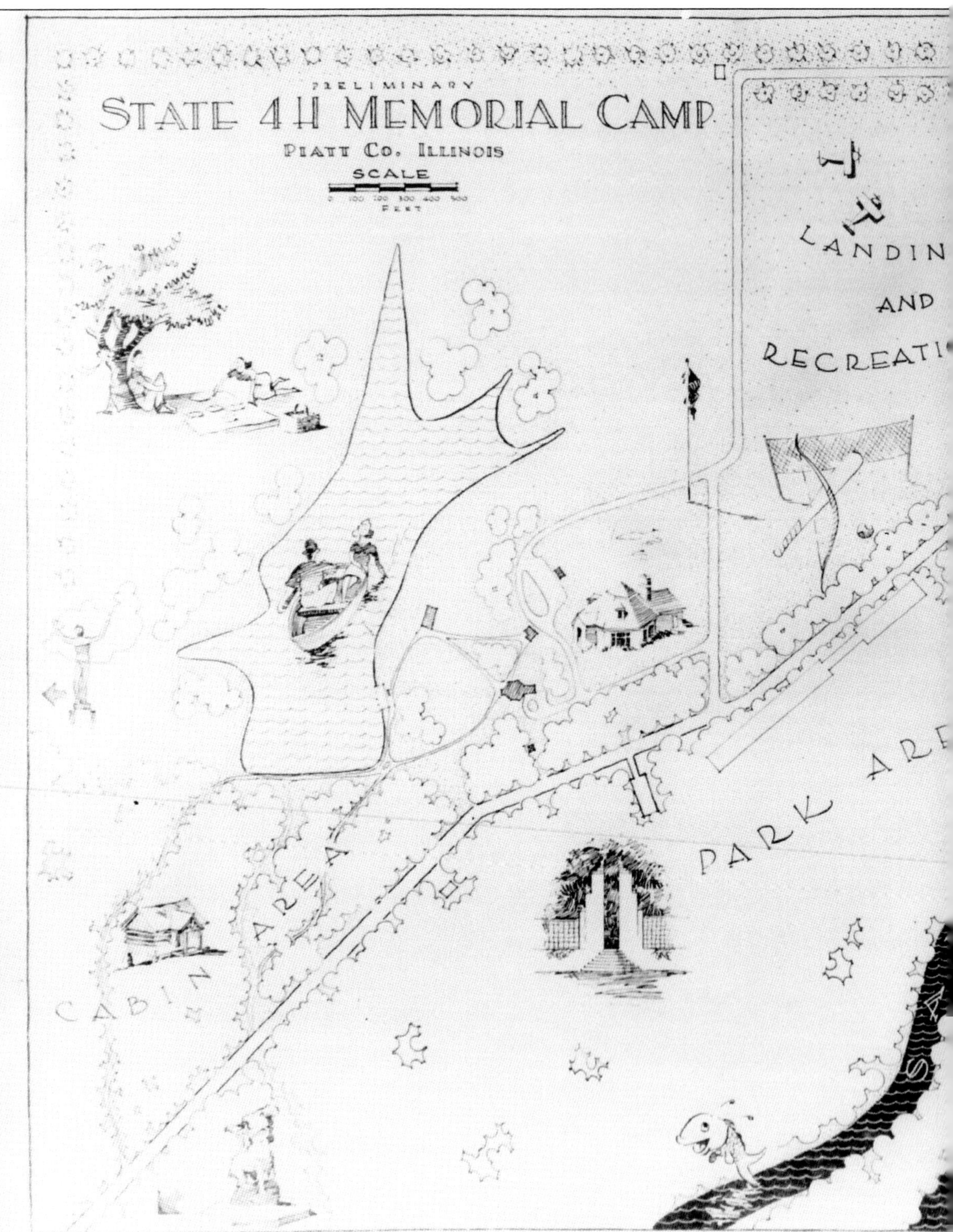
PRELIMINARY
STATE 4H MEMORIAL CAMP
PIATT CO. ILLINOIS
SCALE
0 100 200 300 400 500
FEET
LANDIN
AND
RECREATI
PARK ARE
CABIN AREA

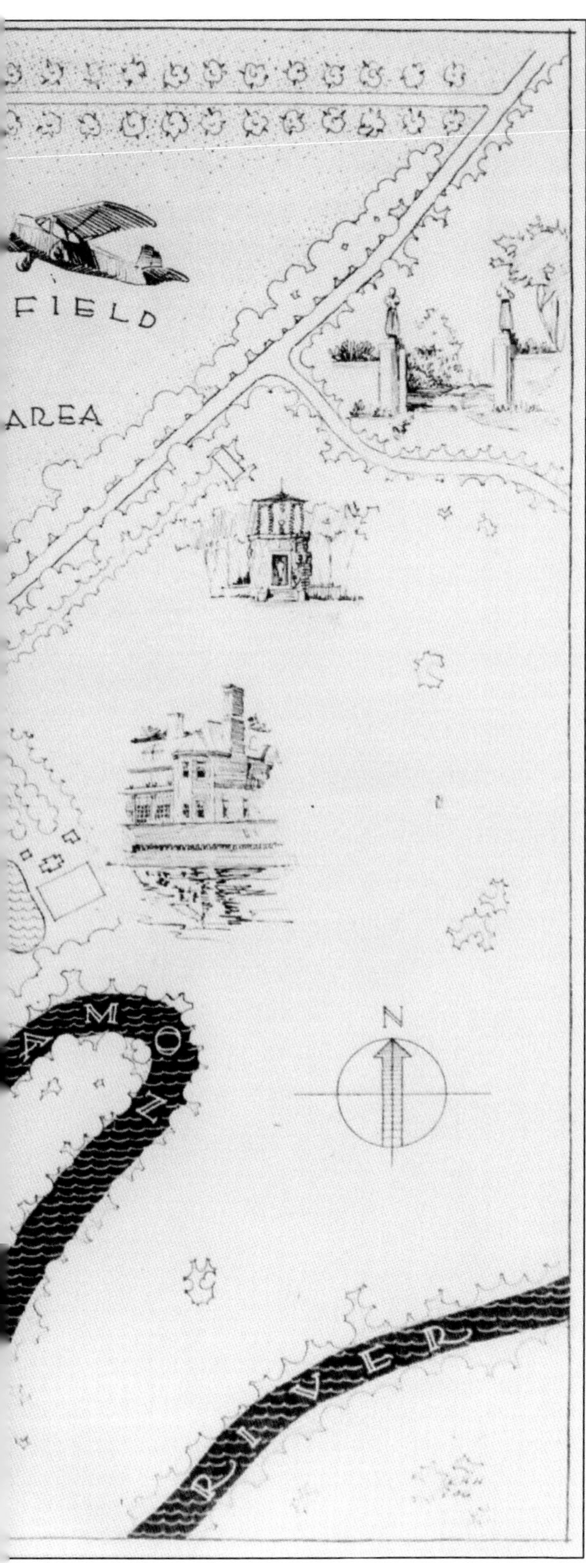


This map from 1946 outlines preliminary details of land deeded to the university and 4-H Memorial Camp. The right side of the sketch shows the entrance, the fu dog garden, mansion, sunken garden, and centaur. The left side shows the cabin area, a lake, and housing. A landing field for planes existed at one time. The camp's boathouse was built on part of the foundation of another barn. As sketched, a lake forms the central axis of the 4-H Memorial Camp. In November 1949, funded through donations, concrete work on a dam was completed, creating the 16-acre lake, which measured 20 feet at its deepest. The donation agreement notes that if the 4-H camp ceases to exist or is unused for more than a year, the land may revert to be part of Allerton Park and Retreat Center. (APL.)

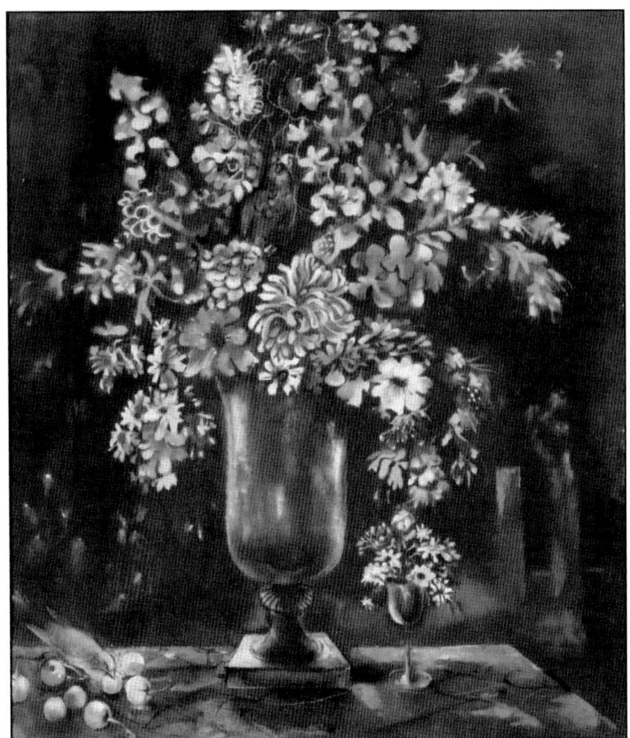

Although the University of Illinois owned the Farms after 1946, Allerton still visited and added art. In 1951, he commissioned Rainey Bennett, an Art Institute artist, teacher, and painter he had befriended during the Depression, to produce four paintings for the mansion's Oak Room, with each painting depicting a view of the estate with foreground flowers and estate statues in the background. (MH.)

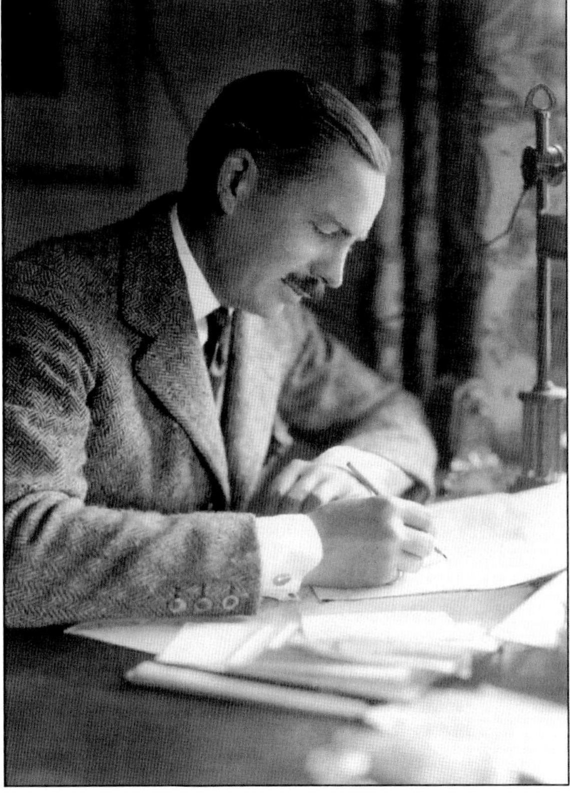

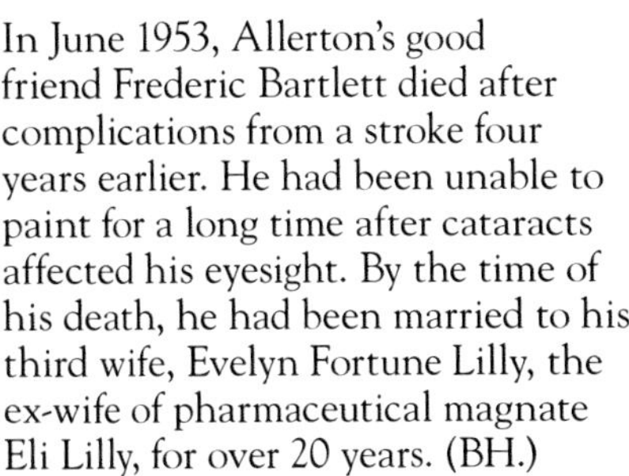

In June 1953, Allerton's good friend Frederic Bartlett died after complications from a stroke four years earlier. He had been unable to paint for a long time after cataracts affected his eyesight. By the time of his death, he had been married to his third wife, Evelyn Fortune Lilly, the ex-wife of pharmaceutical magnate Eli Lilly, for over 20 years. (BH.)

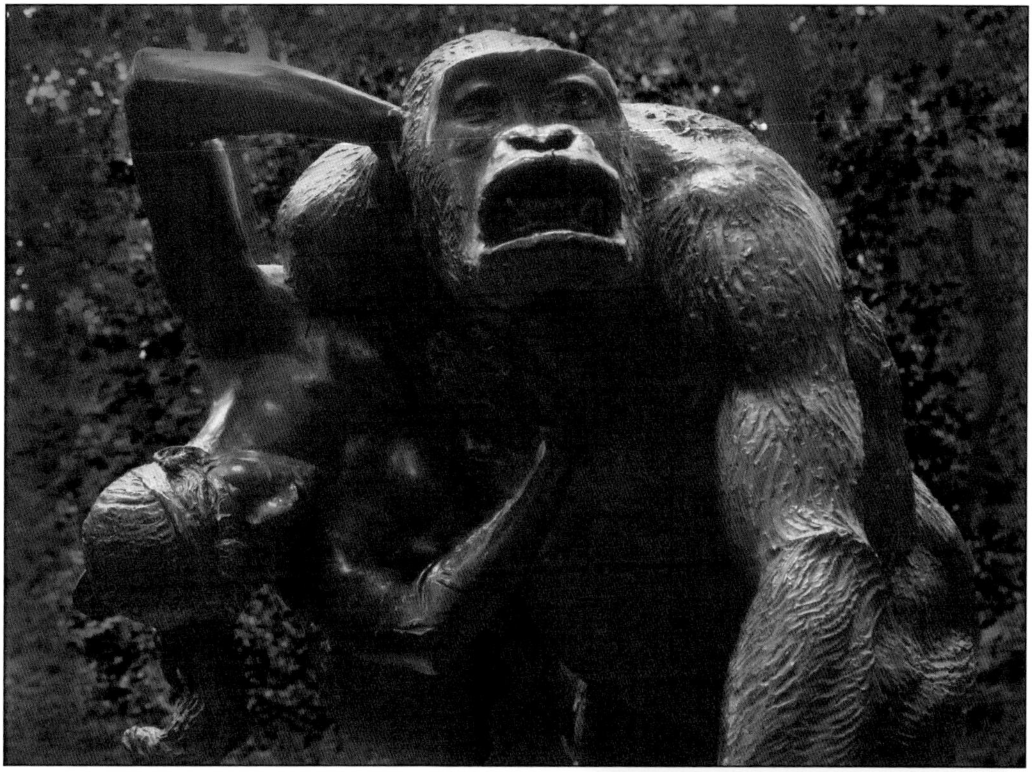

In 1937, the University of Illinois purchased the contents of the studio belonging to artist Lorado Taft. Inadvertently, two pieces by Emmanuel Frémiet were included in the shipment. The two pieces—*Gorilla Carrying off a Woman* from 1887 (the only casting) and *The Bear-Cub Thief* from 1885 (also known as *Le Dénicheur d'oursons*, the second of two castings)—languished in storage while the university arranged for the owner to donate them. The donation was finalized in 1959, and they were placed near walking trails at the Farms. Allerton and Gregg despised both pieces, thinking them ugly. In the 1980s, both wound up at the Krannert Art Museum until the autumn of 2016, when they returned to Allerton Park and Retreat Center. (Both, MH.)

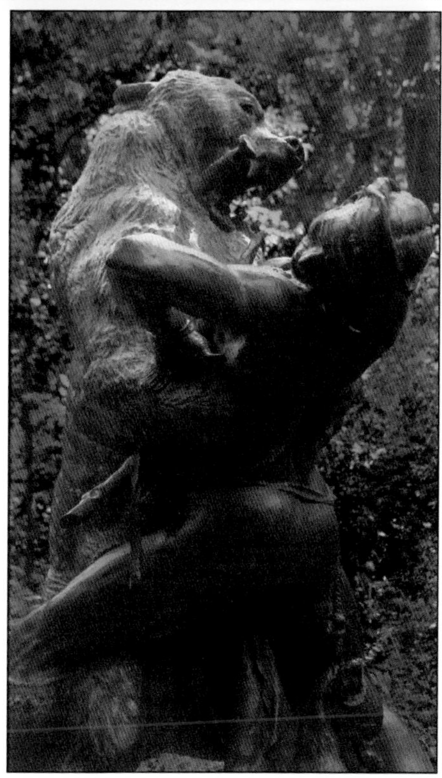

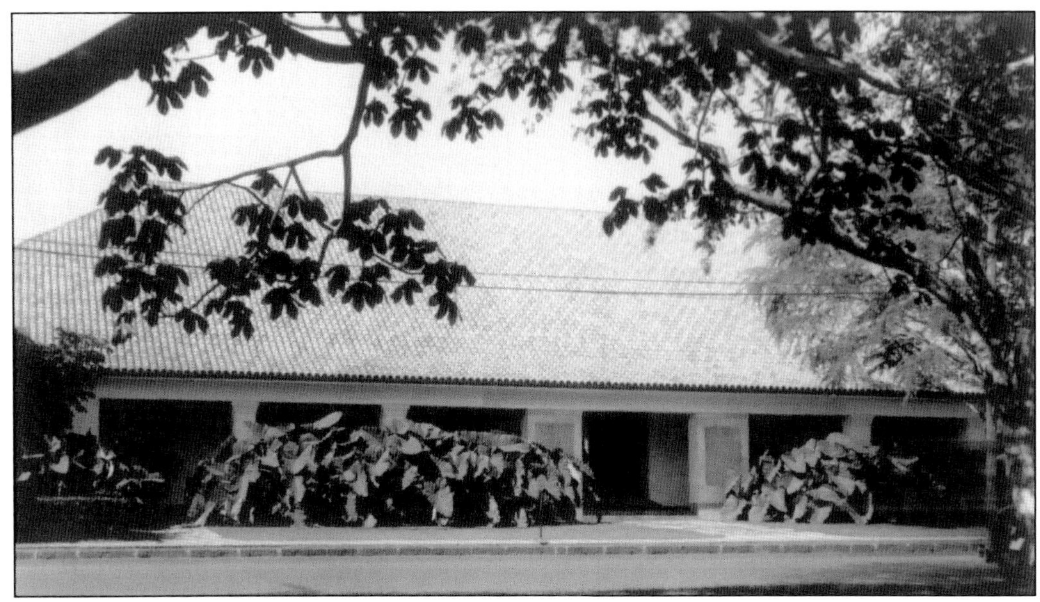

During his time on Kauai, Allerton made a number of donations to the Honolulu Academy of Arts, including works by Impressionists and Post-Impressionists, as well as a seventh-century Buddha, a thirteenth-century Japanese scroll, and a twelfth-century Shinto deity. In 1955, he helped fund the construction of the museum's Art Research Library. After his death, this library was named after him. (AO.)

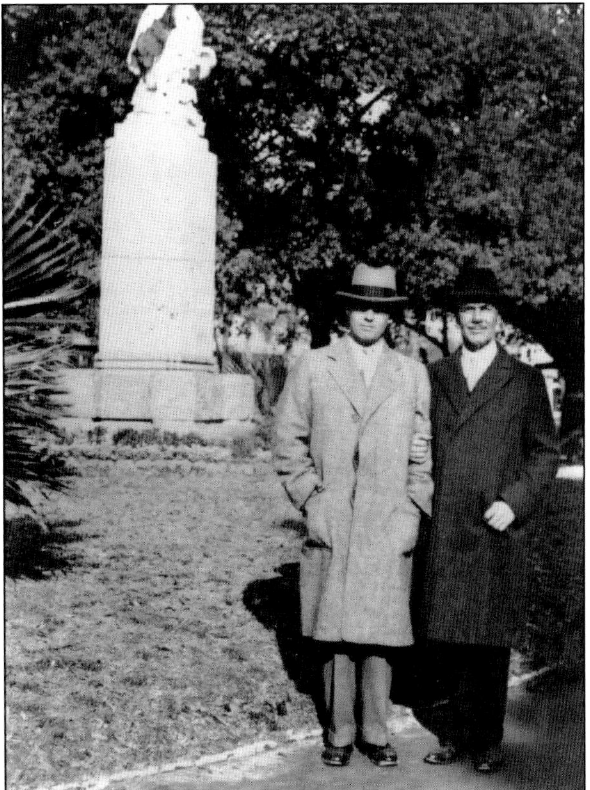

A few years before Allerton purchased the property on Kauai, prior to conflicts erupting overseas, Gregg (left) and Allerton (right) were photographed in Europe, possibly in Germany. In 1959, the Illinois state legislature revised a law, 750 ILCS 50, to take effect on January 1, 1960, allowing adults to be adopted. On March 5, 1960, then-87-year-old Allerton officially adopted 60-year-old Gregg. (APRC.)

In 1961, Allerton and Gregg were still traveling, first to Japan, then Washington, DC, and to San Francisco to see the Leningrad Ballet. In 1962, they spent the spring in Rome, Spain, and Portugal before visiting the Farms. Gregg (left) and Allerton (center) chat with Elmer Priebe in the brick wall garden. This would be Allerton's last visit to his old home. (APRC.)

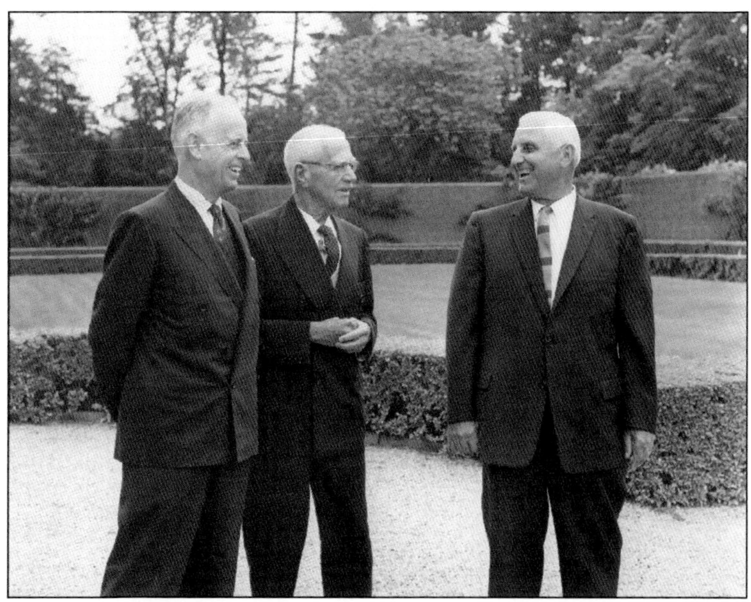

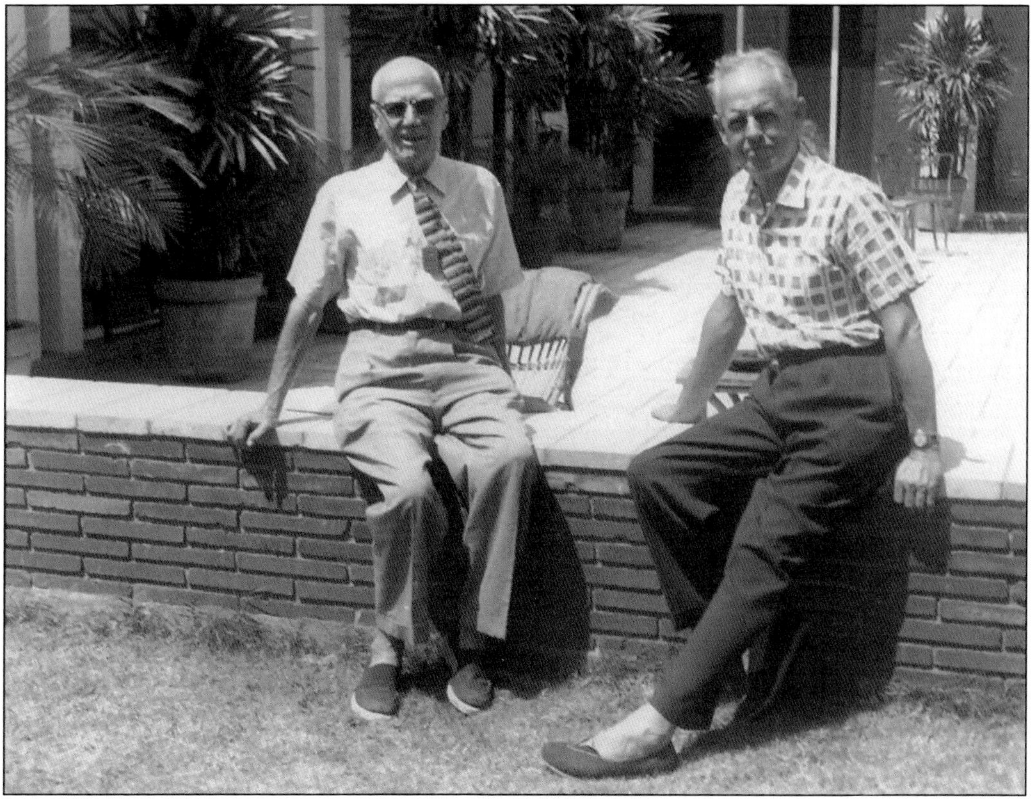

On December 22, 1964, Allerton (left) died from coronary thrombosis after suffering a fractured hip. He left most of his estate to Gregg (right). Gregg died in May 1986, with bequests to the Honolulu Academy of Art and Chicago's Art Institute, but bequeathed Lawai-Kai to the Allerton Garden Trust with the First National Bank of Chicago as trustee, directing the Pacific Tropical Botanical Garden to be the estate's manager. (KHS.)

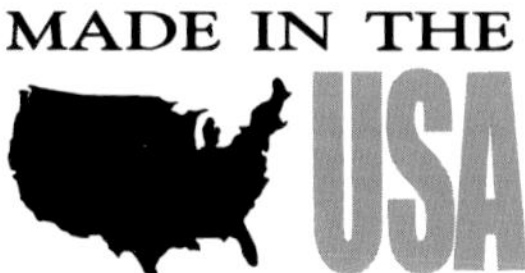
MADE IN THE
USA